A Heart of Souls

A helping hand on your journey through life

A Healer of Souls

A helping hand on your
journey through life

Dawn Paul

BOOKS

Winchester, UK
Washington, USA

First published by O-Books, 2012
O-Books is an imprint of John Hunt Publishing Ltd., Laurel House, Station Approach,
Alresford, Hants, SO24 9JH, UK
office1@jhpbooks.net
www.johnhuntpublishing.com

For distributor details and how to order please visit the 'Ordering' section on our website.

ISBN: 978 1 78099 355 3

A CIP catalogue record for this book is available from the British Library.

Design: Stuart Davies

Printed and bound by CPI Group (UK) Ltd, Croydon, CR0 4YY

We operate a distinctive and ethical publishing philosophy in all
areas of our business, from our global network of authors to
production and worldwide distribution.

CONTENTS

I would like to dedicate this book to three very special people.
Firstly to my father, John Edmund Hopkins
(6 October 1942 – 23 August 2010), who was possibly the best
person in the whole world (even though I am biased). I love
you so much; you are forever in my heart. Your bravery was
beyond measure, and I feel blessed to have been born to you.
My spiritual journey started because of you, and it will
continue because of you, and for all those like you. I know
you are with me.
Secondly, to Don Manuel Q'espi – a Q'ero elder – my guide and
inspiration. Thank you for the love you brought into the world
and for everything you have done, for me and for everyone.
I hope your wish came true.
And finally, to my dear friend Sahar Huneidi, thank you *so*
much for everything. Without you, this book would not have
been possible. I cannot tell you how grateful I am for all your
support and guidance. You are always in my heart, dear sister.

Introduction

Welcome to *A Healer of Souls*. I have written this book especially for you! It is my greatest hope that you may find something within these pages which will help you along your journey through life in some way. Although I am a shamanic healer, this book is not about any particular branch of spirituality, nor is it devoted purely to shamanism. Rather it is a book about my own philosophy on life and *general* spiritual principles which make sense to me and, more importantly, which *work* for me and for my clients. This book does not ask you to believe in anything and it does not recommend you follow a particular spiritual or religious path. Instead, after Part One, each chapter focuses on the 'common themes' which my clients seek assistance with. Each chapter is then divided into three parts, all related to the chapter heading. Firstly, in the 'Memories' section, you will find details of my experiences in relation to the chapter subject. In the 'Practice Notes' section you will find related client case studies, and then in the 'Notes' section, the guidance, information or understanding I try to bring to a client during a healing session.

If you are wondering what sort of person would come to see me then the answer is simple – every sort of person, ranging from 7 months to 90 years! My work as a shamanic healer brings me a wide variety of clients with an even wider variety of issues – from sexual abuse to spiritual struggles, from depression to disease. Men, women and children from all races, backgrounds and religions seek assistance – from all over the world. My hope for this book is that, if you find yourself struggling with one of the 'common themes,' you may find some answers within these pages, find a different vantage point from which to view your situation, or at the very least, you will know that you are not alone!

It is important for me to make it clear here that in respect of the title of this book, I am well aware that no one can *heal* another person, for it is up to each of us to take responsibility for our own personal healing. When we seek healing from another, it must be understood that that person is there to *assist us* on our journey, to remove the obstacles which block our way, and show us a new way forward. However, the title of this book has special meaning to me. Cutting a long story short, I received it as a core identity, or soul name, from a group of people with whom I had attended a very intense personal development workshop. At the time I received the soul name of 'A Healer of Souls,' I was working as a corporate pensions consultant for one of the largest banks in the world, so I was completely mystified as to why the words rang so true to me. In fact, the moment I heard them, I felt as if a rocket had exploded into my chest. But it wasn't until some years later, when I was rather forcibly brought to the shamanic work (more on that later!), that I understood it, and when I was asked for a name for the book, it was the first thing that came to mind.

While it is of course easier to refer to the work as 'healing,' rather than as 'an intervention,' or 'assistance,' I would like to make it clear at this point that before I start working with clients, I always make sure they understand that it is *their* healing journey, *not* mine. I ask clients to imagine I am creating a car for them; I am also providing them with the keys, and the fuel. But it is ultimately they themselves who have to take action in order to arrive at their desired destination by making the necessary changes in their lives – or in their thinking.

Please note that this book is the result of my thinking and realizations *at the time of writing*. We are all rapidly expanding in consciousness, awakening more and more every day. Time itself is accelerating, and the pace of life gets faster and faster. So here is a snapshot of my thoughts and my philosophy, *today*. I am not claiming to be enlightened or to have all the answers, but I have lived my whole life searching for the answers to *my* many questions. Not long ago I came to the conclusion that truth can *never* actually be fully known, because we can only understand things pertaining to the level of consciousness we have attained at that very moment in time. But be assured that in simply considering the concepts within this book, you are at least a step nearer to finding **your own** truths. This is one of my main goals – just to get you thinking and to question your own thinking. And if some of these chapters *do* resonate with you and assist you in some way, then I am honored to have been of assistance to you. May you blossom and bloom and live in bliss and harmony – and like the hummingbird, drink from the sweet, sweet nectar of life.

In *munay* (love and compassion)
Dawn Paul

Part One

A Little Bit about Me…

I have experienced difficulty in just *being* here ever since I was a tiny child – even at that young age I seemed to possess the knowledge that 'this' was not the 'real' reality. Additionally, I always felt pushed forward by something which was relentless – I was never able to fully rest or just 'be' – so my spiritual search started at a very young age. I have had many jobs, all of which have involved working with the public in some way or another, but my main focus was always to find my spiritual path.

In my early twenties I studied Transcendental Meditation (TM) which I practiced for about eight years. Towards the end of this time period, I found that while sitting in the meditative state, an immense and hugely powerful energy would surge through me and out of the palms of my hands. I had no idea what this was, but eventually someone told me that it was healing energy, and that I should learn to channel it. This led me to Reiki, something I had never heard about at the time. I studied three different lineages, achieving my Master level and the 4th degree, but I quickly came to the conclusion that for me, I wanted something that went deeper. I was aware that people felt better for a few days after a Reiki session – I had experienced that myself – but I wanted to find something that would allow the client to **permanently** heal their issue as far as possible, and to move forward into a life of happiness and freedom, liberated from their past. Yes, I could see that it is beneficial to bring in healing energy, but I felt it was rather like trying to 'wallpaper over a rubbish tip,' as the emotional baggage remained within, along with the behavioral patterns. I wanted to find a way to remove the old 'heavy' energy before bringing in the Light, and bring profound and lasting relief to my clients.

After many years of searching, I came across Native American Indian shamanism and felt strongly drawn to it. I attended a course and felt reborn! Spirits danced through me, spoke to me and encouraged me for all they were worth. Sadly, I failed to listen to them – and the wisdom of my own heart – and I allowed myself to be persuaded that the shamanic path was not for me after all. Highly confused (and pretty annoyed) I then went on a *huge* spiritual search over the course of around eight years. If I am completely honest, I would say that I became pretty much obsessed with finding my true calling. On several occasions, wracked with frustration, I even gave up the search altogether, but the nudge was so strong I quickly reverted to it.

Eventually though, I became *totally* disillusioned, angry and frustrated and had no option but to admit defeat. I had been working as a senior corporate pensions consultant for a large bank for years and had done little else with my life other than work at the bank and search for my path. Exhausted, I gave up, and went on a much-needed holiday to Peru.

How It All Began...

I had been drawn to Machu Picchu for years but, for some reason, had never managed to get there. Machu Picchu is cited as one of the new Seven Wonders of the World, and is often referred to as 'The Lost City of the Inca.' A mountain rising to just under 8,000 feet above sea level, covered in 15th-century Inca ruins, it surely is a sight to behold, and breathtaking in more ways than one.

As so often happens when one is on a spiritual path, as soon as I admitted defeat and stopped trying to find my path, it found me. For during my visit to Machu Picchu, quite unexpectedly, I received a powerful and mystical vision which was to change my life forever. I had climbed to the highest point at Machu Picchu to see the Intihuatana stone – also known as the 'hitching post of the Sun.' I was feeling frustrated as I had only caught the last two minutes of a talk about the stone, and the crowd was being shown out of the area down some steep and crumbling steps. I was the last to leave the enclosure, and as I cautiously made my way down the ancient steps, something red caught my eye. Startled, I looked up and saw that I was surrounded by about twenty Inca, all staring intently at me, red cloaks blowing in the strong valley winds, with feathered helmets on their heads and what appeared to be spears in their hands. Having previously enjoyed a trip to Rome that same year, and seen locals dressed up as gladiators and centurions posing for photos outside the Coliseum, I assumed that the Inca before me were a similar sort of tourist attraction, which to be honest I was a little upset about. But as I was able to focus my attention more fully onto them, I noticed that they were fading in and out, as if they were being tuned out on an old-fashioned television. I stopped dead in my tracks right there on the steps. I looked around to see if anyone else was close by, and amazingly, given the 400 visitors a day who visit Machu Picchu, no one was around. I could just make out a friend sitting against a rock in the distance but that was it.

Fearing my knees would fail me, I wobbled my way to the bottom of the stairs. An Inca was standing a short distance away from me, but he was dressed differently to the rest. Apart from a slit in his helmet exposing his deep black eyes, he was completely covered in golden armor. And he was immensely powerful, so powerful that I could barely stand in front of him. I kept subtly pinching myself to make sure I was not dreaming, but there was no doubt he was there, right in front of me, and I was wide awake.

I will admit it, I was pretty terrified, but something in me knew that I must maintain eye contact with him. The charge from his eyes was so strong that when his gaze met mine, a blue ball of electricity formed equidistant between us which crackled and sparked in mid-air. Tears flowed from my eyes and my knees shook, but I maintained my stance at what I hoped was a respectful distance. I had *no* idea what I was supposed to do – or who he was – so I just stood there, bravely fronting up to him, holding my own.

Suddenly his armored arm shot out and he pointed directly at me. His voice boomed, 'You must follow this path – and we will help you!' He then pointed to another Inca on the plateau below us, and indicated I was to go to him. Again, this Inca was powerful but dressed more traditionally. I stood in front of him, again having no idea what to do, and was pretty alarmed when he made a grab for my throat! He wrestled something out of me, threw it into the wind, and then indicated I could leave down some uneven steps down the side of the mountain. A sharp stone dug into the underside of my foot and when I looked down at it, I saw that instead of my sturdy walking boots, I had a pair of black leather Inca boots wrapped around my feet. This stunned me and I realized it was a sign I had been here before. The winds rushed up from the river valley below and plastered me against the side of the mountain. I could barely catch my breath. But then suddenly the wind died down and I heard a voice saying I could go now, and that was it! I was completely dazed, but it was a truly amazing experience and I will never forget it as long as I live.

On returning to the UK, however, I soon found that I had a very hard choice to make. I had spent many years praying and searching in order to find my path – now, it had found me, in no uncertain terms. But I needed to take time off work to start my training. I had no idea what had happened to me at Machu Picchu, but I knew one thing for sure: whoever that shiny golden Inca man was, I did *not* want to disobey his command and deep down I knew it was very important that I followed his direction. I asked my boss for unpaid leave so I could begin my studies, but this request was refused, leaving me with no option but to resign and leave a six-figure job and all the security it brought. Of course everyone at the bank, my friends and my family thought I was crazy, but now I had a direction, a very clear indication of the path I should take, and I could *not* ignore it.

Two years after resigning from the bank I read a wonderful book about the Q'ero – the medicine people of the Andes – entitled *Masters of the Living Energy*, by Joan Parisi Wilcox. My mouth gaped open as I read the following paragraph, which Joan has kindly allowed me to reproduce for you. (Note: the word *apu* refers to the 'Lord' of a holy mountain and a *paqo* denotes a person on the Andean medicine path.)

> When an apu determines that a paqo has acquired personal power commensurate with the apu's own power, then it may call that paqo into service. The call most often comes in the form of a dream or vision during which the apu talks to the paqo, offering to be his or her master and teacher. For a paqo, to receive the call of an apu is to receive an *estrella*, which is the Spanish word for 'star' ... To be called by an estrella means that a paqo has found his luck, his guiding spirit. Since the spirit of an apu cannot be seen directly, it often appears in the guise of an animal or person. Its most common animal appearance is as a hummingbird, bull, condor or puma. It most frequently appears in *human form as a man in white or shining clothing* that comes to a paqo in a dream, or, less frequently, in a vision ... But each call does not have to be answered. Paqos are free to refuse to accept an estrella, although to do so can imperil not only that paqo's health and even his life, but also may adversely affect his family.

I realized that what I had seen at Machu Picchu in my vision was *not* an Inca chief or king after all, but the holy mountain Machu Picchu itself, in human form, calling me into service as a shaman! And after reading the last paragraph, I was very glad I had followed my instincts and left the bank. Having said that, it has not been an easy journey at all and I have been deeply challenged at every step – in every aspect of my life. Someone once told me that of all the spiritual paths to take, the shamanic path is the hardest, and I know now that they certainly were not joking! But I wouldn't change anything; this is who I am.

I now work worldwide helping people to put their past behind them and assisting them to take steps closer towards wholeness, and I feel honored to be able to assist people on their journey through life. My personal opinion is that no other therapy is as effective as shamanic healing; as far as I am aware, nothing else really reaches the core issues quite so efficiently. Throughout my years of practice I have witnessed many powerful and often miraculous healings which I perceive do not come from me, but through me. I truly love my work and I feel blessed to have been called to this ancient and wonderful tradition. It may have been a long and arduous journey, but it has been worth it!

Shamanism

As you will have read, I first came across shamanism many years ago and instantly fell in love with its power and its simplicity. Shamanism is the system of belief and healing of the first peoples of the world, such as the Native American Indians and the Australian Aborigines. It is at least 40,000 years old, therefore it is older than any religion, yet it is not a religion in itself. There is no holy book, no one to worship, no rules, no restrictions, and it is without dogma. Instead, it simply maintains that humans can, and should, have a direct relationship with God – no priest, guru, or other intermediary needs to be involved. It teaches that man can live in direct communion and harmony with the Earth and with nature.

Personally, I perceive the shamanic path as one of great beauty, and true beauty can often be found in the simplest of things. Shamanism offers us the glory of creation, in all its forms. The shamanic viewpoint is that God, or 'Great Spirit,' is not restricted to the heavens, but that His hand and His essence dwells in *everything*. Each person, animal, river, tree, flower, mountain and stone has a spark of Divinity in it. A shaman strives to live respectfully and in harmony with the world around him, in acknowledgment of that Divine essence. The Divine spark in all things is perceived as a form of consciousness, a consciousness that can be tapped into, listened to and understood.

Let me give you an example of this. I remember once being in the Amazon jungle with a guide. He told me that scientists would visit from the West to learn about the plant medicine which grows in great abundance there. The scientist would ask, 'But *how* did the shaman *know* what the sap of this tree could do? How did they *know* that a cupful could kill parasites in the digestive tract? How did they *know* that the leaves of the same tree could be mulched down and used as a compress to bring down joint swellings?' The guides would reply that the shaman knew because he would simply *ask* the trees or the plants what they could do to help, and then they would listen for the answers. This may sound crazy to you, and to the scientists, but when we are in balance and harmony with nature, *nature speaks to us*. A shaman works hard to gain that balance, and that level of communication with nature, by living harmoniously with the land, by honoring the land through ceremony, by aiming to live harmlessly, and by remaining in balance with nature.

I have worked with the medicine people of the Andes and observed them giving an offering or gift to a plant before picking a flower from it, whether the flower was to be used in a healing ritual, or simply to be put in the brim of their hat as decoration. If they wish to drink beer or wine, they first spill a little onto the Earth, or Pachamama as they call her, as a gift of thanks before drinking themselves. Additionally, such is their loyalty and love for the Earth that after harvesting their crops, huge celebrations take place in the villages, honoring the Earth for its bounty and generosity. As a community, despite their poverty, they will sort through every ear of corn until the finest two cobs are found and these are then buried back in the land as a prayer of thanks and a request for future abundance. Likewise, permission will be sought from the Earth before constructing any roads or buildings, as in the Oriental cultures.

The honoring of the Earth and of nature is common to all shamanic traditions. For example, Native North American Indians usually carry out elaborate ceremonies and rituals before hunting. They do this to ask permission of the soul of the beast they expect to slay and to thank it for the sacrifice it is making, and afterwards a dance and ceremony will take place to help the soul of the animal pass into the next world. These are the old ways of the Earth, and sadly, over time they have gradually been lost. We need to bring those ways back. We need to stop living so aggressively, so harmfully, so *horribly*, for our *own* benefit, for the benefit of our children and also for the benefit of the planet and *all* those – human, animal and elemental – who dwell upon it. Living this way should not be seen as 'going backwards;' rather it should be seen as living *intelligently*. Anyone can see that living the way we do is going to result in disaster, one way or another. Surely the test of true progress is that we are all happier in our lives than before? Despite all the gadgets and technology, our relative wealth and the facilities we have at the touch of a button, can we really say we are *happy*? I don't think that we are; in fact my sense is that as a population we are becoming consumed by depression.

There are a lot of misconceptions about shamanism and it can often be perceived as dark and scary. I am not going to tell you that there is not a dark side to it, because of course there is a dark side to *everything*. There are whole villages given over to sorcery in Peru, and the shaman there will dole out curses and then alternatively lift them as requested by members of the community – in fact they often find themselves undoing their own work! It is just a job to them. It needs to be remembered that there is polarity in everything and also *in each and every one of us*. There is a dark side to most organized religions, as we all know, as well as a dark side to business, science, medicine – to anything in fact which involves power. Power is power; it just *is*, and it can be used for good or evil. It depends absolutely on whose hands the power is in. For example, imagine a knife – it can be used to kill or wound, or alternatively it can be used to perform life-saving surgery, or to create beautiful food. It all depends on who holds it. It is our job to use our intuition when seeking out assistance on our healing path, and to listen to it.

In all my spiritual endeavors, I have always worked on the side of the light, and I will continue to do so. My belief is that love and light will always win out against evil and darkness – and I find a lot of love in the shamanic traditions. Because shamanism is not a religion in itself, people can add it onto their own religions. I have worked with many medicine people in Peru who carry crucifixes in their medicine bundles – of course Jesus is probably the most famous shaman of them all! This works incredibly well with clients as well – it does not matter if they are Christian, Catholic, Muslim, Sikh, Hindu, Jew, Buddhist, agnostic, or atheist; the benefits of the tradition are available for all.

One of the best features of shamanism is the focus on the *collective*, the good of the community, the whole, rather than on the individual. In ancient times, each community had its own shaman. This person acted as a priest, doctor, counselor/adviser and also as a bridge between the human world and the spirit and natural worlds. If your baby was sick, you went to the shaman. If your crops were failing, or your animals were sick, you went to the shaman. If you were unlucky in love, you went to the shaman. If you were desperate for rain, off to the shaman you would go. Usually the shaman would live a little way out from the community, but would be entirely supported by the community, so he would receive his home rent-free, and all his provisions from his people, in return for his (or her) services.

The role of shaman would normally be passed down through the family line, or alternatively nature would select the new shaman for the community. In Peru and in many other traditions, it is usual for the new shaman to be chosen by being struck by lightning (and, of course, surviving). I saw many medicine people in Peru who had lightning craters in their heads, missing ears and scarred faces. One of my guides was not only struck by lightning, but was also *taught* everything he needed to know by the lightning; all his medicine ways and knowledge were 'downloaded' into him in that instance! Imagine that! I am *so* happy that I received an *estrella* vision instead of being struck by lightning!

Generally, shaman source their power from power places, natural objects, totem animals or teacher plants which are local to their environment. For example, the shaman of the Reindeer Tribe in Mongolia (detailed in Rupert Isaacson's marvellous book *The Horse Boy*) work with their reindeer power animals. The Altomesayoks of the Q'ero Indians of Peru, from whom my tradition originates, are aligned and apprenticed to mountain spirits, or the *apu* as they are known locally. Some shamanic lineages may work with the spirits of a sacred lake or river. Most of the shaman of the Amazon jungle work with the spirits of 'teacher' plants such as the *Ayahuasca* vine. Other hallucinogenic teacher plants utilized in shamanic traditions are the San Pedro cactus, Peyote buttons (mescaline), and psilocybin mushrooms. These powerful plant substances are not used as recreational drugs but are instead ingested in order to attain 'hypnogogic' or trance states in which valuable teaching, knowledge and information can be obtained. The plants are viewed as sacred teachers, and they are greatly revered – feared almost – and great care needs to be taken in the rituals of harvesting and preparation.

Shamanic practices are very similar across the many different lineages. Somehow, the shaman of old received similar information to each other – despite being separated by vast distances. Basic practices generally include the clearing of the *energy body* (or aura) of a person through whipping, rattling, drumming, dunking in freezing lagoons or under waterfalls, or through the use of fire. One of my teachers once told me that a tribe in the Amazon heal people by rubbing the person with wax, spraying them with alcohol and setting them on fire! Amazingly, this does not result in any harm to the person because of the skill of the shaman and the utilization of trance states. However, I *do not* suggest you try this at home!

Fortunately for my clients, I prefer to use a rattle in order to break up heavy energy – which we call *hucha* – in a person's energy field. Of course a rattle is a traditional gift for a baby. This is because the sound of the rattle alters brain-wave activity in the child's mind, thus enabling the baby to become more peaceful and fall asleep. I, and many other shamanic healers, particularly of the Native American Indian traditions, use a rattle to 'journey' with. The repetitive and rhythmic sound of the rattle is used to alter brain activity, enabling the achievement of a *hypnogogic* state – a state between sleep and wakefulness – allowing us to 'journey' or *travel in our minds* to other worlds, dimensions, or realms of consciousness.

Of course there are other tools which are used for journeying and these tend to be typical of the shamanic lineage or tradition the shaman belongs to. Many traditions use the rhythmic beat of a sacred drum; others may use the monotony of a chant, prayer, or song, a whistled tune, the ringing of a bell – or even an ecstatic dance. Journeying is the main work a shamanic healer carries out for a client. The aim is to achieve heightened states of consciousness – during which information and knowledge can be obtained, for the benefit of the client. This is how the medicine person gains access to the *core issue* of a client, rather than purely listening to the 'story' the client presents with. Another common theme across the many lineages of shamanism is the concept of the 'Three Worlds.' They are as follows:

- The Middle World – This is this world, the everyday world, which is called the *Kay Pacha* in the Quechua language (the language of the Inca, which is my lineage).
- The Lower World – This is the world beneath this one, which exists inside the Earth. This world is normally accessed by journeying through the roots of a tree, or alternatively through a cave or a lake. I need to stress here that this is *not* a hellish dimension at all; it is just another dimension, another entire world below this one. This is the place to which our lost soul parts normally return – to the safety of Mother Earth – as well as representing the realm of the subconscious and also the unconscious. In my tradition this is known as the *Uhupacha*.

- The Upper World – In my tradition this realm is known as the *Hanaq Pacha*. This world exists above the Earth, in the heavenly dimensions. It extends through various layers of the upper dimensions, which all have different themes and increasingly higher vibrations. Again these dimensions are accessed through journeying; the most common way is by entering a tree and traveling up through the branches, or by taking flight with a power animal. A tree is utilized in many shamanic traditions and each shaman normally finds his or her own power place and access point into the different worlds.

In addressing the healing needs of the client, the first step is to clear the heavy or intrusive energies from the client's energy and/or physical body, and then bring the person back to wholeness through a process that is also common through many shamanic lineages, called 'soul retrieval.'

Delicate Souls

Our souls are delicate, like slivers of glass, and they can shatter and splinter as a result of severe emotional, mental, spiritual or physical shock, trauma or pain. Normally a pattern of soul loss becomes established between the ages of 0–10 and then it becomes ongoing. Often the initial loss forms a 'pattern repeat' and more and more parts become lost, resulting in the person feeling like an 'empty shell.'

To make it easier to explain this to you, imagine, if you will, an orange – all those juicy segments connected to each other within the thick skin of the orange. Now, imagine that the orange skin or peel represents the human body, and the orange segments are the soul *and also* units of vital energy. If the person is happy and safe the segments remain within the peel, but if someone experiences trauma then this can result in some segments leaving the orange skin. To give an example, if a child is sexually abused by a parent, then this is unbelievably traumatic for the child and soul loss will most definitely occur. Assume that three segments of the orange leave, which results in a lack of vitality, or energy, within the physical body. The abuse will then set up a pattern of abusive relationships and negative events, and as the child grows, segment after segment leaves the orange, until there are only a few segments left within it.

The effects of the soul loss on the person will range from depression and low energy, to problems with the immune system and disease, poor energetic protection, difficulty feeling anything, and problems finding their place and purpose in the world. In short, they will feel like something is missing, because something *is* missing – those aspects of the soul. Often when people go on a 'big search' – perhaps for the perfect job / partner / their real mother / their purpose in life / their spiritual path etc – what they are actually looking for is those soul parts, those lost aspects of themselves.

Although this may sound scary, soul loss acts as a type of protection mechanism. The soul knows it is delicate, and it will leave the physical body to return to the safety of Mother Earth in order to ensure its survival, and also to allow the person to cope more easily with what has happened to them, by 'dumbing them down' a little, or – in some cases – a lot. The best example I can give of soul loss (although admittedly it is not a very pleasant one) can be seen in articles in magazines where a woman describes being raped. The victim will often describe the event as follows: 'I was completely detached from the scene, and seemed to be watching everything happening from above my body.' This is because she actually *is* watching herself from above, as she will have completely left her body in order to distance herself from the event. What happens then is that not all of the soul (or spirit) returns to the body, because if it did, it would bring back the memory of the event and this may be too difficult for the woman to deal with. So some of her soul re-enters the body and the rest of it returns to the safety of the Lower World.

A large part of my work involves journeying down to the Lower World in order to retrieve those segments and return them to the body – to put them back in the orange skin, as it were. This process is repeated until the person feels good and whole and starts to move forward in their life. It is an amazing process and hugely beneficial to the client. I have heard it said that as a process it is equivalent to many years of psychotherapy. It makes a huge difference to people and also they benefit as their energy levels, immunity and vitality levels increase, plus the character traits that the soul part contains are returned to them.

To my mind, no other therapy is as effective as shamanic healing. Why? Because it quickly highlights the core issue as I mentioned previously; it also improves physical energy levels and immune system function by clearing heavy energy from the energy field. It works on *all levels* of a person's being, which is important because we receive trauma on all levels of our being. It enables the client to become free of conditioned or ancestral responses, helping them to break their patterns, and most importantly, it helps to restore a person to wholeness through soul retrieval *and* encourages a person to move forward in a new, healed identity; it allows them a rebirth, you could say. And in my view, healing doesn't get much better than that!

Not only do I strongly believe in the value of shamanic healing – perhaps because I have benefitted from the healing methods myself and found them to be hugely powerful and transformative – but also I believe in the value of living shaman-ically. Living shamanically is about living with respect to the old, ancient ways of relating to the Earth, about being in harmony with nature, with our animal friends and, of course, with each other. Can you *imagine* how marvelous life would be if we all lived like that? What a positive impact it would have, not merely upon the Earth – but in everyone and everything!

The most important shamanic principle is *to live with respect for*

ALL *living things*, which includes such things as rivers, lakes, trees, plants, winds, insects, rain, and even rocks and stones. If we lived with respect for all things, would crime be possible? Imagine it. If everyone on the planet lived by just this one rule, then we would not need to spend billions on weapons, armies, defence and intelligence services. Those billions could be put to better use – perhaps looking after our brothers and sisters abroad and at home who have fewer resources than us. Or it could be spent on finding clean, green energy sources and solutions for cleaning up the planet for the benefit of all our futures. Or alternatively it could be spent on the much-needed improvement of our healthcare facilities.

We, as a population, would be happier; therefore, thanks to the mind/body connection, our health would be better. We would be living in more natural homes, in more natural clothes, with more natural cleaning products for our homes and bodies, because we would respect ourselves and the planet. We would be kinder to each other and give and receive more love and nurturing. We would have a closer relationship to nature and to spirit and to each other; we would live in closer contact with each other, and community spirit would reign once more. We would suffer less depression. We would be more fulfilled as individuals as we would choose work that is more fulfilling and less driven by financial need; we would be able to live on less as we would be living simpler lives, and because we would be happier generally, we would need less 'stuff' around us to fool us into thinking that the stuff is going to make us happy. (It doesn't, as perhaps you have already worked out.) There would be less hatred in the world, as everyone would be loved and respected, regardless of race, color, religious belief or sexual orientation.

It is important to remember that the Earth and everything around us is a reflection of us. If we are happy and full of love for ourselves and for others, everything, including the Earth, will be happier.

In this new world, we would be kinder and more thoughtful and balanced in the choices we make regarding food, alcohol and drugs. The food that we did eat would be from local farms using organic farming techniques (as chemicals harm the Earth, animals, fish and of course us). Animals reared on the farms would live in better conditions and would be treated more respectfully in recognition of all they give to us, and they would therefore be happier, so ultimately they would give higher quality meat or by-products. Our relationships would be better, more caring and loving. Parents would give their children the love, support and encouragement they need in order to grow into happy and fulfilled adults. Just think about it: how good would it be to honor one another and in turn be honored back – simply for who we are? Remember that when we are once again living in harmony with nature, all the positive forces of nature will live in harmony with *us*. Doesn't it sound dreamy…

Is it possible? Well, of course it is! Everything is possible. Will we do it? Well, I think that if we don't do it, things may have to get so bad that we have no option but to change our ways. When will we have had enough of living the way we are doing currently? How bad will it have to get before we all move forward towards change? We *can* all make those changes, *now*. We don't have to wait for someone to tell us to do it. It's up to us. It is the dream of my heart, and I think we all deserve it – don't you?

Part Two

Main Chapters
As detailed in the Introduction, the following chapters are based on the *most common issues* which the majority of my clients have struggled with.

Each chapter is then split into three parts:

- The first section, 'Memories,' details my experiences.
- The second section, 'Practice Notes,' provides one or more client case studies.
- The third section, 'Notes,' provides notes, teachings and information.

The information in each section refers to the overall chapter heading.

1. Pre-Birth and Birth

Memories 1.1

I am energy, I am light and love, and I am one with the Divine. I am formless, fluid, full of grace and I live in a world of timeless beauty.

I know it will soon be time for me to once more descend into matter, into being-ness. So many times have I made this journey. But I do not fear, for I know I shall in time return to this place of light and love. I do not fear, for I have prepared for my journey well. I have chosen my parents and they are good – perfect in fact for my next incarnation. I have already chosen the circumstances of my life into which I will be born and the many experiences I have to come – and I am ready and willing to accept them. I do not fear because I have purposefully chosen these lessons, for the continuing evolution of my soul, because that is really all that matters; that is what life on Earth, the spiritual descent into matter, is all about. I do not fear, as I hope to bring understanding and wisdom to my soul from the experiences of this next lifetime, and as difficult as they may be, through it all, I hope I will remember who I am, outside of the illusion of 'reality' – outside of the illusion of being human.

I am ready to leave, calming myself with the knowledge that I will return home in what will seem the mere blinking of an eye – after all, a human lifetime is so unbelievably short! I begin my descent; I am peaceful and at ease, flying through the stars like a comet. I look forward to what lies in front of me, to the joys of the physical, the joys of all the senses. I long for the experiences that having a human body allows – the caress of a lover, the colors of a sunset, feeling the cool wind on my face and warm water on my body.

I am closing in now and am surprised to feel a resistance building within me as memories flash unbidden into my consciousness, reminding me of the many trials of lifetimes past, of pain and loss and suffering. The stars streak past as my velocity increases. I try to force my focus onto the many joys of physicality – the sunsets and the kisses

– but I am dismayed to feel the first tinglings of homesickness as I descend into matter. Alarm strikes as I feel aspects of my self, my soul, my very being-ness, start to splinter, to shatter away from me, to return home without me.

What have I done? I fear the loss of connection to the Creator; I am fearful of forgetting who I am. But all too soon, I pass through the Veil, and my memory of home, of my connection to Source energy, of all those past lives, is wiped clean, snatched from me like a leaf in the breeze. I find myself somewhere warm and dark. I feel held, and temporarily, I feel safe. I sleep.

And then, all too soon, I am born, forced, pushed out into a blinding dazzle of light, of roughness, of noise and, once again, separation. I am inspected, prodded and poked, and finally wrapped in a rough blanket and held tightly. Cautiously, I open one eye – a blurry, pale face peers back at me. I recognize that face from somewhere… ahhhh, I remember now – she is the one I chose to be born to. And so it begins…

Practice Notes 1.2

The story of childhood abuse I have just heard is the worst I have ever encountered – and that is saying something! I press my lips together and force my face to remain neutral as I look at my client. I know I must try to remain neutral, but I can't help wondering how a mother could do such things to her own flesh and blood. My client is in her early fifties and she is the nicest person one could ever wish to meet. Her life has been unbelievably traumatic and it seems she has been thrown more than her fair share of trials. Trauma and drama have been almost relentless for her, a savage continuum. She has come to see me because she wants to put an end to these harsh, repeating patterns and move forward to grasp the happiness she now knows she deserves.

I look down into my hands. I know what I am about to say is true, as far as my spiritual understanding goes, but I am not quite sure how she will take it. To suggest to someone that *they* have scripted their lives to ultimately assist in the evolution of their soul is not always well received. I must choose my words carefully.

I look her in the eye and smile, and tell her that in the greater scheme of things, everything is perfect. Always. I tell her there is a bigger plan, that we are much more than we know, and that we are not being punished by some outside source, or the Divine, but that *we* choose our life lessons, and the hope is that we deal with them from the position of our true selves, our Higher Selves, not from our ego minds and our humanness with all its frailties. I tell her that it is a generally accepted spiritual principle that *we* choose our parents and the circumstances of our lives.

She glances up at me sharply and for an instant I wonder how she will react. Then she smiles beatifically. In her soft warm voice she tells me:

'I know this. I do. Although of course it has taken a very long while for me to understand it. I have never told another living soul this, but I shall tell you, because I know that you *know. I remember*. I remember being *up there*. I *know* I chose my parents. I remember I was given a choice. I was shown a lovely couple! They were driving a car somewhere in the countryside; they were bright and happy, full of laughter. I could have had a wonderful life had I been born to them.

'And then I was shown another couple, in a cold and horrible house. The images of that life accelerated – fast-forwarded, if you like. I knew how life would be with them. I knew about the beatings, the poverty, the lack of love and the mental, physical and sexual abuse. I saw it all, exactly how it has been. I knew exactly how life would be with them, and yet I *chose* them to be my parents. I know that sounds crazy, but I did it because I don't want to come round again. I want this to be my last lifetime. I wanted to experience everything I possibly could in this lifetime, so I don't need to come back. And I knew that the woman I chose to be my mother was the person who would best enable my learning, by providing me with the necessary experiences. I knew that she would be my biggest abuser, but also my greatest teacher.

'What depths that woman has driven me to! Oh my, the things I have learned! And you know… I really did forget for a while. Who I was. I became a victim for a while – a *long* while actually. I became lost in the illusion of my humanness. I do love her, you know, because ultimately she is the one who has enabled me to learn. Does it surprise you to know I love her? I do; I love her and I forgive her. For *everything*. I still see her – we don't get on too badly at all now. There is no other option. I am at peace with it all; I just want to clear myself and move forward in life.'

I am stunned. I always knew that my clients would be my biggest teachers, but I am awed by this woman's compassion and understanding. I have never felt so humbled in the presence of so much grace.

***

Jasmine lies on my couch. She is very still as I guide her on her journey. I ask her to follow the golden cord along the line of her life in order to find out where her difficulties started. Her face, previously calm, starts to show signs of strain and distress. Tears shimmer down from beneath her lashes.

'Where are you?' I ask her gently.

'I am in the womb,' she replies. 'I am in the womb and I'm afraid. I don't want to be born; I don't want to come out into this world. I'm not wanted. Already I know I am not loved. *I feel it.* Not only from my mother, but from my father also. They resent me already – and I'm not even born! I know already, in my tiny baby heart, that this is not right. It is not how it should be; it is not how I want it to be. I want to stay in here, in the womb of my mother. Or go back to where I came from. I feel a pain within me, a deep sadness. This is where my pain started. All the way back, at the very beginning.'

'Fast-forward a little,' I whisper. 'What is happening now?'

'Oh no! I'm being born! I can't help it – I'm being squeezed out! I have no control. Harsh hands grab me, the lights blind me, and I can't breathe. I'm rubbed with rough cloths, wrapped tightly – I can't move! I'm being handed to her like a parcel. She looks at me and I look back, *willing* her to hold me, to love me. But she jerks her head away to the side and breaks eye contact. She doesn't want me, so she holds me reluctantly, limply. I feel unsafe, as if I may fall. The feelings and the energy of rejection are already in my heart – and they are growing fast.'

Notes 1.3

I will never forget the first client detailed in the Practice Notes to this chapter. Her wisdom and capacity for compassion were nothing short of holy, given her personal history. However, for many of my clients, this level of understanding has not been reached. I have seen clients in their *eighties* who still use their mother's or father's behavior towards them as an excuse for their own unfulfilled or unhappy lives. (Note please: although I am using the examples of parents in this chapter, this content can be applied to anyone who has an impact on your life, either positive or negative.)

I have come to the understanding in my own healing journey that circumstances cannot change and the past simply cannot be rewritten. However, a different vantage point *can* be taken, to give a new and higher level of understanding of any life situation. In some instances, mere education on this fact alone has been sufficiently healing to assist a person to move forward in their life. For example, imagine being in a small valley surrounded by mountains. Your life, and the understanding of your life, takes place within the confines of the valley. You see what is in front of you at face value and you react to it emotionally. This is how we as humans tend to act all the time.

'This is how it is,' we say. 'My life is like this.'

But how different would it be, if we agreed to drop our 'stories' and instead climb one of the mountains? The view of our life when viewed from different heights and different angles may seem another story altogether as we ascend further up that mountain. Additionally, when we are high enough so that we can see *all* the events happening on the other sides of the mountains – like the intersecting cogs whirring around in a clock – we can see from our lofty vantage point the absolute perfection of life.

Further still, what would our life look like if we left the mountain peak and ascended to the level of the 'Higher Self' (the greater part of us that resides outside of ourselves, the part that knows who we are, what we have come to achieve in this lifetime, who we have been and who we will become in the future) – or the level at which God resides? Maybe from that point, when we can see all the myriad intricacies at work, we can truly see the truth in what has become my favorite saying:

EVERYTHING IS IN DIVINE AND PERFECT ORDER – **ALWAYS**

For I have no doubt from my studies, my personal experiences and from my clients' experiences that I have been honored to share, that we do indeed *choose* who we are born to. I do appreciate that this statement may be a very bitter pill to swallow if you have experienced a difficult start in life. But I would ask you, just for a while, to try to park your emotions to the side and consider the possibility that you may have been living in the valley instead of upon the mountain peak.

Most of us live in the valley, all the time. It feels safe to have boundaries and good to have someone to blame for the fact that our life may not have gone the way we wanted it to go, whether we blame our parents, life, God or the Universe. It takes a vast amount of courage to look ourselves in the eye and admit that maybe, just maybe, we were wrong about all that. And once we begin the journey of our soul – our spiritual search for under-standing and light – once we take up permanent residence on the mountaintop, then our life can appear to be very different indeed. Deep peace and healing are available to us once we have that new understanding, once we shift our vantage point.

Imagine this for one moment. You are a soul, a spirit, residing in another, higher dimension, which has a different relationship to time. You have lived many, many lifetimes already and have had many, many experiences while in incarnation (in physical form). You know that in order to get off this cycle of life and death... life and death... life and death... you need to experience *everything*, complete your life lessons and most of all, to *learn from them*. You are contemplating your next incarnation on Earth, and decide that the lesson you most wish to learn in this future lifetime (for example) is that of Unconditional Love. You also understand that it is unlikely you will achieve this learning via a happy and blessed life! You understand that you are going to need to experience some challenges along the way, in order that you can demonstrate this Unconditional Love.

You state your wish for your coming lifetime, and look down at Earth, searching for the very souls who can gift you this lesson of Unconditional Love. You spot a likely couple and know that you will obtain the learning you wish to receive if you are born to these people, in the circumstances in which they are living, or will be living in, by the time you are born to them. You also know that these people carry a particular vibrational resonance which, when combined during the act of creation (lovemaking), will provide you with just the right vibrational resonance you wish to be born into. This vibrational resonance will, like a magnet, attract to you the experiences you wish to have – both positive and negative.

Who knows... maybe these people agreed to act out these roles for you before *they* incarnated, just so you could have the learning you desire. Rather like the actors in a drama series, perhaps you all got together in some cosmic Green Room to decide on your roles and your scripts. Perhaps *you* handed the scripts out. Perhaps *you* even *wrote* the scripts and created the characters in your very own series. Perhaps they agreed to take on these roles because it fitted in nicely with the things *they* wanted to experience as souls. Maybe you all signed a contract to assist each other in this way. You have all 'learned your lines' and are all aware that you have clean and clear understanding of your roles and the lessons you wish to learn in this dimension.

You *hope* that, once incarnated, you will step out of the blindness and illusion of your humanness and remember who you are as a soul, and instead of falling into the human trap of victimhood, you will remember what it was that you wished to learn and experience here, and *why*. Once you look at your life experiences, figure out what it might have been that you wished to learn or experience before incarnating (i.e. Unconditional Love), you can then move on from your past, unencumbered, with *gratitude* – not hatred or loathing – for those who helped your soul to achieve its goals and learn its lessons.

Just for a minute, imagine this to be true, and then from your soul's perspective, look at your own life and ask, 'If this was the case, looking at my life, what could it have been that *I* wished to learn? Given all my experiences, what contract might I have written? Taking out the emotional aspect of my life, and standing back, what might have been the purpose of this lifetime, if I were to take complete and total *responsibility* for it? Why would I have chosen to create this "story"? What might have been the ultimate purpose of it all?'

When we can find an answer to these questions, something marvelous happens. *We can stop being victims.* We can stop blaming God – or others outside of ourselves – for the challenges we have faced in life, and look at our lives from a vantage point of responsibility and ownership of our *own* power in creating *our own* reality. We can also have the new understanding that we created our particular reality not to punish ourselves, but for our *ultimate benefit* on our soul's journey. And once we recognize the gift of the lessons we have learned, we can *truly* put the past behind us, pull ourselves up and get on with creating lives of joy, laughter and happiness – because those qualities, the positive things in life, are *available to all of us*, regardless of our past or current circumstances. In fact we owe it to ourselves to do everything we can to create such lives! It is all possible; *we* are indeed the Creators of our lives – we can create a good life for ourselves just as easily as we can create a bad one, and boy, are we experts at creating bad situations for ourselves! (I've been quite talented in that area; more on that later.)

Make no mistake about it: from a human vantage point the above questions are tough ones to answer. They require us to step outside of our pain, our emotions and our *need* for our *story* – for that is what it is, a story – before we can see clearly enough to find the answers. It is often said that the biggest illusion is that of our humanness. If we shift our understanding again, and see ourselves as the truly eternal beings we are, then, as souls on an epic journey, we can see why we may have chosen to have a few short years in conflict in order to get a step closer to where *we* want to be in our evolution. What if, for example, as souls, we were billions of years old? What sacrifice would, say, 80 human years of struggle be in the grand scheme of things? Or 800 years of struggle? It would pass in the blink of an eye to the beingness we truly are.

So many people weep and moan, 'Why, WHY did this happen to me?! Why would *God* do this to me? Does He *hate* me that much?' (And I think that if we are honest, most of us have vented this way at some point – I know I certainly have!) But shift your vantage point again, and consider, 'What if God has nothing to do with our lives at all?' I don't mean that there isn't a God (or whatever name you call the Divine), but the understanding I have come to in all this is that God is there, loving us, and observing us and waiting for us to go Home to Him / Her / All-That-Is (I will refer to the Divine as 'Him' for ease) when we have completed our soul's journey, so that He may know Himself. He is interested, fascinated even, in our progress – or our lack of progress – but He does not interfere; He does not judge us and He certainly does not create conflict for us. He gave us free will, and He is *very* interested to see how we use it.

Assuming this is the case for one moment, how would it be for you if you knew that God had not punished you or created all those bad things in your life? How would it be to know that *you* created them, for *your* ultimate *benefit, in the larger scheme of things?*

Now I know some of you will be railing at this, saying, 'Are you CRAZY? Are you telling me I *chose* to be blind/disabled/abused etc in this lifetime?' But look at it again through those mountaintop eyes. What if a) you knew you were eternal, b) you had already lived a thousand lifetimes, and c) you wished to experience say, blindness, because the lesson you wished to learn in this lifetime was to look within, or receive another perspective on life, or even to allow someone else to give *you* Unconditional Love as part of *their* soul's journey?

Many clients come to see me because they have been traumatized by their parents in some way. I tell these people a story that I was told by one of my teachers when I was in Peru. He told me that the Inca believed we all have two *true* parents and two parents only. Our true Mother is the Earth, whom the Inca called Pachamama. She gives us everything we need: food, water, shelter, beauty, nature, oxygen, minerals, crystals, jewels, etc. Our true Father is the Sun, called Inti Taita, and he waltzes with our Mother through the Universe, bringing us energy and light. He is always there, above us somewhere, even if we cannot see him. The Inca medicine people also said that our biological parents therefore are just that – biological vehicles to provide us with a physical body. A body which exists on a vibration we need it to be on, in order to attract to us the lessons and experiences we need on a soul level.

There is a very nice meditation I teach my clients and I would like to share this with you. Take your time with it. You can do it in bed if you like.

Lie down and imagine being cradled by your true mother, Pachamama Mother Earth. Feel her enclose you and keep you warm, like a tiny seed in her arms. Feel the love she has for you and spend a few moments thinking about all the beautiful things she creates for you.

Then feel the light of your true father, Inti the Sun, shining down sparkles of light and energy upon you, warming you and encouraging you to grow.

Take a few minutes to feel nurtured in this way, held between your two true parents.

The meditation above is also very comforting when a person has lost their parents, or is separated from them in some way. In fact I do the meditation myself, when I need to feel held and supported! Try it for yourself, if you feel it may help you.

Another important aspect to remember when considering parental relationships (or any disharmonious relationship) is that of the natural law of karma. It is important to understand that we stay in the same soul groups when we incarnate; however, our sexes and our roles change. Imagine I have a daughter in this lifetime. In a previous lifetime she may have been my mother, or father, or even my brother or sister, my uncle or even my boss. I have seen many clients who have been abused by their parents in some way come to a realization through past-life regression that in a former life, *they* held the role of the abuser, and in this lifetime they are simply receiving karmic payback for that.

Perhaps you don't believe in past lives – many people do not. Interestingly, however, when working with clients' 'chakras' (the seven energy centers of the body, seen as vortices or wheels, which are generally acknowledged in many Eastern healing traditions – more on these later), many very quickly find themselves in past-life situations – even if they don't believe in them! For me, past lives are a given; I have always believed in reincarnation and the subject is simply not up for debate. Even if I did not believe in past lives myself before starting this work, my work with clients would have taught me otherwise!

So, we have looked at the importance of viewing our lives through different eyes and also from different vantage points in order to gain greater understanding, and also *why* we chose to be born to certain people. Also we have briefly touched on the workings of karma in our personal relationships. So let us look at things from yet another perspective – the purely human perspective.

When we are small children, we think of our parents as Gods. They are huge beings, we believe they are always right, and we have an innate desire to be loved by them and for that love to be shown, verbally or physically – preferably both. We want to be told we are loved unconditionally, that we are good enough, and that we have done well at whatever it is that we are doing. We also need, more than anything, physical touch and comfort, such as hugs and kisses. Hugs are *essential* to our wellbeing, whatever our age! When we are little, we assume that our parents know everything, and also we assume in some way that they have been to special parenting schools and therefore know exactly how to be perfect parents. (Actually it always amazes me that people do not learn how to be good parents; after all, it's one of the most important jobs we can ever do! Maybe they should teach it in schools; my guess is that it would be of far greater benefit to society than learning trigonometry!)

Our hurts and pains as children affect us deeply; they blind us, in fact, and they also reside in us in that same childlike fashion. Even if we are grown, mature – perhaps with children or even grandchildren of our own – we continue to hold on to our woundings and very rarely do we question them. We continue to be stuck in a child's understanding and logic when considering our parents' past actions, no matter how old we are.

I remember feeling very frustrated with my mother because she would not answer *all* my very many questions to my satisfaction. She would often seem bored and sigh, 'I simply don't *know*, Dawn.' I used to get very upset and assumed she was fobbing me off. What I failed to take into account is that actually, I used to ask about a hundred questions a day! (And I still do!) It must have driven my mother mad! Or alternatively, I would feel that my mother would perhaps act in ways that I disagreed with, and I often felt hurt by her as a child. But when I look back, with an *adult's understanding*, I can see the reality of the situation. My mother was only 21 when she had me! That means when I was ten, far from being the fount of all knowledge and the goddess of perfect parenting that I wanted her to be, she was only 31! I used to get upset because the answer was always 'No' when I asked for this, that or the other, but as an adult I realize that it wasn't because she was being mean – we just simply couldn't afford the things I wanted.

I also used to feel very upset because I saw so little of my father – but now I understand that he worked all the overtime he could and worked weekends too so that we could make ends meet. When I ask clients to look at their childhood issues with the understanding of an adult, it is clear to me that they have never done this before. This is because *that inner wounded child* still lives within us, so it is *vitally* important for us to heal those inner children as well as ourselves. Again, healing can come from taking a different vantage point on our *perceived* hurts.

Sadly, our parents did not go to a special school in order to learn how to become super parents. They tended to bring us up the same way that they themselves were brought up, and given that *their* parents didn't go to super parenting school either, the results of our upbringing can be seriously lacking indeed, but not necessarily because of any *intentional* mistreatment by our parents. Again, this issue for clients intrigues me, as no consideration ever seems to be given to their own parents' upbringing. Yet when I ask clients if they know anything about it, they often comment, 'Oh, my father had the most terrible childhood; he was beaten regularly and was never shown any love at all by his father.'

When I reply, 'So, do you think that may explain why he was unable to express the love you were desperate to see? Did he show his love in other ways, other than consuming you in hugs and kisses every day, which is how you wished to perceive that love? Is it possible, conceivable, that he *did* love you very much, but just had no idea how to show you, because he never experienced it himself?' At this point my clients often raise their eyebrows and exclaim, 'How funny! I never thought about it like that! I guess it makes sense.'

Whether we like it or not, our parents are behaviorally conditioned and often carry deep wounding from *their* childhoods. I am not asking you to make excuses for your childhood traumas, neither am I trying to belittle them in any way, but I have noticed that we take things *so personally*! And maybe we shouldn't.

The following is a typical and very regular conversation which can be heard in my healing practice:

'My mother didn't show her love for me when I was little, therefore I am scarred for life. I now suffer from very low self-esteem and I have no self-confidence. All my relationships with men have been abusive. Clearly, I am not lovable; that is why she couldn't love me. She ruined my whole life. Everything is her fault. I have failed in life because of her.'

I ask, 'Did you have brothers and sisters?'

'Yes, I have two brothers and one sister.'

'Did she treat them the same as you or differently?'

'She treated us all the same. One of my brothers is alcoholic because of it. My sister never married because of it.'

I then put this scenario to the client: 'Imagine if I was born to your mother. Do you think she would have treated me any differently?'

(Long pause) 'No, I don't think she would have treated you any differently.'

'How about anyone else you know? Do you think she would have given them the love they needed?'

'Er... no.'

'So is it correct then for you to believe you are unlovable? Or is it more likely that your mother, for whatever reason, was *simply unable to show or demonstrate love*, full stop?'

(Very long pause) 'Well, *maybe* it would be more correct to say that she couldn't love, rather than saying I'm not lovable. I do know she had a very traumatic childhood herself, although she never really talks about it, which may explain why she was that way. I haven't really thought about it like that before.'

Please, if your childhood was less than perfect, just take some time out now to consider the points above. Be brutally honest with yourself and try to push any emotion to one side for a moment so that you can see clearly. It can help if you write the following questions down and then write your thoughts and feelings down underneath.

1   What is the *actual truth* of your childhood?
2   If another child was born to your parents, would they have treated them any differently?
3   Did your parents actually have the capacity (or the resources) to act the way you ideally would have liked them to?
4   How would it feel for you to simply accept that your mother or father had some parenting or emotional deficiencies, rather than assuming that *you* were lacking in some way?
5   If you could accept these deficiencies, and stopped blaming your parents for the way that you are, how

different could your life be? How different could your personal relationships be with others?

6 Given then the assumption that your parents would have treated *any* child the way they treated you, doesn't that mean that, as such, there is nothing actually 'wrong' with you?

7 If you let all the emotional pains regarding your childhood go, how would that improve your own parenting skills?

8 In what ways are you mirroring your parents' behavior with your own children?

9 What would you need to believe about yourself in order to change your behavior towards your own children? Are there other models of child-rearing you could consider other than your own dysfunctional parents?

10 What did you need as a child? The chances are, your children need the same things. Can you rise up out of your past and be the parent that you would like to have had?

11 How much have you continued your parents' abusive behavior towards yourself? How much do their voices still ring in your head? Think about how they treated you – are you treating yourself in the same way? If they failed to love and nurture you, have you managed to correct this in your treatment of yourself? Or are you as guilty as them, or even more guilty because you have maintained that behavior for longer?

12 Can you bring yourself to forgive them? Not to condone their behavior, but to forgive them in order to free yourself from your past?

13 Can you forgive yourself for carrying on any abusive or unloving behavior towards yourself, or others?

14 Imagine you grew up with *perfect* parents. How would your life look now? Who would you be? How would you

be different, act different? Is there anything actually *stopping* you from being that happy and fulfilled person? Do you not deserve that happiness and fulfillment?

15 How hard would it be to put all blame and resentment behind you and go out and create the best life possible for yourself?

16 How much do you like having someone else to blame?

17 Does it figure that having a difficult childhood means your life has to continue to be difficult? Is it a must? Or could you simply decide to make the necessary changes to your life *now*?

18 Are you trying to indirectly punish your parents for your difficult childhood by failing in life in some way? Who are you *actually* harming by acting in this way? Will becoming a complete and utter failure (or making yourself ill in some way) suddenly make them love you? If they couldn't do it when you were a child, do you think they are going to start magically loving you now?

19 Do you feel that if you get on with your life and become happy and successful, your parents will be 'getting away with it'?

20 When will *you* have suffered enough?

Again, take your time with these questions, and really think objectively. I do appreciate they are tough, and they may 'push your buttons.' I know how desperately we all like to cling onto our 'stuff,' but really, if your life is not going the way you would like it to, maybe it is time to drop the blame (whether your parents are guilty or not!) and take responsibility for your life. What about your responsibility to yourself? We all deserve to live happy and fulfilled lives. All of us. That life is there for you too, if you would just like to reach out and grab it. But first you need to make a decision. In order for you to reach out for your new and happy life, you first need to empty your hands of whatever negativity, or incorrect beliefs or blame, you are holding on to. Be assured that holding on to your stuff *does not serve you in any way.* Don't forget who you are! You are the Divine made manifest, so honor yourself as that. Your life is in your hands... whatever your beginnings.

2. Home

Questionnaire before Reading Chapter 2

As I mentioned in the Introduction, the chapters in this book are related to the main themes which concern the clients who come to see me. It needs to be remembered, however, that clients are drawn to certain therapists because they are in vibrational resonance with them in some way, and this is the same for the clients who come to see me. So, while the contents of this chapter concern a theme which runs *very* strongly through my healing practice, this will not necessarily be the case for other healing practitioners. Therefore I have devised a questionnaire in order for you to ascertain whether this chapter will be relevant to you or not. Of course you can read it if you wish, because even if it does not concern you it may remind you of someone that you may know, and it may help you to understand them a little better.

Alternatively, you may skip this chapter altogether. I appreciate that its contents may raise a few eyebrows, but this is a *very* real issue for many of my clients, even though the vast majority initially have no idea why they are the way they are. As a percentage of the population, this issue affects very few indeed, maybe only 1%. For this reason I considered omitting this chapter altogether; however, I reconsidered because this book is partly about my journey, and the issues raised within this chapter have caused *me* the most heartache in my life. Also, for the clients it *does* concern it is also the biggest issue in their lives, and yet often they are unaware of what is really happening to them and who they really are. Such is the struggle that such clients face every day with this issue that many of them tell me they have considered committing suicide, *so it is for this reason* that I have included this chapter.

Have you always felt different to everyone else, tried to fit in but never managed it?	YES	NO
Have you always been *treated* differently to everyone else?	YES	NO
Do you feel you have to study other people so you can behave like them, and copy their actions?	YES	NO
Do you often feel superior to others in some way, without having any real reason to feel this way and despite the fact it makes you feel awful?	YES	NO
Can you 'see' into other people very easily and understand what is going on with them?	YES	NO
Have you always had a sense of being 'special' in some way?	YES	NO
Can you look at a work project, for example, and be able to tell instantly if it will work out or not?	YES	NO
Do you have problems with bosses? Do they seem somehow threatened by you? Do you get held back from promotions etc?	YES	NO
Do people react to you quite strongly? Do they either become convinced you can help them or alternatively find you quite a threat?	YES	NO
Do you find that people do not want to hear your problems at ALL, and expect or need you to always be OK?	YES	NO
Can you find the solutions to problems very easily?	YES	NO
Do you feel that not many people are like you?	YES	NO
Do you have a large family and lots of friends but still feel very isolated and lonely?	YES	NO
Do you always feel like you are 'playing a role' or 'acting'?	YES	NO
Are you very sensitive – to other people's emotions, loud noises, bright lights, crowds, the news or bad vibes?	YES	NO

Do you often get treated badly by people you thought were your friends?	YES	NO
Do you have a poor relationship with your physical body, e.g. have food or weight issues?	YES	NO
Do you have a tendency to be ungrounded, i.e. disconnected from the Earth, 'daydreamy'?	YES	NO
Do you have a very 'busy' head, i.e. lots of thoughts and chatter going on all the time like lots of radio channels all playing at once? Do you find it hard to be 'present' (in the moment)?	YES	NO
Do you find it hard to be interested in things of 'this world' such as hobbies, sports etc?	YES	NO
Are you very interested in things 'out there,' e.g. spiritual things, evolution, astrology, astronomy, science fiction, channeled material?	YES	NO
Do you prefer to be indoors (preferably upstairs) rather than outdoors?	YES	NO
Do you feel trapped, either in your home location or your role?	YES	NO
Have you always felt very homesick, even if you live in the town of your birth?	YES	NO
Do you struggle in personal relationships, particularly marriages, and feel that your partner just does not 'get' you?	YES	NO
Do you feel that you are meant to be doing something in particular – that you have some great purpose?	YES	NO
Do you rarely feel at ease?	YES	NO
Do you like a challenge and are you fantastic at organizing and getting things done, often in record time?	YES	NO
Are you very concerned about the meaning of life, why we are here, all the 'bigger picture' stuff?	YES	NO

Do you have odd occasions when you feel tremendously powerful?	YES	NO
Do you have unusual dreams, visions, or experiences?	YES	NO
As a child, did you have regular nightmares or were you very afraid of the dark?	YES	NO
Are you super-conscious about your safety, e.g. do you like to sit with your back to the wall in restaurants and do you always make sure that you know where the doors, windows and exits are?	YES	NO
As a child, did you have a very strong feeling that you were adopted?	YES	NO
Do you get accused of being 'intense'?	YES	NO
Have therapists suggested that you may have been sexually abused in the past, or do you feel as if something similar has happened to you, where you were powerless and someone abused you, but you have no memory of it?	YES	NO
Do you look at the world and think, *It's all wrong; this isn't how it is meant to be?*	YES	NO
Do you feel a very deep connection to the Divine/God?	YES	NO
Are you often surprised by the harshness and lack of thought or lack of love or kindness shown by other people?	YES	NO
Do you feel like a fake, all the time (not just at work)?	YES	NO
Do you often feel overwhelmed, particularly in places like supermarkets?	YES	NO
Do you have phobias about 'bodily' functions, such as vomiting?	YES	NO
Do you suffer or have you suffered regular panic attacks?	YES	NO

If you answered 'YES' to most, or all of these questions, then this chapter is for you.

If you answered 'NO' to most of these questions then you can skip this chapter if you wish.

Memories 2.1

I am standing in our small, tidy kitchen; my mother is kneeling before me, tugging me into my tiny duffle coat, struggling to force the toggles through the loops. She smiles at me, her three-year-old daughter, and tells me it will be good for me to get some fresh air, and put some color into my permanently pale cheeks. I study her closely as I often do, in a very detached way. I watch the lines of concentration on her face as she tries to arrange my badly co-ordinated fingers into the correct holes in my glove. I try to help her but it only seems to make matters worse.

Finally I am dressed; she opens the kitchen door and helps me down the steep step into the garden, tells me to play for a while, then goes back into the kitchen, closing the door behind her to keep the heat in. I narrow my eyes against the strong biting wind and watch as decaying leaves cartwheel their way across the small sodden lawn. I hear the ominous howl of the wind as it squeezes down the passageway between our house and the next. The skin on my cheeks contracts with the coldness; icy fingers creep into my tiny bones. The normally forlorn tree at the end of the garden now dances its crazy dance, denuded arms flailing, framed against the sullen, smoky, somber sky. I watch the gunshot-grey clouds speed silently by, racing to get wherever it is that clouds go. Perhaps, I think, they are unaware that there is no destination for them, no end, no home, just constant journeying.

I exhale deeply and watch my breath escape before me in white curlicues. And in a moment I recognize a crushing feeling in my heart and I accept it. For I know. And the sadness and pain of that knowing is almost unbearable; it rises from my gut into my throat as if it had the strength to snatch the very life force from me. I look around, desperate in my panic, as if I need to grab on to something to stop me sinking away, falling into the earth, into isolation, but there is nothing there. Our house is only a few yards behind me but it feels miles away, almost in another dimension.

What is it that I know, you ask?

I know that this is not my true home, that I do not belong here, even though I was born here, and have remained solely here in my three long years of existence. And if you are reading this, in all likelihood, it will be because you feel the same.

Practice Notes 2.2

Elizabeth sips her tea, her sharp, deep-green eyes surveying me over the rim of the cup. I enquire as to why she has come to see me. She believes there is something seriously wrong with her and she has not been able to get to the bottom of it. She still feels terribly upset about the death of her father which happened a few years ago, and also she believes she is obsessed with an ex-boyfriend she went out with in her early twenties, even though she is now happily married and has a son.

She is also plagued with the deepest sadness that she simply cannot shake off. She has seen many therapists, none of whom were able to help her, in an attempt to try to sort this out. She has been taking anti-depressants which have had no effect at all. In her desperation, she has come to the conclusion that she is mentally ill in some way. She has not found any answers despite her comprehensive search and has come to me in the hope that I can help her.

I think for a while, curious about her need to hold on to these two obsessions for dear life. I ask her to close her eyes and to imagine how she would feel if I told her I could give her a magic pill that could instantly take away the obsessions about her father and her ex.

She bolts upright, tears springing into her eyes. 'Oh no, you can't do that! NO...! I can't allow you to take that away from me.'

'Why not?' I ask her gently.

'You can't take those things away from me, because if you do... then I will be just the same as everyone else.'

'Aren't you the same as everyone else then?'

'No, no, I'm not! I don't know why, but I'm not. I never have been. I am not the same as them, no matter what I do or how hard I try – and trust me, I try really hard. And I don't get treated normally either; everyone seems to want my help with their problems, but no one is there for me when I need help. I have so much trouble with girlfriends; they can often be very cruel to me, for no reason. I can't fit in. And sometimes, I'm ashamed to say it, but I sit with friends and I wonder, *What am I doing here?* It's like I'm pretending, ALL the time – pretending to be, well, *human*. I study people, and try to be like them, copy them – what they are wearing, what they say, how they act. I don't feel like I belong. Anywhere.

'I love my husband, but he isn't the same as me. I don't know what I mean by that, but he is different from me; even he is aware of it. He refers to it sometimes. And sometimes he says I scare him; he thinks I have super powers or something like that. I can see things clearly – but people at work accuse me of being negative, not being a team player. I *know* certain projects won't work, and I know what needs to be done to make them work. But they don't want to listen. I don't know how I know these things; I just do. I don't find the work hard; I can be really efficient – sometimes I even impress myself.

'My colleagues are OK, but they treat me strangely; it's like they think I'm above them in some way. And to be honest, I do feel that I am different to them, but then again, there is no reason for me to feel like that.'

I ask, 'Do you feel superior to your colleagues, even though they may be above you?'

'Yes!' Elizabeth cries, looking embarrassed. 'Yes, I do. But not just with my colleagues – with everyone! Strangely I feel, in a way, superior to most people – and that's a horrible thing to say, isn't it? I know it is. But it's true, and it's very distressing! Because *why* do I feel superior to other people? There is no reason! I'm not really clever, talented or rich. But I *do* feel it. In my being, in my bones, in my soul perhaps. I can't explain it; it makes me feel awful inside because I shouldn't be like that.'

I pause for a while, and then ask, 'I know this may sound like a very strange question, but how do you feel about the Earth and nature?'

Elizabeth starts to color up and tears start to stream down her face. 'I love nature – I do really, it's lovely – but I find it very hard to be outside, *in* it. I don't feel part of it. I seem to want to be indoors all the time; even if it's sunny, I'll tend to stay indoors, upstairs preferably, in my bedroom – I like it there.

'As for the world itself, well… it's just not right, is it? What's going on? Why is it so wrong? What is wrong with people – can't they *see* what they're doing to each other, to the Earth? It just seems too harsh, being here. It seems alien to me somehow. I can hardly watch the news; it upsets me too much.

'And I can't seem to find my place in the world. I like my job, but I always feel I should be doing something specific, something *better,* but I don't know what that is.'

'Do you have any interests, Elizabeth? Any hobbies of any sort?'

'Er, no, not really. I just don't seem to be interested in a lot of the things that other people do; I don't see the point in them, I guess. I find it hard to find things I'm really interested in – oh, apart from astronomy! I'm really interested in that.'

'So, would you, for instance, be the type of person to call a radio show, to enter a competition, or ask for your favorite record to be played?'

Elizabeth looks at me blankly. 'No, it would never, ever cross my mind to do something like that. Things like that are for other people, not me.'

'And would you say you were highly sensitive?'

'Oh yes, I am – too sensitive in fact. I get hurt so easily and I can sense when things are going on with other people. I know instantly if they're in pain, or if they're sad or upset. And I don't like loud noises, or bright lights. And crowds – I find crowds hard work and I try to avoid them. I get overwhelmed very easily, say if I'm out at a party, and all of a sudden I'll want to go home. There seems to be too much to take in and it makes me very tired.'

'And do you feel tired?'

'I feel *so* tired. So tired and weary. In my soul, I think. It all seems like too much effort, a *huge* effort, just to do simple things, just to be. Sometimes I think about dying, about the blessed release of it, about not having to *pretend* anymore – how nice that would be! And I know it's a terrible thing to say, because I have so much to be happy about! And I would never, ever do it. I could never put my son through that, or my husband. I know you think I'm probably mad, but I'm not; I am *not* depressed. Honestly. I'm just tired, and sometimes, it all seems so hard, and I just want to go home.'

'Home?'

'Yes, home. The place I belong.'

'So, that place – home – isn't here on Earth then, Elizabeth?'

'No, no, I don't believe it is.'

Notes 2.3

If you answered 'YES' to most of the questions in the question-naire, then the likelihood is that, like Elizabeth and regardless of your actual age, you are what I would call a 'Starchild.' If this is the case, you will feel the resonance of these words and the words which follow in your heart and soul, even though your mind may be fighting the logic of it – or the lack of logic of it!

I know the following may sound crazy, but try to let that

judgment go. Remember, your body has all the answers and knows truth; your head has only that which has been learned, along with your conditioning. If you want to know if something is true or not – and this goes for *everything in life* – try the feel of it in your gut, and in your heart, for your body never lies.

So, what is a Starchild? Let me start from the beginning in trying to explain this theory. I truly believe that 'our' universe is not the *only* universe. I think there are many, and that they are all connected, in the same way that bubbles are connected to each other when we have a bubble bath. The bubbles are complete in themselves, but attached to others, with a thin membrane between them. Now imagine that a complete universe is held within each bubble. This is how I envision it. So, yes, the scientists are completely right: we may be the only life forms in our *galaxy*. But what about the other universes out there?

Not only that, but what about the other *dimensions* which exist? As an example, we believe that we alone live in the third dimension along with the plants and animals etc, but I see quite clearly that the elemental world and the spirit world can enter it too; it's just that most of us can't see them or communicate with them. But just because we can't see them does not mean they do not exist. So I believe that there are many other civilizations out there, ranging through the full vibrational spectrum, from the highly evolved to the lowest forms of intelligence. We haven't (apparently) found them yet because a) we are searching for them with *our* technology, which is probably millions of years away from theirs, so it is a bit like trying to view an atom through a magnifying glass, and b) I think we are expecting them to be like us, made of matter with physical bodies. I *do* believe that some have physical bodies, particularly those of lower vibration. My experience of them is that they are more like spirits: they are made of energy. This is why they can travel huge distances at massive speed. They can appear and disappear in an instant, perhaps in many different places at once.

But we must ask ourselves – are these other races *separate* from us? They are certainly different, but are they separate, and therefore *not of God*? My theory is that 'we' – i.e. humans and extraterrestrial (ET) races – are *all part of God*. I believe that God (or any other name for the Divine that you wish to use) wished to truly know Himself. In order to do this He sacrificed some of His energy to carry out a great experiment. He divided this energy into a gazillion units – souls – and scattered them throughout the universes. Some of those souls *originally* came to Earth, and others went to other planets, dimensions and star systems.

I believe that some of the souls who were sent to other star systems, dimensions and universes, did very well indeed. They evolved very quickly, became enlightened and returned in bliss back to the Creator. And others, such as ourselves here on Earth, well, we struggled a bit, we became blinded by the material world and by our physical desires, and perhaps we didn't do as well as we could have done. Some of us have indeed woken up, and 'reconnected,' but others still live in denial of who they truly are – an aspect of the Divine. I think that others, in different star systems, did far, far worse than us here on Earth, and as a civilization they are still completely disconnected from that Divine spark within. They are focused on power, on survival at all costs, on possession and manipulation.

So, just as there are differences between human beings as to the levels of consciousness attained, so too can this be seen among our star brothers and sisters. Therefore what I am suggesting is that there are intelligent beings in other star systems, but that essentially we are all from the *same source*. These other beings may have different bodies than ours because bodies are defined by one's environment. Indeed some may not have bodies at all and they just exist as energy, as we are, at our source.

So where do the Starchildren fit in? I believe that Starchildren are those whose original seeding (from the Divine) initially came not to Earth but to one of the more highly evolved star systems.

Instead of reaching an enlightened state, and then returning to the Creator, they may have volunteered to assist other civilizations, who were not doing so well, to reach higher states of evolution. At some point – after perhaps having many series of lifetimes in other star systems – they incarnated as souls on Earth to bring their light here. Not just for one lifetime, but for a series of life-and-death cycles.

I do appreciate that this sounds crazy, but remember that I am writing this chapter because this is an issue which *many* (completely sane and functional) people come to see me about. I would say the vast majority of my clients are 'Starchildren' even though they may not actually be aware of it – although actually, many appear to have figured it out for themselves and will talk about it quite candidly. I would like to make it clear that if I suspect a client is a Starchild, I do *not* impart this information to them, *unless* they are truly suffering and struggling in life.

When required, I ask them the questions detailed in the questionnaire. They very often answer 'YES' to *every* question. They say, 'Yes! This is exactly how I feel and how I have always felt, right from being a child!' When I gently try to explain my Starchild theory to them, very often they have a huge physical reaction and many immediately burst into tears in recognition of the truth which resides deep within their souls. Other clients stare at me and say that, as crazy as it all sounds (and I do of course acknowledge that it sounds crazy), they kind of knew it was something like this all along but didn't understand it completely, or they were scared to admit this truth to themselves. When I tell them that it is the same for me, that I feel the same way they do and have always done so, for the first time in their life they feel truly understood, accepted and acknowledged. Most of all, they feel able to be themselves, without having to *pretend* anymore. They don't need to explain themselves, because they are already understood.

When we carry out the shamanic journey processes and I

guide the clients to trace their ancestry, many report being as ancient as the stars themselves and of having thousands of lifetimes in other dimensions. Many also have memories of being around in the time of Atlantis, a civilization which is believed to have existed many thousands of years ago here on Earth.

When clients attain this level of understanding, it does not necessarily make life any *easier* for them – they will still struggle with the things they struggled with before. But great benefit can be found in knowing that *there is nothing actually wrong with them.* They are not different because they are not good enough in some way, or because they don't try hard enough, or are not simply likeable; they are just *different. That is all.* They have a higher vibratory rate and a higher level of consciousness than the vast majority of people, therefore they will not *resonate* (be in easy relationship) with the vast majority of people. Because of this they will naturally, whether they like it or not, be treated differently – or even with suspicion. This is because the majority of people *sense* there is something different about them, but cannot put their finger on it; therefore, this makes them uncomfortable.

Whether you like the idea or not, my sense is that at some point in the near future, it will become clear that ET races do visit Earth, and have done so throughout history. I was interested to hear that the Vatican recently confirmed that it was 'permissible' for us to believe in extraterrestrial life – and who knows what the Church authorities know? The Church itself has hugely supported the science of astronomy since the 18th century. There are Vatican Observatories in the Pope's summer residence in Italy, and also at Mount Graham in Arizona, which is run in partnership with the University of Arizona. The Vatican Observatory is, according to Wikipedia, 'the oldest astronomical research institute in the world.' So we now have permission to believe – right from the top! I also read an article on the internet which alleged that MIT – the Massachusetts Institute of Technology, a private research university in the United States devoted to science and technology – actually held a five-day conference devoted to the subject of alien abduction, so maybe all this ET stuff is not as nuts as you think!

An image came to mind the other day regarding space travel and the huge distances involved. The image was of a standard garden hosepipe, unrolled so it lies straight. Imagine that one end is 'A' and the other end 'B.' Assume that each millimeter in between the two points A and B is a year in time, or even a light year (which is only 5.87 trillion miles apparently). So there are many, many years or miles between points A and B, *if* the hose is laid out straight. But, if you picked up end A and then end B and brought those ends together, then the two points would be very close indeed. Like the bendy hosepipe, I believe ET races have technology which can similarly bend time, to bring the points A and B in space closer together, and to create portals and doorways in time.

The question is: If we accept that Starchildren exist, why do they come to Earth? And the answer to that is… I am not completely sure. (I didn't ever say I had all the answers!) What I have noticed more recently, however, is that many appear to have an angelic lineage and angelic qualities. My sense is that Starchildren have either signed up to have a life cycle here on Earth, or they have been required to come here for some reason. *Only*, I feel, when those lifetimes come to an end, can they return 'home.'

Sadly, many Starchildren feel suicidal due to the intense problems that arise for them simply trying to exist here. Imagine, if you will, how an angel would feel, living here on Earth, trying to pretend to feel 'normal' and fit in, when inside they feel anything but. Suicide, however, is not an option, *at all*, as we will just find ourselves back here again in a new and more difficult lifetime.

I think Starchildren are here to help in some way, to bring a higher energetic vibration to Earth, to bring in light and wisdom and a *remembrance of Heaven to Earth*. Remember, we are now in the year 2012, deemed by some to be the end of the world as we know it (more information is provided on this later in the book). It doesn't take much intelligence to see that we are in deep trouble and cannot carry on the way we have been doing. My sense is that the Starchildren have come to help us through what may be the most important time period in the history of the Earth. My sense is we are going to need all the help we can get over the next few years and therefore the new children currently being born are indeed of a much higher vibration and intelligence.

You may think that such people are few and far between, but believe me, there are a lot of them around. Some clients are very aware of why they are coming to see me. I had a new client, a lady in her sixties, booked in to see me a couple of days ago. As normal, before she arrived I carried out a card reading for her, as this helps me to know what I need to focus on during her healing session. I use a beautiful set of cards called OSHO Zen Tarot. The first card that flew out of the pack was the 'Existence' card. The picture on the card shows a woman sitting in a large leaf on Earth looking up into the stars, so I knew exactly why this lady was coming to see me.

When she walked in and commented on how still and light the energy was in the house, I knew the cards were right. I also knew that I didn't need to beat around the bush with this lady – she knew exactly who she was, so there was no need for me to tread carefully or for small talk. As she sipped her tea I smiled at her and came straight out with it. 'You aren't from here, are you?' I said gently.

'No, I'm not,' she replied, smiling in relief at having found someone who could understand her. 'And I can tell you, I don't like it here *at all* and I can't wait to go home. Every day I wake up annoyed to find that I'm still here, that I still have to *pretend*. I'm quite angry actually; because I'm pretty sure I didn't come here out of my own free will. I'm angry at God for sending me here. In fact I've really fallen out with Him over it. But having said that, I have been pretty lazy really and I know I haven't done what I came here to do – which is why I've come to see you. While I'm here on Earth I guess I might as well get on with it!'

Not only are there many Starchildren already here, but also the percentage rate of them coming through is ever increasing with each new generation. I believe that there is a correlation between Starchildren and conditions such as autism. My sense is that these special children have come to be *our* teachers, to show us the ways of love, ways of being beyond materialism, and to usher in a bright new world of peace and harmony.

Interestingly, in this regard I have just had a look at prevalence trends for autism on the internet and found a posting of a report from the California Department of Developmental Services stating that in the four years between December 1998 and 2002, cases of autism nearly doubled, from 10,360 to 20,377. Autism used to be a rare disorder appearing in as few as 1 in 10,000 births. Food for thought perhaps?

So, how does it feel to be a Starchild? I can tell you from direct experience: it's not easy. There lies within us a terrible homesickness, a homesickness which defies explanation. Many people affected are in happy relationships, with lovely children; they enjoy good jobs / successful careers or businesses, own nice homes, and are financially secure. They often have everything that one would wish for, but they are besieged by a kind of depression, a yearning for another place. Many feel like outsiders: looking just like everyone else, yet feeling so different on the inside. Imagine being so sensitive that you find ordinary existence unbelievably challenging. The biggest problem is that of heightened awareness, which can often make Starchildren feel overwhelmed and overloaded with information. In short, this makes life very difficult for the individual. They tend to feel out of place *whatever environment they are in*. Of course this makes personal relationships very difficult. Feeling misunderstood at a core level does not make for an easy relationship!

If you feel you may be a Starchild and you are feeling very isolated and sad, fear not. There are many people who feel just the way you feel, all living normal lives, but feeling just as isolated. You can find them – you will know them when you see them – and you can become friends, because you will instantly have a feeling of resonance, of same-ness.

Many Starchildren tell me that they just want to feel 'normal.' The very best suggestion I have for them and for you is: *Don't even bother trying.* You are not 'normal' and you will never be 'normal.' And please, I am using the word 'normal' here to suggest being like everyone else. Having said that, you are not *abnormal* either; you are just you, and it is much better for you to just accept and love yourself. Please believe me when I say that there is nothing wrong with you; you are just vibrating at a higher rate and you probably have a higher level of consciousness than the majority of the population. I am not saying that you are better or worse than others; you are just you, *perfect* as you are. There is no need to try to change yourself or to mimic others; just be you. Don't hide your special light away – the Earth needs it. Similarly, don't feel pressured to 'Save the World'! Just find joy in your own life, just save yourself and be as happy as you can be, and let your light shine. Just be content with being.

It also helps to do work you enjoy and which is in alignment with who you are. Please bear in mind that it *doesn't have to be something 'spiritual.'* You don't have to give up your job and go and sit on top of a mountain, and you don't need to become a healer – just having your energy here on Earth *is enough*, so simply focus on finding work you love.

Most of all, do your best to enjoy every moment of being on this beautiful planet, this *jewel* of the Universe. Every day is precious, and the Earth needs you now, more than ever.

I am aware that many of you will have found the subject of this chapter challenging, to say the least. But I know the extent of the suffering which all Starchildren go through, and I see the huge grief and pain which resides in such people and the huge desire to end their life because of the difficulties they encounter simply existing from day to day. Therefore I made the decision to include this chapter, despite any potential ridicule which may result from it, with the view that even if the information provided here helps just one person, it will be well worth it.

Due to the fact that isolation is the main problem experienced by Starchildren (even though they may have many friends), many clients have suggested I should start up a forum where Starchildren can get together, so they can make friends and remember they are not alone in the world. Therefore I have set up a Yahoo Group specifically for this purpose. If you would like to join this email group – providing you have answered 'YES' to the majority of questions in the questionnaire – please send me an email headed 'Starchild' and I will add you to the list. My contact details are at the back of this book.

3. Why Am I Here?

Memories 3.1

I lie in bed, reading yet another 'spiritual' book, which is what I do every evening after returning home from work. In fact the pile of books at my bedside is so big, I have to climb over it. I am not reading for pleasure; *I am searching for clues.* I am pretty sure that I will be able to figure out what I am supposed to be doing with my life. I know it is something specific, but quite different from the norm, and it is definitely *not* being a pensions consultant for a bank! That much I do know for sure. But what is it? What could it be? Every book leads me down a rabbit hole, and every book leads me to at least three more books. How will I ever read them all? *I will not be happy until I find what it is I am meant to be doing!*

I have been doing this for years now, yet I am still no further forward. It feels like I am being pushed by some invisible hand to keep searching, to not rest until I know. My eyes start to droop. It is very late now. I try to keep reading on, but I can't concentrate anymore. I throw the book down onto the pile in frustration. Another day wasted. Another day not doing what I am meant to be doing.

Practice Notes 3.2

'I need to know what my purpose is, so I can get on and do it,' my client tells me. 'I've been searching for years, but I cannot find it. I've tried many things. I worked in TV, I had my own jewelry business for a while, then I worked in fashion, which I enjoyed for a bit then got bored of, then I traveled for a couple of years, then I went back to TV but it still wasn't right. So I got a job in PR, but it was really bitchy and not at all what I thought it would be like, so I left there. Then I decided I would be an actress, but that didn't go so well, so I went into writing, thought about journalism for a while. But I think I suffered from writers' block, although some of my stuff was pretty good, even if I say so myself. After that, I decided to study book-keeping but it was really boring so I stopped that. I'm so frustrated.

'Can you tell me what my purpose is? I'm so fed up with searching. I just want someone to tell me what it is. A psychic told me I would be a garden designer but I don't really like gardening, or being outside, or getting dirty. But do you think she's right? Should I give it a go perhaps? Do a course? What do you think? It's making me really miserable, all this. I just can't relax. I'm constantly looking for something – searching, I guess. It's driving my parents mad! They can't understand why I keep having all these jobs. What do you think? Could you ask my spirit guides what it is, please? They will know, won't they? Won't they? I just want to get on with it. I've searched so hard.'

* * *

Another client looks at me earnestly. 'In the last few years I guess you could say I've been on a spiritual journey. I've studied Reiki and I love that, and I love reading all the books. I've decided now that I want to be spiritual. You're so lucky! You know what it is you were meant to do! I wish I could be like you. Perhaps I should do what you're doing? What do you think about that?

'What am I doing now, you ask? I work in a bakery. That isn't very spiritual, is it? Making buns! No, I definitely need to leave my job and do something *spiritual*. Just can't figure out what though. Or do you think I should just concentrate on becoming enlightened? How long will that take? It takes a while, doesn't it? I really want to find out what it is that I came here to do; can you understand that? Because then I can be happy, and everything will be perfect. Everything will be easy then, won't it? And I will be happy. I can't wait! And it's important, isn't it, to do something spiritual?

'I've read about all this 2012 stuff, about all the changes that will be coming. It's not long now, is it? I'd better hurry up and find my thing, hadn't I? I'm getting so frustrated! What am I doing... making cakes when I should be saving the world in some way! It's terrible, isn't it? I mean I quite enjoy my job, but it's not going to save the world, is it?'

Notes 3.3

I felt quite embarrassed to write the Memories section of this chapter! But I can't deny that I did it. Looking back, I think I have been searching all my life if I am honest, but the search became almost frantic for about ten or so years. I let everything go, pretty much – exercise, housework, diet, socializing – all in an effort to find what it was that I was meant to be doing! If there was a way to go about finding one's purpose, I probably did the *opposite* of that. I made the biggest mistakes I could have made when it comes to this topic. I fell into the largest trap, which is that of looking *outside* of myself for what resides *inside* and trying to figure it out *logically*.

A spiritual search is governed by the ego mind, which does not have the answers. The body, the heart, has all the answers, so instead of searching we need to be quiet enough to hear the song of our heart. I went about it the wrong way, both in my approach and in my understanding of what our purpose is. I think I thought that God had a secret note on a big board in Heaven that said, 'Dawn Paul is meant to do X' – and all I had to do was search around hard enough to know what was written on that secret piece of paper. What I absolutely failed to realize is that a) there was no secret note, and b) even if there was a secret note, God would *not* have wanted me to use all my precious Earth time searching for my purpose while neglecting myself and my home at the same time! Yet I didn't want to think about all of that. I was on a mission, you see, and I was determined to succeed in it. Oh, how foolish I was!

Many clients come to me asking what their purpose is in life.

Some are as tormented by it as I was. Or, as a result of the healing work we do together, clients are opened up to the spiritual realms and then they decide they want to give up their jobs and 'be spiritual.'

What I failed to see back then is that we *are* spiritual, *all* the time! We *are* spirits having a human experience. It doesn't matter really, what we do for a living; it is a matter of *how we live*. We can work in industry or on the Stock Exchange and still bring in light to our roles and everyone we come into contact with. If we make cakes in a bakery, we can hold light within ourselves and put love into the cake mixture! Dr Masaru Emoto shows us in his marvelous book, *The Hidden Messages in Water*, that water can react to intent, so why not put the intent of love into a cake mixture? Why not smile to all the customers and *be* joy while you are serving them their cakes? Why not just *be* love, whatever it is that you are doing work-wise?

If I had succeeded in my searching around in Heaven for that secret piece of paper, I would have found two words on it: 'FIND JOY.' That is all. I am completely convinced, through all my years on my own journey and in my experiences with others on their journeys, that this is all the Divine wishes for us. To find *whatever* it is that brings us joy and bliss and take it back to Him when we are done here. Whether that is origami, train spotting, oil painting, cake making, or being a captain of industry, a fund manager, or a spiritual guru… as long as it brings us joy, that is good enough for Him. And trust me, this has been quite a painful realization for me!

If I repeat this realization to clients, they frown and say, 'Well, it's alright for *you* – you're doing something spiritual! What about me? What I am doing isn't going to save the world, is it?'

I then tell them that if I die now and go to Heaven this is quite likely the conversation which will ensue:

God will ask: 'What have you done, child of mine?'

I reply, 'I have healed fifty thousand people, Lord!'

'I asked, what have *you* done, child?'

'And I answered that question. I have spent my life healing others, and I have healed fifty thousand people!'

'I asked, what have *you done*? What are you bringing me? Where is your joy, your bliss? What have you created? What have you loved to do?'

'Well, I didn't have any time to have any fun or be creative because I've been busy healing fifty thousand people!'

'Not good enough – try again!'

And I will be sent back down to Earth to do things differently in the next lifetime!

So it is not what you do; it is *how* you do it, and how aligned you are to joy while doing it.

Remember, we are on a journey, and that journey is not fixed. The quality of the journey affects the eventual destination – because it is a moveable feast, if you like. We should not label ourselves: 'I am a shamanic healer.' 'I am a doctor.' 'I am a baker.' Yes, you may be those things now, but to define yourself by your role makes it harder for the Divine to guide you towards finding your bliss.

Additionally, do not make the mistake of thinking that working in a 'spiritual' field will be easy, or even that it is necessary at all. I see many clients who have been sexually abused, and they say to me, 'As soon as I'm better, I'm going to train as a therapist and specialize in sexual abuse, to give something back.' Or someone who has suffered a disease such as cancer will want to counsel people in similarly bad health. But this is not necessary! For example, if you have suffered sexual abuse, and healed the effects of it, then you should do whatever it is that would bring you *joy*. If you can *truly*, hand on heart, say that counseling people with a similar history to you would bring you joy, then go right ahead; but otherwise, steer clear and move on.

I remember seeing a client once who told me that after

working with me, she now felt so much better that she had decided to devote all her spare time to acting as a support person to families of people suffering from multiple sclerosis, because her own mother had suffered from this debilitating disease. This client was a lovely lady, who had experienced a highly traumatic childhood, and she was doing her best to come out the other side. She looked me straight in the eye as she told me that she could not wait to start her training, she was so looking forward to being of service, and she absolutely knew that this was what she wanted to do.

I asked her, 'Do you think it will bring you joy?'

'Oh yes!' she exclaimed. 'Absolutely.'

And then I shocked her and said, 'No.'

Her face fell. She looked like she was about to burst into tears. She spent some time going on about how she really, really wanted to do this and how she knew it was the right thing for her to do. I stayed quiet. After a while she became subdued. I told her that she should only offer her assistance to these people if she could say, hand on heart, that her only motivation was to be of service to them and their relatives with MS. I told her that if she was seeking to *gain* something via this act of 'service,' then it was not a pure intention and it was actually quite selfish to utilize suffering people for her own ends.

After a while she started to cry and nod her head. She told me that she wanted to offer her services in this way so that she could start to feel good about *herself* and to effectively pull a blanket over her guilt concerning some of her past actions. She thought that offering her services would help *her* to develop some much-needed self-esteem. I gently explained that she needed to heal her guilt and develop her self-esteem and leave the family support role to someone who had clearer intentions.

I asked her whether this role would have really felt like joyful service to her, and she told me that it would not have done, and she would have struggled with it, if the truth were told, as it would have brought back a lot of unpleasant memories about her past. I asked her what would be joyful to her and she said that she loved to dance and would like to take classes. This action was more in integrity with who she was and was a much better use of her time. I would like to point out that I do not normally offer such strong opinions to clients, but when she left my house she was so light and free it was a joy to see!

I am not saying that we should not help those less fortunate than ourselves; what I am saying is that we should not attempt to heal *ourselves* through our clients or people who need our unconditional support and selfless giving. If you are considering going into one of the healing professions, be very honest with yourself and ask, 'Why?'

Over the years I have seen many clients, in particular Starchildren, put themselves under tremendous pressure to 'Save the World.' We cannot save the world; we can only save ourselves, by aligning ourselves with love, peace and happiness. Having said that, the world is a reflection of us, so if we are love and peace, then in a way we are saving the world! Not being able to save the world comes as quite a harsh realization to many people, including myself. But unless saving the world is our destiny – in which case it will all happen naturally – then we are going to cause ourselves a huge amount of stress and frustration in the long run. And please, do not underestimate the wonderful effect you would have on the world if you were to reside in inner peace and harmony.

It is said that when one reaches enlightenment, all one needs to do is to sit next to someone in order to positively affect them. However, we can still affect others positively without being enlightened. Try it for yourself – if you are coming home from work on the train, close your eyes and meditate. Align yourself with peace and harmony and radiate love out from the center of your being. Sense how everyone in the carriage (maybe even everyone on the train!) is affected by this. When I do this, if there is a lot of chatter, unrest and agitation, I notice that gradually the noise levels die down, people turn off their mobile phones, put down their books and newspapers, and more often than not within a few minutes either everyone has nodded off to sleep, or they are just sitting peacefully looking out of the window at the passing scenery. We are powerful beings, and we can heal in many, many ways.

I would also like to refer to the assumption that working as a healer in some way is 'easy.' I can only speak of my experiences, although I know friends that work in the same or similar fields would agree with me, when I say that working as a healer is probably the hardest thing I have ever done in my life. Not necessarily in respect of dealing with clients, which has probably been the easiest aspect, but I can tell you that I have been pushed more than I ever dreamt possible. In fact when I felt like I had been squashed against the wall of my outermost limits, and in no way could go a millimeter further, spirit pushed me about another 50 miles!

I have faced huge challenges, in business, in romantic relationships, in personal relationships, on my spiritual path, in my family life, and in life in general. Every time I thought I had a grasp of my work, my life, and what it was all about, everything would change and I would be forced into new and deeper understandings. There have been times when I wished with every cell of my being that I had never left the bank! I have been through hell and back and out the other side, and it has been exhausting. So think about this, if you are expecting an easy ride! Do I regret following this path? No, not at all. If I had known at the outset what it would entail, would I have had the guts to go for it? No... I would have run a mile.

So, enough about the do not's – what about the do's? What would I have done differently regarding trying to find my purpose? If I had to do it over again, I think I would have tried to feel more, and think less. I was continually trying to use logic and reason to work out my purpose, but these things need to be *felt*. I would have accepted while I was working at the bank that although I knew ultimately that was not the work I was put on Earth to do, I would enjoy each precious day I was there and not allow myself to be miserable. I would have tried to bring light to the situation I was in, and accept *what was*, trusting that when it was the time for me to know my purpose, the Divine would reveal it to me in some way. And I would have had much more chance of hearing that Divine call if I was well balanced, healthy, and looking after myself properly.

I should have also liked to have been calm and centered enough to use my free time to perhaps be creative in some way, to trust my intuition more, and most importantly, to go inside and meditate and allow my Higher Self to guide me. If I had been less preoccupied with my search I would have perhaps been more self-aware and been more observant of the messages around me. Because in retrospect, I can see now that the Universe *was* giving me messages, *all* the time. I was just too caught up, confused and frustrated to see them. The Universe will try and assist you – honestly! You just have to be grounded and centered enough to take notice and be observant.

Recently I was told that I was meant to be doing something as well as my shamanic healing. Remembering my past mistakes and vowing not to repeat them (a sure sign of madness!) I simply prayed to God. I asked Him, 'If I am meant to be doing something else, something on top of my shamanic healing work, please show me what it is *very clearly* and more than once, so I really get it.' In my head I thought that perhaps it was something like studying nutrition, or bodywork – something associated with my healing work. I was very shocked that over the course of the very next day *and the next four consecutive days*, quite unintentionally I ended up in artists' studios. Five of them! What a sign that was! They don't come much clearer than that! So, my first recommendation for you is to *ask*, not search. Pray to your God, your guides, or your Higher Self, and ask to be shown very clearly what your purpose is, and to remain very observant afterwards.

I would also suggest taking a good, hard, long look at yourself and what you *do*. *Yes*, I worked for a bank as a corporate pensions consultant, but what did I *actually* spend most of my time doing? When I look at my daily experiences in retrospect, it becomes very clear. I would invariably find myself in the Ladies' Room, when one of the other office workers would come in, in tears for some reason, and I would spend time helping and talking to them. When I went out to see corporate clients, many company employees would come and see me in my pensions 'surgery' (as we called it), and ask me questions about their pension benefits for about two minutes and then ask for my help in their personal life. And when I look right back, to being just age five at my infant school, I can remember my teacher telling me all about her problems! And at junior school they used to nickname me 'Marjorie' after a famous agony aunt, Marjorie Proops. People have *always* come to me with their problems or questions. Always.

So, ask yourself, what is it that you have always *done*? There will be some clues for you here. Maybe you have always drawn, or written or been able to sort out people's business problems, or loved looking at architecture? Maybe you have always been passionate about animals, the environment, or food? Or maybe your mind has always been on travel, or on how you can make your home more attractive? You will find clues in your *passions*. I have always been passionate about truth, about seeking answers to life's questions, and about trying to help people as best I can.

A few more questions that may help you:

- What do you become completely absorbed in? What things do you do that cause time to fly?
- What fires you up – what do you love to talk about?

- Conversely, what drives you mad? For example, if badly run businesses drive you crazy then maybe you are destined to become a business consultant. If badly designed premises drive you crazy, then maybe you need to look at architecture, or interior design.
- Are you an indoor, or an outdoor person? Big clues can be found here!
- If you won £10 million today, what would you do tomorrow and the day after?
- What would you do for free?
- What things did you enjoy as a child?
- What is your idea of fun?
- Imagine waking up in the morning; how would you ideally like the rest of your day to be?
- Who do you admire? What do they do?
- What do you find easy that other people seem to struggle over?
- What subjects did you look forward to at school?
- What did you want to do before someone told you to follow the family tradition, or to 'be responsible'?
- What do you like to do in your free time?
- If you could do *anything*, what would it be? Remember, nothing is impossible.

I remember once seeing a man who had a very good job in the film industry. Many people would have loved his job. During a soul retrieval session, I brought him back a gift of a quill (pen). He burst into tears and just could not stop. Eventually he told me that he had always wanted to be a writer. He was passionate about it. One day, when he was young and at school he went to see a careers advisor. He told the careers advisor that he wanted to be a writer, and writing was his greatest passion. The careers adviser told him that this type of career would not be an option for him, as his test results had shown that he was 3% outside the margins of an acceptable score and therefore he would not be able to follow his dreams. (What a ridiculous thing to tell a child!) So that was it: his dreams were crushed and he *never* wrote another word! Even as a middle-aged man, he had believed in the words of the careers advisor and failed to follow his dream.

Instead of looking at it so negatively, he could have said, 'Well, I'm 97% of the way there. I will organize extra tuition for myself and prove this man wrong!' Or he might have worked out that passion would always be more powerful than skill. But we are so negatively aligned that we often just give up on our dreams without a fight. What was *your* dream? What if it *is* possible, after all? Never give up on your dreams.

Finally, I would suggest that you do not look for your purpose, but simply allow it to come to you. It will find you; be sure of that.

4. Life Can Be Chicken **** or Chicken Salad

Memories 4.1

I am propelled out of a deep, dreamless sleep by the sound of my bedroom door opening. This morning, the sound sends vicious needles of white-hot pain spiking through my head. Squinting briefly with one eye, I make out the outline of my brother standing in the bright light of the doorway.

'Urggh!' he exclaims. 'It stinks in here.'

I groan and mumble through a foul-feeling mouth and tell him to go away. I am lying on my right side, facing him. He asks me what time I arrived home from the club the night before and I don't answer – mainly because I have no idea myself and also because I think it is none of his business. I vaguely remember going to someone's house after the nightclub closed and I remember that there was a drinking competition and I won, again, but that is all. I realize I actually can't remember how I got home. I start to feel annoyed at his questioning; he is my kid brother, after all – what does he know? He doesn't understand how I feel or what I am going through! All I want is to be left *alone*, by everybody, *forever*. Is that too much to ask?

I mumble again for him to go away. He starts to lecture me; he goes on and on… how worried my parents are about me and why am I ruining my life? *My life is already ruined – doesn't he understand that?* Anger and intense annoyance rise up within me, and I raise my head up off the pillow so I can shout at him. As I start to do this, something warm and gloopy stretches out between my face and the pillow. Shocked, I bring the side of my face back down into the mushiness, so that he does not see it.

'Just leave me alone,' I croak weakly.

'It's *your* life,' he mutters as he turns and leaves; then as a sign of his annoyance he slams the door hard into the frame, which sends further splinters of light searing through my head.

As soon as I hear him stomp down the stairs, I cautiously start to raise my head off the pillow. The higher I raise my head, the colder the goo on my face feels. I can't work out what it is, but it feels horrible. Now that I am a little more awake, I realize that the right side of my face is also stinging. Cautiously, I manage to sit up, and the room tilts and glides unsteadily around me like oil on the surface of water – I can't hold on to it, can't focus on anything. Nervously, I wipe at the side of my face, and I feel soft squishy lumps come away onto my hand, as if my face itself is melting. I stare at this for a while in the half light, and then the chilling realization hits me: I have vomited in my sleep.

Fear grips me as I realize that I could have easily choked and died in my sleep and known nothing about it. I am 19, and I could have easily died last night. My brother or my parents could have walked into a very different scene this morning – what would that have done to them? How would they have coped? Perhaps the only thing that has saved me is the fact that I fell asleep – or more accurately lapsed into unconsciousness – while lying *on my side*. The shock of the realization of what could have happened makes me tremble. Maybe I will stop drinking now.

Practice Notes 4.2

Molly is in her late sixties. She is attending her first appointment with me, so I ask her to tell me why she is here. She smiles and tells me that she has written everything down and that her notes are in her handbag, which she starts to rummage around in. Many clients do this, as it is easier for them to think about what they want to discuss in their own environment and write down a few bullet points. But I am stunned when, instead of pulling out a sheet of paper from her bag, she pulls out a whole ream of paper as thick as a telephone directory! My eyes open wide in surprise – I can't help it. Molly carries on chattering, something she has not stopped doing since she walked in.

'... I have told *sooooo* many people my story that in the end I thought I might as well write it *all down*. I can guarantee you, you will never in your life have heard such a story as mine! I know you doubt me, but I tell you, mine will beat them all, hands down! My life has been a *complete* disaster. It's so terrible and sad that no one has been able to help me! All the therapists I've been to see – and trust me, there have probably been *hundreds* over the years – have told me it's the worst story they have ever heard!'

Without stopping for breath, she starts to read the notes, line by line. They are intricately detailed, like a novel, and her story begins when she is just a few months old. I have to politely interrupt her and tell her I don't have time to hear her whole story, but I would like to know what it is she wants to work on overall. She looks annoyed at the interruption and continues to read.

I interrupt her again and tell her that we will be working towards getting her *out* of her story, not further into it, and that I would like her to put her notes away. I also tell her that no one can ever really 'heal' another person, that all I will be doing is facilitating and supporting her in *her* healing work. She looks even more annoyed and clutches the stack of paper to her chest and repeats again that I really must hear it *all*.

I know then, that she is lost. I will not be able to help her because she is too attached to her past, to her story, to her pain, so much so that she sees herself as some sort of celebrity as a result of it. Clearly, despite her pleas for assistance and healing, she has no intention of doing her own inner work, which is why she has failed to move forward in the past.

I eventually manage to get her to stop reading her notes and we get down to doing some work. As she leaves, I know I will never see her again. A few days later, she calls, provides a weak excuse, and cancels her next appointment.

* * *

Sabrina tells me that since her last session she is doing much better. Although it is clear that she has taken our work on board, she has not taken *any* action regarding moving forward. She tells me she feels unable to let go of the past, and that she constantly has her mother's hurtful comments playing over and over in her head which stop her going out and creating the life she wants for herself, which, given that she is in her late forties, is not a good place for her to be.

We start work and I take her on a guided shamanic journey, using the gentle rhythm of the rattle to help her to relax and fall into the space between wakefulness and sleep. As I take her deeper into the journey, I ask her to find a symbol of her past, of her emotional wounds.

'I see it as a great big heavy black backpack. It's weighing me down.'

'How does holding on to this baggage aid you?'

'It keeps me safe. It's a great excuse for me not to do the things that scare me; it stops me moving forward and therefore I am safe... safe and in my place.'

'Is this *your* place or the place your mother put you in?'

'God, yes, it's the place my mother put me in. It's not my place at all! I'm much better than this! I've held on to this baggage for so long, it's my whole identity. But... if I let it go, who will I be then? I'll disappear; there will be nothing left of me.'

(This is a very common place to arrive at when addressing a person's healing needs. They want to die to their old self, but fear that doing so will leave them without any identity at all. Therefore it is necessary to help the client to find their new, healed self, their future self, through further journeying. Once this new 'them' is known, they are able to step into it and embody it.)

Once Sabrina found her healed, reborn self, this helped her to build herself a new identity and rebuild her self-esteem. She tossed the backpack – the burden she had been carrying all her life – over a cliff without a moment's hesitation. She smiled, and told me she felt free and light – for the first time in her life.

Notes 4.3

'Life can be chicken **** or chicken salad.' I first heard this line in a movie and it has stuck with me ever since, because there is great truth and wisdom in it, even though it may be a little crude. It is a fact that we cannot control negative circumstances and situations which happen to us. But what we often overlook is that we *do* have the ability – and the power – to *choose* how we react to these events internally. Sadly, our usual reaction is to fail to recognize we have options and only see the negatives in the situation facing us and act accordingly.

This option to act differently, to try instead to see the positives in any given situation, is beautifully expressed in a well-known Zen story, which I will recount for you.

One day a monk is walking along peacefully when suddenly a tiger leaps at him and gives chase. The monk runs as fast as he can, but eventually he comes to the edge of a cliff and he has no choice but to jump over the edge. Miraculously, as he is falling, he manages to grab on to a vine. While dangling in mid-air he looks up to the cliff top and sees the tiger peering down at him. He looks down and sees a rocky ravine far below him. Then he looks at the vine he is holding on to and sees a mouse nibbling away at it. But then... what joy! He spots a juicy berry growing off the vine! He picks it with his spare hand and pops it into his mouth. Mmmmmmmmmm, it is delicious!

This monk shows us that he is utilizing his *choice* as to what he is aligning himself with, even in the direst of circumstances. He is also showing us that while the tiger is in the past and the ravine – and his imminent demise – in the future, he is only focused on and aware of the *present moment*, and in that moment, he chooses the most positive thought he can possibly have, which is to focus on the deliciousness of the berry.

If we are present and accept *what is* without judgment, always aim to find the positives in any given situation, and trust in the workings of the Divine no matter what faces us, then quite simply we cannot go wrong. These are the things that the various spiritual texts have been telling us to do for thousands of years. Of course, as with most spiritual requirements – in fact, as with most things in life – it sounds very easy, but *living it* is quite a challenge!

Let me give you a personal example. When I was 17, I received the devastating news that I would never be able to have children. This was a massive blow for me because being a mother is something I had wanted to do since I was about four. It was all I was interested in really and my entire upbringing had been focused on me growing up to be a loving wife and mother, to the extent that I had not been career focused at all. When the doctors told me that that life would now be an impossibility, I was heartbroken. My parents did not know what to do and I was left to deal with the news myself as in those days there was no counseling or support available. I really wish I had known the chicken quote back then, because unbeknown to me, I *did* have options available to me at the time – I just could not see them, nor did I realize I had a choice as to how to react to that news. I didn't even imagine there could be a chicken salad route!

What could this have looked like? Well, maybe I could have taken some time out to deal with the news and mourn the loss of the life I thought I would have, because obviously it is important to grieve – for a while. Then I could have reassessed the potential positive opportunities in the new life I was now being presented with, and decided on the best way forward. I could have gone back to studying, perhaps worked towards going to university (I didn't really even know what university was – I had a very sheltered life!), found a career I loved, and built a very different but good life for myself.

But of course I didn't do that and instead I went down the chicken **** route. I felt shattered (and had most definitely suffered soul loss – more on that later), like my whole life was over before it had even begun. I *chose* only to see the negatives, and instead I became lost in an alcoholic fug and worked all day and then in the evening and had only a few hours' sleep each night. I couldn't bear to be on my own and I couldn't bear to think – about anything. And I carried on drinking heavily until I was about 22. I was already in a difficult situation, *but I made things even worse.* Did going down that route actually make my situation any better? No, of course not – it just made things a whole lot worse.

Some people are chicken salad people – they will *accept* whatever challenge occurs in their life; they will deal with the challenge as best they can, call in the help they need, and do everything they can to move forward and try to remain positively focused.

On the other hand, people who take the chicken **** route are those who take the traumatic event (or the 'challenge' as I prefer to call it) and drown in it. They will use it as an excuse to make many more bad decisions, thus furthering their suffering in life, and further reinforcing their identity *as a victim.* Their situation will consume them and their every thought, and they will cling on to it for dear life, like a life raft in a stormy sea. The challenge then becomes their 'badge,' their identity. You can often recognize these people as they have a tendency to tell you their personal stories a mere few minutes after first meeting them. Been there, done that.

My question to you is: Which type of chicken do you go for, and which option do you think is the *best* one to take? Here are a few questions for you which should give you some valuable insights.

- What challenges have you had in your life? List them if necessary.
- How have you handled these challenges in the past? Using the salad approach, or the **** approach?
- If you used the **** approach, did this actually make things any better, or did it actually make things worse?
- If you had instead taken the chicken salad approach to life, where do you think you would be now?
- If you are continuing to take the chicken **** approach, what do you think the eventual outcome of this route will be? *Is that what you want?*
- What past trauma or difficult memory are you still holding on to and keeping alive?
- *Why* are you still holding on to it?
- *Who* would you be if you did let go of it?
- Is your identity caught up with your challenge/trauma – does it define who you are?
- How do you see yourself now, and how would you *like* to see yourself?
- How do you allow others to see you and how would you *like* others to see you?
- What would you need to let go of, in order to move forward?
- Are you achieving your absolutely *fullest* potential? If not, *why not*?

I know this is not particularly easy, but please, take some time to question the beliefs you have built your identity around. Look at yourself honestly in the mirror; look into your own eyes. Ask yourself, 'Who am I really, without my story? How do I want my life to be? Is anything actually, truly, preventing me from seeking happiness and a life I love?' Please also bear in mind that you can be a multi-millionaire and still see yourself as a failure and a victim! I have seen this many times with clients. Many wealthy people do not feel worthy of their success, and can even be afraid for their success to be seen.

What would happen if you imagined that all your issues and past and current problems were red helium-filled balloons... and you simply let go of them and let them float away? What would that feel like to you? Does thinking about letting go of the balloons feel good, or, like the lady mentioned in the Practice Notes, do you feel resistance to doing it? If so, *why*? Are you holding on to those balloons because there is a *gain* for you somewhere by holding on to them? Perhaps you want to punish someone, or make them take notice of you? Or do you crave pity and sympathy? Who are you *really* punishing by holding on to those balloons? Take time out here to do this exercise and really pin down what is keeping you stuck, because once you know what it is, you can address it and move forward.

It is normal to feel scared about letting go of an identity you have had for a long time – even if it is a negative one – but there is no need for you to suffer and be burdened with your past for the rest of your life! All that needs to happen is for you to create a vision of the new, positive, future 'you,' the not-only-healed-but-fulfilled you, so moving forward without all your stuff is not so scary.

It is important to remember that our *judgment* – about ourselves, our situation in life and about the things that have happened to us – is based on 'position and polarity.' In many spiritual traditions, including the Christian tradition, polarity in all things is acknowledged. For example, there is good and bad, male and female, high and low, light and darkness. In the shamanic tradition, we are advised to take the middle path, because this is where the magic happens. Non-judgment particularly runs through the Eastern Buddhist teachings.

An understanding of the importance of non-judgment is essential in life; rather than saying, 'X is good' or 'Y is bad,' it is better to not judge anything – it just 'IS.' After all, how many times have we had a 'bad' experience and many years later it has turned out to be a complete blessing? How different would our lives be if we stopped judging and instead said, 'Neither good, nor bad, just so'?

My life has certainly been very different to how I *expected* it to be, but I have learned so much and had such amazing experiences which I would not have had if I had just been 'married with kids.' The only decision we have to make, then, is what to align ourselves with in any given situation. As the Buddha said, 'All human problems arise from not accepting what *is*.'

One of my guides has an expression: 'Expectation is the mother of all disaster!' which is an excellent saying! I see so much expectation with clients:

'He was *supposed* to love me!' they wail.

Or, the most popular: 'My mother *should* have loved me!'

Well, your mother *didn't*, or *couldn't* love you for some reason! But – and please think about this carefully – does this really mean that there is anything wrong with you? No, it does not. So deal with it; deal with what *is*. So many people keep trying to change *what is* and it is futile, a complete waste of time!

Our pasts *do not* have to determine our future – not at all! In the shamanic world we have a saying: 'I am what I speak, not what I have spoken.' And that is so true. It means that I am who I say I am, in this moment. Yes, people are unloved as children; yes, people are sexually abused; this is sadly *what is*. But doesn't that person, who has had such a hard start in life, *deserve that the rest of their life is as great as it can be*? Don't we ALL deserve to have happy lives, regardless of anything else?

I have made big mistakes, huge ones, so I am certainly not attempting to be 'holier than thou.' But my hope is that you can learn by *my* mistakes and, if challenge strikes, then you will remember these words and know that you have a *choice*. Reaching for the gin bottle / drugs / pills / sex isn't going to make things better. Only *you* can make things better. *You have complete and total responsibility for the quality of your life.*

I often explain the benefits of being a chicken salad person to clients, and it is clear that although they say they get it, they don't *really* get it. They make comments like, 'I really tried hard at that happy salad thing you told me about. I did really well, then my husband got made redundant and I got really upset.'

To make it very clear, what follows is an example of the differences in *thinking* between a chicken **** person and a chicken salad person.

Chicken **** Alignment

1 Wake up in the morning, feeling a bit anxious perhaps due to a bad dream – *focus on the feeling of anxiety… is something bad going to happen today?*

2 Make your breakfast, burn the last piece of toast – *get really angry, throw burnt toast around kitchen, swear a lot, decide today is going to be a bad day.*

3 Get stuck in traffic, realize you are going to be late for an important meeting – *start getting very frustrated and angry, beep at a few bad drivers because it makes you feel better, bash steering wheel a few times, get very hot and sweaty.*

4 Meet up with your girlfriend at lunchtime, who tells you she has fallen in love with someone else and is leaving you – *go mad, shout at her, tell her you didn't care about her anyway and she is rubbish in bed. Stomp out of the restaurant, narrowly avoid getting hit by a bus. Give the driver the two-fingered salute.*

Chicken Salad Alignment

1 Wake up in the morning, feeling a bit anxious, perhaps due to a bad dream – *meditate on the feeling, see if you can apply the anxiety to anything at all. You can't. Center and ground yourself, visualize all heaviness disappearing down the plughole as you shower. Put on some uplifting and relaxing music while*

you make yourself a nice healthy breakfast. Remind yourself of your blessings and focus on a happy memory in order to shift your bad mood – and your brain chemistry.

2 Make your breakfast and burn the last piece of toast – *put the toast in the bin, open the door to let out the smell. Calmly figure that obviously you were just not meant to have toast today for some reason, and have cereal and fruit instead.*

3 Get stuck in traffic, realize you are going to be late for an important meeting – *stay calm and peaceful; after all, you cannot do anything about the traffic jam. Pull over and make some calls explaining the situation; get someone in the office to cover for you if possible. Practice staying in your center. Trust that everything is perfect – maybe your clients are in the same traffic jam and will be similarly delayed. Play your favorite music on your stereo. Clear your mind and breathe.*

4 Meet up with your girlfriend at lunchtime, who tells you she has fallen in love with someone else and is leaving you – *thank her for having the grace to tell you face to face. Calmly accept **what is**, and trust that everything is in Divine and perfect order. Understand that if this is happening, then clearly she is not the one for you and you are a step closer to finding the right girl. Thank her for all the happy times you have had together, and for all that you have learned from your relationship. Tell her you are glad that she has found true love and that you wish her every happiness. Give her a hug goodbye and part on good terms. Take a deep breath, trust, center yourself, and accept what is.*

Now this may seem like a bit of a tall order, but is it impossible? Ideally it is the way of living we should be aiming for. Chicken salad people usually address their own personal healing work, and have a great relationship with themselves, as they *self-source* their love and happiness. Therefore, any external relationship is icing on an already happy and whole cake. Having said that, of course you may feel sad at the ending of a relationship, but if you are whole and balanced as an individual, this sadness should not last for long. So, I hope you can see now that being a chicken salad person has nothing to do with events, but with how you *choose* to deal with them.

Joy and happiness are NOT brought to us by *things or circumstances*, such as lottery wins or handsome new boyfriends. They are *internal* states of being. For us to truly have love, peace, joy, happiness and security, we must generate these feelings from *within ourselves*. They are *chosen options*, decided in each moment, and we do not need to allow *anything* to move us away from our alignment with them. If situations arise which would normally see you going off the rails, **break your pattern**, and retrain your brain out of its pattern of negativity and drama. When faced with a challenge, simply say, 'Is that so?' *This is the way to finding inner peace.*

Contrary to popular thought, living in peace does not mean that you no longer have any problems; it means that you deal with your *challenges* differently. Many people look at the image of Buddha's face and say that they would love to have that level of peace and serenity. They – incorrectly – assume that because the Buddha is enlightened, he is no longer faced with challenges or trauma. But this is not the case at all! The Buddha may exist surrounded by chaos; however, *he does not allow himself to be shifted out of his internal alignment with peace and serenity by external events.* He is aware he has a choice and he chooses peace, love and serenity.

The first part of moving forward into joy is *consciously* monitoring your thoughts and moods. If you find they are leaning towards the negative then it is necessary to *consciously* 'reframe' your thoughts in order to alter your internal state and raise your vibration towards a joyful one. Our emotions are *not* meant to control us; we are meant to control them!

For example, if I wake up in the morning feeling down after a bad dream, I will work hard to *consciously* shift my emotional state by thinking of my happiest memory until I feel better. Similarly, if we have a negative thought, we can imagine erasing and rewinding the negative thought and recording a positive thought in its place, as if we have a video player in our head. Reframing is a very important tool on the healing path. We very easily get into habits of negative thinking and those thoughts go round and round in our heads – so we have to consciously stop them. This is hard work, but it can be done.

There are other reasons people fail to move forward in life. I learned about an interesting concept in my life-coaching training called 'The Upside Gain.' Many people hold on to their stuff because they *benefit* from their dysfunction in some way, and trust me, this can be very addictive indeed. Now you may be thinking, *How can anyone benefit from being in a bad situation?* But it is generally accepted in the psychological professions that if a person has a continued dysfunction, there is a *gain* lurking around somewhere. Dysfunction keeps us stuck. And stuck = *safe*. Dysfunction can also equal receiving lots of sympathy and attention. People consciously desire a new and shiny life, but unconsciously, they are terrified of it, because their whole identity is wrapped up in their dysfunction, in their old way of being. They end up in a kind of very uncomfortable and unpleasant place – which is actually a *comfort zone* to them because they *know that place so well*.

I think the usage of the term 'comfort zone' is widely misunderstood, as it implies that the zone one finds oneself in is pleasant – but this is not the case at all. I think a better term to describe this state would be a 'Known Zone.' Ever heard the saying, 'Better the devil you know'? Well, herein lies the root of the reason why so many people stay stuck in places they would really rather not be in.

Often, it takes some digging to uncover the reason a person fails to move forward or achieve their goals. I remember once working with a female client who was clinically obese. She had tried every diet going for years but she continued to gain weight. After a lot of prompting and digging on my part, we finally uncovered the reason why she found it impossible to lose weight. What was it, do you think? A slow metabolism? A fat gene? A thyroid problem? Lack of willpower? Or the fact that she hated having sex with her husband, who only fancied her when she was slim? Correct. If *that* issue could be resolved, then the lady would be able to lose weight, no problem. But boy, did it take a lot of work for her to figure that out!

I explain to clients that it is important to *really* get to the core of what is going on. If you imagine a target symbol, with the main issue such as weight loss being at the center, then before the weight loss can be addressed it is necessary to find out what the issues are in the circles around the bull's-eye. In this client's case, working from the outside ring towards the middle, the first ring is sorting out the sexual problems, the next ring is to address any lack of self-love issues, the third ring involves addressing actual diet and exercise issues, and then the goal of weight loss can be achieved – and more importantly – maintained.

A dear friend attaches the following quote – which I believe is from Carl Jung – at the end of all her emails: 'I am not what happened to me; I am what I choose to become.' Isn't it great? We are not our pasts; we CAN let the past go and decide who we are, what we would like to have in our lives, *and then we can go out and get those things or achieve those goals*. We can transform ourselves into the beautiful butterflies that we are meant to be and take flight. Are you ready to fly?

A few years ago I visited a National Trust property which had a butterfly sanctuary in its grounds. People were able to go into a humid greenhouse full of plants and butterflies, and stand there while the butterflies flew around them and often landed on them. While I was there I learned something very valuable which I had not fully comprehended before. I learned that a caterpillar in the cocoon does not simply *turn* into a butterfly, bit by bit. It does not start to sprout wings and antennae; instead, it is gradually dissolved until there is *nothing left of its original form* – until only a *liquid* remains! Its previous identity has to be *completely* destroyed, and *only* from that point on does the magic occur, does the butterfly – oh, so slowly – start to materialize. This is why the butterfly is such a deserving symbol of transformation, because it has been **totally** transformed from its previous identity.

And this is the process we have to undergo on our healing journey or spiritual path – whether our goal is to simply heal our past, or work towards achieving enlightenment. (More on that later.) Yes, it does take a certain amount of courage to go on a healing path – everything can change, and very often it *needs* to change – but you don't get to be the beautiful butterfly without going on the journey, and even though it may be arduous, of course it is worth it in the end!

Here are some important points to consider:

1 **You** will need to be willing *to shift and to change your life.*
2 You will also need a huge amount of willpower, as it takes significant effort to break habits and negative mindsets and patterns.
3 You will need to *take responsibility* for your past actions – this means no longer blaming anyone else for the place you now find yourself in. Recognize your part in any situation you find yourself in.
4 A decision needs to be made at some point whether you are going to seek assistance in your healing journey or not. I know of many people, including myself, who have thought, *I can deal with this; I don't need any help,* but a good healer or therapist can provide the mirror that we need to clearly see ourselves – plus they can challenge us to grow beyond our own image of ourselves.

5 Ask yourself whether you are gaining *in any way* from the situation you find yourself in.

6 Commit to invest in yourself and your healing. You may need to see more than one healer or therapist, and this can start to get expensive, but again, remember you are investing in you, *your future and your dreams*. The Universe will assist you in this where possible.

7 Be willing to step outside your comfort zone. KNOW that whenever you step outside your comfort zone (or your Known Zone), it *will* feel very unpleasant and feelings of anxiety will always arise – this is normal! I have seen so many clients take a few tentative steps out of their comfort zone, and the moment the unpleasant or anxious feelings start they scurry back into it and into their old ways of being and behaving. You may feel anxious, you may have butterflies in your tummy, things may be difficult and you may feel scared, insecure and unsure of yourself. Again, THIS IS NORMAL. It is simply your body's way of telling you that you have stepped outside your comfort zone; it just wishes to alert you to this fact, in case you were not already aware of it. Here is an example just to be clear. I live on a road which has a convenience store at the end of it (very useful, I must say!). Now, if I run out of milk or bread, I just grab my keys, go out the door, walk up the road, and get what I need without any problems at all. However, imagine that for some reason I hadn't left my house for three years. The action of popping up the road for some bread is then going to be a major issue, and there will be a huge feeling of anxiety as I take the journey. Not that there is anything *wrong* with going to the shop to get bread – there is nothing dangerous about it – but my body will create the anxiety because I am out of what is known and things are *different*.

My best advice is to just keep moving forward one day at a time – all you need to do is take baby steps in the right direction and you will get to where you want to be.

What sort of chicken will *you* have today?

5. The Energy Body and the Physical Body

Memories 5.1

I am seven years old, and lying on a hospital trolley. I am scared and have a terrible pain in my tummy. A man in a white coat is telling me how he is going to give me a scratch on my arm and that this will make me go to sleep. He says that when I wake up, something called my 'appendix' will be gone and so will all the pain. He makes the scratch and cold fizzy liquid goes into my arm. He starts to count, 'One, two, three, four, five, six…'

Suddenly I am wide awake, but unsure of where I am. I look around and notice that I appear to be hovering high in the corner of a big, pale green room full of big shiny things and bright lights. I am just below the ceiling, but I can't see anything of myself such as my hands or my feet. It is like I am nothing more than a pair of eyes!

I try to shout but I cannot make a sound and no one seems to notice me. I see doctors and nurses below me, all wearing green dresses and face masks, but they do not see me. Instead they appear to be very busy, working on a little body which is lying on a big table.

I try to get a better view of the body and recognize – with complete and absolute dispassion – that it is mine. It appears that I am on the big table, but I am not; I am here!

Suddenly, everyone below me starts to panic and rush around; they are all shouting at each other. I watch, interestedly, as they grab my body and roll it onto its side. I wonder – what on earth are they doing?

I am back in my bed on the ward, and have finally stopped being sick now. A tall doctor approaches my bed; he tells me that he is the doctor who performed my operation. I tell him that is good, as I have a question for him.

'Go ahead,' he says, nicely.

'Why did you tip me over?' I ask. The doctor's head jerks up from his papers and he looks at me with his mouth open.

* * *

It is the dead of night and I am lying – almost frozen to death – in a sleeping bag and a tiny tent 16,000 feet up the Holy Mountain Ausangate in Peru. My mouth is bone dry due to the lack of oxygen, but the water in my water bottle is frozen solid, like my body. I start to wonder in fact if I will make it through the night, and indeed, whether my efforts at even getting up here in the first place have been in vain.

Tomorrow, I am supposed to be undergoing an initiation, which will be in two parts. Firstly, I will be required to strip naked and stand beneath a glacial waterfall while a shaman beats me with a swatch of mountain reeds – this is intended to remove my old 'energy body.' Then I am to jump into the sacred Jaguar Lagoon, a *glacial lagoon*, and swim in it, in the hope that the spirit of the lagoon will gift me with a new, clean energy body. I feel like such a *coward*, but I know I won't be able to do it! I am terrified that the shock of the extremely cold water will cause me to have a heart attack. I whisper my apologies to the mountain spirit of Ausangate that I am so sorry, but I can't take the risk of that happening. I am not afraid of death – I just don't want to die tomorrow.

But then, softly, sensuously, a peace comes over me. I don't feel any warmer, but I feel safer, I feel held. Suddenly, a vision appears in my mind. I see myself swimming in the Jaguar Lagoon – but within a golden bubble of light. I see that the protective bubble is a gift from the Apu – the spirit of the mountain. There are no words but it seems to be telling me that it will protect me from the cold while I am in the freezing water. I then know I *have* to go into the lagoon, I have to go through with the initiation, and I have to trust the mountain spirits, for this is part of my journey.

* * *

Night falls quickly in the Amazon, and a wet chill oozes into the black air under the bright stars. The jungle is stilled – not a sound emerges from it – in contrast to the cacophony of sounds heard in the daytime. I am sitting cross-legged on a thin foam mattress by the river, with the contents of a large glass of bitter Ayahuasca – a powerful psychotropic vine – raging through my system.

Pandoro, the *Ayahuascero* – a Master of the Vine and of herbal medicine – kneels before me, staring at a place in front of my body, about a foot from my chest. He looks concerned. He roughly pulls open my coat and all the many layers I have underneath in an attempt to keep warm. He takes a few deep pulls on his pipe and blasts my bare chest with his fragrant smoke. He then squats on his haunches in front of me, and puts his hands on my head, as if he is initiating me. He prays with great fervor. I feel a whirring in the energy over my chest, and some sort of release. I am not sure what he is doing, but I trust him so I allow the process. My chest starts to feel lighter, freer.

The next day I ask my teacher what happened. He tells me that Pandoro saw an energetic *imprint* of lung disease in my energy field and removed it for me in order to prevent me from suffering lung disease in the future. I go to Pandoro and thank him profusely for his assistance and skill.

* * *

'How can I help you?' asks my osteopath, who is also a master of energy and martial arts.

'My head isn't on properly,' I say.

'Oh yes, I can see that,' he says smiling. 'Everything is energetically pulled over to the right.'

I am relieved that he has such amazing energetic vision. A doctor would have locked me up if I had said this. But my face feels pulled over to the right, and I keep feeling like I am going to topple over. My osteopath applies his ancient tai chi techniques and works hard on my energy field to bring it back over my head properly. The movements in his fingertips are infinitesimally small, yet I feel each subtle movement having an effect.

Finally, he steps back. 'How does that feel?'

I scrunch up my face. Everything feels back in the right place. I ask him what he saw in his inner vision when he worked in my energy field.

He tells me, 'I was shown a vision of you as a young Egyptian woman. You had been tortured and were nearly dead, so you were thrown into a deep pit. On the way down you cracked your head on the left side, which killed you instantly. It appears your body has decided it wants to have that memory and experience healed; hence it has made you very uncomfortable so you now address the matter.'

As I leave his office I catch sight of myself in the mirror as I leave. Nothing looks any different than it did before, but I sure do *feel* different!

* * *

I am lying on a massage couch, thinking how very lucky I am. My friend's boyfriend is studying to be an osteopath and has asked if I would be a case study for his massage practice. This is my third session with him and all I can say is that it is quite marvelous! He is very gifted and his strong hands work the stresses and strains out of my muscles, while the warm summer breeze wafts in through the open door. He turns my head to the right and works on the tense muscles in my neck.

Suddenly – BANG!!! It is as if fireworks have gone off in my head. I see myself as if from above on a medieval torture device, like a rack. Men surround me; torches light the dim, grim room. I am bound to the rack and in extreme agony as they plunge instrument after instrument into my belly, tearing away at my flesh.

As quickly as it came, the vision goes, but my body is inconsolable and wracked with sobs. I realize a deeply held imprint of torture which has been held in my energy field has been triggered by the touch of my masseur; he has not done anything wrong – I will try to tell him this, as soon as I can stop crying.

Practice Notes 5.2

Sara lies on the couch in front of me. I try to see her clearly but it is as if she exists within a dark cloud; even if I squint it's like she is barely there. She has told me she has a lump in her breast which is growing rapidly, and that she is scheduled for surgery.

I start to work on her and as I use my rattle to break up the heavy energy within her energy body, I freeze inside. This does not feel right at all. It feels like I am trying to shake a rattle in a vat of lumpy tar – even the sound of my rattle seems muffled. I can feel unusual undulations in her energy field which are so deep they have connected to her physical body – hence the manifestation of the breast lump. I know I am not meant to allow personal feelings into my work, but nevertheless I swallow down a lump of concern for this lovely young woman. Interestingly I notice that as if to mirror my concerns, the wind and rain outside are hammering forcefully upon the window, as if they are trying to get in.

I explore her energy field more deeply, and find similar dark masses all along the length of her spine, like viscous black pebbles. I adjust my state of consciousness and get on with the job in hand, focusing on clearing all of the heaviness from her field. It is hard work, but I make good progress. The spirit of the weather works with me; the more heavy energy we clear, the lighter the day becomes.

Eventually we finish. The rain has stopped now and it is bright and sunny outside. Afterwards, when she is back on the sofa, it is as if I can now see her properly; the black cloud has gone.

* * *

Nicky lies on the couch; she looks serene yet troubled. She has endured neck pain for over ten years after suffering whiplash sustained in a car accident and takes a huge amount of painkillers each day, which are causing her other problems. I am not a medical practitioner of course, but I am fairly sure that it is not usual for whiplash to still be causing problems ten years later.

I start to track her, to journey into her, in order to find what is really going on. The sound of the rattle changes my state and psychically I can see that there is some sort of long wooden pole, about the circumference of a lemon, going in through the back of her neck, on the diagonal, pushing out through the front of her throat, and extending out a couple of feet in front of her. I cannot see if there is a blade at the end of it, or if it is fashioned into a point. I realize that this is something that had killed her in a past life; the energy of it has become hardened, and has remained in her energy field all these years and is now causing her pain in the physical. My guess is that once the pole has carefully been removed, her 'whiplash' injury will disappear.

* * *

Keeley suffers with tremendous physical problems below her waist. She has been in continual pain for years and has had many operations on her bladder, bowels, womb and pelvic floor, all to no avail. I ask about her personal history. She tells me that her parents split up when she was 6 months old. At the age of one, she was given to her grandmother and an aunt as her mother couldn't look after her. At four, her mother took her back, as she had remarried.

Keeley tells me quietly that her mother's new husband sexually abused her, continuously. He told her it was quite normal but she must not tell anyone about it. She recounted how she used to float up out of her body while it was happening, as she could not bear to be 'in' it at the time the abuse was happening. Even though she was so young, she sensed what he was doing was wrong. At 15 she terminated a pregnancy, which may or may not have been her stepfather's child – she didn't know for sure as she had zero respect for her body and was sleeping around at the time. At 17 she tried to commit suicide.

A couple of years later she met a man and married him and had three children by him, all girls. He became domineering and violent, and she eventually left him after suffering many years of abuse. A few years later she met and married a kind man, but her eldest daughter never recovered from the breakup of the first marriage, and after many difficult years, she killed herself.

* * *

Zach is deeply relaxed on the couch. I use the sound of the rattle to change my perceptual state and ask to be shown the reason why Zach's ankles have both started to degenerate. This problem has defeated the medical profession for years and Zach fears he may be crippled forever. I have asked Zach about his life; he appears to be a massive procrastinator and for some reason he cannot seem to move forward in his life.

The moment I shift my perceptual state and look at Zach's ankles with my inner vision, I see that there is a complete break in energy, nerves, bones and blood vessels across each ankle. It is as if his feet do not exist. I see a flash of a past-life vision, and I see Zach as a soldier. I am not sure what type of soldier he is, or where he is from, but I do get the sense that he has been abandoned in enemy territory and that he is wounded. I then see the scene fast-forward and see him being captured by the enemy, and tortured. Both of his feet are cut off; he is in agony but he is not killed.

I have to journey to retrieve his energetic feet and then I use psychic surgery to reattach the muscles and ligaments, connect the nerves and blood supply, and heal the cuts in the bones. I then reconnect the meridians and allow vital life-force energy to flow to Zach's feet once more. He tells me that he can feel the changes, and his ankles now feel strong and his feet feel part of him again.

* * *

Hilary is different from many other clients I see, for her life seems blessed. Despite this fact, she tells me there has always been inside her a deep, painful sadness that at times is overwhelming. There is always a tear in her eyes, ready to spring up at the drop of a hat, yet there is no reason for it as her life is blessed.

I use the tone of my voice and the sound of my rattle to take her on a journey. I ask her body to show us what needs to be healed, what memory or emotion is at the source of all this sadness. Suddenly her breathing changes, her body stiffens and tears pour from her eyes. I ask her to communicate with me, to tell me what she is witnessing.

She tells me she sees herself as a man, an Indian chief. He is standing high upon a rocky hilltop looking down upon his village in the valley below, horrified at what he sees. Everything has been lost, destroyed; his people have been killed, all butchered to death. The bloody corpses of men, women and children are sprawled all around, tepees and shelters are on fire, everything is lost. And he was not there to help defend his community! He feels terrible! And I realize that this part of Hilary has been standing on the hilltop staring at this bloody scene for lifetimes, and that this is the source of her great sadness.

The chief will not rest until all the souls of his tribe – similarly trapped in the valley, frozen in time – are taken to the Light. Only then will he allow himself to rest in peace.

As he ascends to the Light, Hilary screams like an animal and contracts her body into a ball. I understand that the energetic imprint of this scene, this devastating sadness that has been with her for so long, is finally being released from Hilary's energy body.

Afterwards she lies there, limp, fluid, relaxed. She smiles and tells me she feels lighter, much more serene and free. At her next session she reports that she feels truly liberated, there are no more tears, and she can now fully enjoy all her blessings.

Notes 5.3

It is difficult to comprehend that we have more than one body, but we do. As well as a physical body, we also have an energy body, a mental body, an emotional body, and spiritual bodies. I do not mean that we have many different bodies as in different aspects of the self, but that we have different types of body over and around our physical form, fitting around us like sheaths, in layers of differing energetic vibration. The physical body, of course, is the one that we are all familiar with, and the only one that is made of matter, the only one that is solid. The rest are electromagnetic in form, so they are often referred to as 'subtle bodies.'

The easiest way to picture the energy body is to imagine a colored egg-shape of energy cocooning around a figure of a person, radiating out from them for about one meter. Within that cocoon are many layers of subtle bodies. It is not just humans who have energy bodies; pretty much everything has one – animals, trees, plants, crystals, rocks – and occasionally even man-made items can have an energy body.

The Q'ero Indians call the energy body the *poq'po*, which translates as 'bubble,' and this is a good way to visualize it. It can also be called an 'aura.' The late American psychic Edgar Cayce, who was known as the 'Sleeping Prophet,' routinely saw colorful auras around people without trying. There is an interesting story about him which is relevant to this chapter so I will share it with you.

One day, Edgar Cayce was in a large department store waiting for the elevator to arrive at his floor. When the doors opened, the elevator was reasonably full of people, but appeared to Edgar to have some sort of emptiness about it. He stalled stepping into the elevator, not quite knowing why, and then became distracted by someone walking close by, wearing a red sweater. The lift doors closed, without Edgar in it... and the lift immediately plummeted to the floor, killing all the occupants instantly. Afterwards Edgar realized what had startled him when the doors had opened – the elevator felt empty because none of the occupants had an aura, as this aura recedes when people are close to death. (Hence I always check that people have nice healthy auras when I get on airplanes!)

You may like to attempt to see your own energy body – have a go! You need to be very, very relaxed and not *try* to see it. It takes a certain softening of the gaze to be able to see in this way. Hold your hand up against something dark, relax your eyes, almost to the point of not focusing, and watch. I can often see a fuzzy glow around my hand and streams of white light, a little like smoke, shooting from my fingertips.

Varying esoteric groups have different names for the different energy bodies and there is a huge amount of information available if you want to learn about the specific layers. But for the purposes of this book and this particular chapter, all that is important for you to understand is that a) we have other, subtle bodies that surround the physical form, and b) importantly, it is the health of these bodies which directly affects the health of our physical body. Note please: just to restate that it is the health of the *energy* body that governs the state of our *physical* body, not the other way round.

It is generally accepted within shamanism that part of a shaman's job is to release disease from a person well *before* that disease manifests in that person's physical being, which is what Pandoro did for me when he removed the energetic imprint of lung disease from my energy field. A shaman understands that all disease is first created in the energy field and gradually tracks *towards* the physical body. This is why addressing our personal healing needs is so important – because the more clogged up our energy body is with toxic emotional debris, the more energy is required to keep that debris away from the physical body.

Conversely, it is also important to remove the energetic structure of disease from the body when trying to cure a person of a disease which has *already* manifested in the physical, to prevent that illness manifesting again. For example, if I had contracted a form of lung disease, I would have needed treatment to remove the disease from my physical body – my lungs – but in order to prevent the condition *recurring* I would also have needed to have the energetic structure or imprint/blueprint of the disease removed. I agree that this all sounds quite bizarre, perhaps because the energy body cannot be seen, but we have all heard of instances where people have suffered pain in limbs that have *already* been amputated. This is because the condition is still thriving – in their energy field!

In addition, it is important that the energy body is healthy and clean as it actually *feeds* the physical body with light energy, so having it all sludged up is bad news on both fronts. This is why many people with a lot of emotional baggage can be tired, unmotivated and depressed. Conversely, someone like the Dalai Lama, who is very spiritually advanced, has a huge, radiant energy field. Sadly, I have never had the honor of seeing him, but I have heard that he lights up the room and his presence is immense. This is a perfect example of the correlation between the state of the energy field and the state of the mind. But what comes first, do you think – an enlightened mind or a lightened energy body?

Depression, in fact, is a common side effect of a very heavy energy field. If we are depressed, we are depressed for a *reason*. While medication can help to block that reason and give us a lift, the depression does not actually go away; it is just masked. Rather than trying to block the reason for the depression, my view is that the trick is to face that reason head-on and clear it emotionally. Depression is also utilized by the body to block out other less 'acceptable' emotions, such as rage, anger, guilt or shame. Additionally, it can be used as a tool to manipulate others and as an excuse to 'bow out' of everyday life.

Sufferers of depression normally run the full gamut of problems: low vibration / heavy energy field, poorly functioning chakras, a sluggish physical body (constipation, bloating, weight issues), low energy generally – all masking deeper issues *and* the utilization of the excuse! So in a healing session, each aspect has to be addressed in turn. Afterwards, the mind lightens up and the depression is lifted. The client then feels more motivated to sort their life out and get on and fix the things they are not happy with, which leads them to feel more fulfilled. Almost effortlessly, cravings occur for more healthy foods, and many automatically give up smoking and drug taking, as they are no longer attracted to things of a lower vibration. Some also give up meat, but please note that this is not always beneficial, depending on your body type. Interestingly, I have also seen previously depressed clients start to become interested in spiritual development, so addressing depression can bring *huge* changes to a person's life!

I am 'clairsentient,' which means that I can sense emotion, pain and discomfort in a person's body – which is a very useful gift to have in my work (not so useful when sitting exams, for instance!). When I am with a client, I work on them until *my* body feels clear and then I know that *their* body is clear, even if I am in the UK and the client is in Australia. In fact, I remember having a telephone session with a client in Australia once and the moment I answered her call my stomach shot up under my ribs, the muscles in my abdomen contracted, and I could hardly breathe because of the pressure against my lungs. When I reported my symptoms to the client, she replied, 'Oh yes, that's how I feel *all* the time – it's one of the reasons I'm calling you.' So clearly I had linked into her *somehow*.

I believe the health of our energy field is instrumental in all areas of our lives, not just our health, but also in our personal relationships, our levels of success, luck, happiness, intuition, peace, and in attracting all our experiences in life. I firmly believe that our subconscious thoughts and beliefs – particularly our negative and limiting beliefs – affect our energy field so much as to attract the experiences which bolster those beliefs. For example, if we have the subconscious belief, *No one will ever love me*, then that thought will create a vibration in our energy field that will ensure we *only* attract to us people that will let us down or treat us badly – or simply be unable to love us for some reason. Then that belief will be proved right... which then goes on to energize the belief more and more and then brings us even worse examples of not being loved, and so on.

You may have read about the popular 'Law of Attraction' which states: 'That which is like itself is drawn' – this law is indeed very powerful. But what I see more and more with clients is that it is not the *conscious beliefs* and desires that are manifested, but the *subconscious beliefs* and *conditioned beliefs* – those which have been passed down to us by parents, family, teachers etc. An example might be: *Money does not grow on trees*. This belief, stored as an imprint and vibration in the energy field, will ensure that the person never comes across money easily! The Law of Attraction is hugely popular at the moment, but it is often misunderstood, particularly the fact that the law operates on our subconscious beliefs. This is the reason why we are not all multi-millionaires living with George Clooney or Angelina Jolie, even though we have read and applied the wisdom contained in the book *The Secret*! It is only when the *vibration* of our energy field is in line with the *vibration* of that which we desire or seek, that we are able to manifest what we want.

I believe that our energy body also affects how other people treat us. It is said that over 90% of communication is non-verbal, but I do not believe that vocal tones and facial expressions solely make up that 90%; I believe that it is the state and vibration of our energy field which governs people's reactions to our communications. And much of that is governed again by our *beliefs about ourselves*. Our projections of the *dis-owned* shadow aspects of ourselves are held in our field, and others – often those closest to us – will play out those shadow roles for us, and often not be aware of why they are saying certain things to us, or being unkind.

So our energy fields are immensely important to us. In fact without one, we would be dead! It is also important as it is our body's main source of defense against negative energies, both from other people, buildings, land, and such things as entities and earthbound spirits. This is why drug usage, which appears to be rampant, is so dangerous – not only for the physical damage it causes but also because it creates huge holes in something that is supposed to act as a protective membrane around us! Therefore, a healthy energy body is going to lead to a healthy and happy body and a healthy and happy mind.

It is our emotions, thoughts and beliefs that have the greatest effect on our energy body – so all the more reason for us to think positively! We particularly need to identify, clear, and reframe any negative beliefs we have and heal any emotional wounds from our past to prevent the formation of a 'pain body.'

A pain body is quite hard to explain, but I will try. Imagine the body of a man standing within a golden aura – an egg-shaped bubble of energy. Within the egg shape, attached to the body, is a dark balloon of energy, containing memories of past trauma, and what we in the shamanic world call 'heavy energy.'

As you now know, according to the Law of Attraction, like attracts like, therefore more trauma will be attracted to the person, resulting in the dark balloon growing in size. Once the pain body gets sufficiently large, like a tumor, it starts to develop its own personality and consciousness – so it is almost like having another person living with us in our energy field. This other person is a fragment of *us*, albeit a very negative aspect of us, which holds all our unhealed pain and negativity. It links into our minds, and aligns us with negative thoughts. The more negative thoughts we have, the more negativity we attract to us, and that dark balloon just keeps filling up all the time and gaining more 'power' over us – so a vicious circle is created. Therefore, it is extremely important that our energy bodies and our pain bodies are healed.

Take the example of Keeley in the Practice Notes. Her problems, at the root, were *not* actually physical; they were all to do with her pain body, and her consciousness was trying to draw attention to her sexual abuse in order that it could be healed. Her doctors had *never* asked about her past – they were only interested in her *symptoms*; but these were not the *root* of the problem, which is why the pains continued despite all her operations. If the root of her problem had been sorted out (i.e. her abandonment by her mother and the sexual abuse) I am convinced her body would have been able to correct her physical problems. I see time and again that when the root cause has been healed, the body can easily correct any physical problem, mainly because it no longer needs to drive attention to the area concerned in order to get it healed! Therefore, the physical condition is *no longer required*. Always remember, your body has *huge* intelligence, and it can heal *anything* – given the right conditions.

The health of the energy body is hugely undervalued and fails to be understood by the medical profession, but its health is absolutely essential to our physical health. Our energy body is so large and so complex that I believe it is still relatively little understood. I have even heard it said that our energy body can extend to over 50 miles from our physical body! My sense is that it can extend *much* further.

In order for us to have good health, it is essential that we keep our energy body functioning at a high frequency. It is important that we understand that *everything vibrates, everything has a frequency.* Again this may sound bizarre, but it is true. Disease vibrates within the lower range of frequencies; therefore if we are vibrating at the same low frequency of disease, disease will be attracted to us, as 'that which is like itself is drawn.' Have you noticed how quickly you become ill when you are depressed or down? Have you noticed how often depression and disease go hand in hand? This is why. So here is yet another good reason to adopt a 'chicken salad' mentality.

So, what increases the vibration of the energy field?

- Positive thinking and an optimistic outlook are definitely top of the list.
- Meditation and a connection to the Divine through spiritual practice comes a close second.
- A connection to the Earth is vital. It is immensely important to be 'grounded,' and in the body, rather than floating around with your head in the clouds.
- Being outdoors in sunshine is wonderful! *Breathe* in that sunshine into all your chakras and your physical body, and fill your energy bubble with golden sparkles of light. (Obviously, that is a little harder if you are here in the UK, but if there isn't any sunshine, *imagine it!*)
- Being outdoors generally is very beneficial, as you will read in the following chapter. The wind is also very cleansing for our energy field, for it literally 'blows the cobwebs away'! Go out for a walk on a windy day and feel how refreshed you feel afterwards.

- Eating foods with a high quotient of light (sunshine) will bring that sunshine into our energy fields. The purpose of the digestion process is to release the light from our food; the more light there is in the food we eat, the better it is for us. Therefore we need to focus on natural, organic foods, things that have been in the soil and grown, rather than on man-made foods – and they need to be eaten as close to raw as possible in order to retain maximum nutrition.
- Exercise is wonderful for our energy bodies and stops them from stagnating. Yoga, tai chi and chi gong are particularly good as they also focus on the movements of energy. Having said that, nothing beats a good night of dancing!
- Sex *can* be beneficial; it just depends who it is with! Remember that energetically, a man dumps his *hucha* (heavy energy) onto a woman during orgasm. That is why a man feels so much better after sex! It is for this reason, ladies, that we need to be extra careful about whom we choose as partners! Our energy bodies have to clear our man's heavy energies, as well as our own, and this can take quite a toll on us energetically!

The following *reduce* our vibration significantly by building up or allowing in heavy energy, and therefore weaken our energy body:

- Negativity
- Fear
- Worry
- Stress
- Depression
- Sugar
- Yeasts (bread/beer)
- Alcohol
- Tobacco

- Drugs
- Sadness
- Regret

What do you crave when you are feeling fed up? Sugar? Alcohol? Does it make you feel better, or worse? When our vibrations are low, we crave things of a similarly low vibration, which makes us feel more down in the dumps, so we crave *more* alcohol or sweet things and before we know where we are, we are chronically depressed – as well as spotty and fat! I have definitely seen a correlation with depression and obesity in my clients. Therefore, it is better to try as hard as possible to be as optimistic as possible; focus on what good things you do have, rather than what you don't have, and do things which *raise* your vibration, such as going for a walk in the park, dancing, or exercising.

The energy body links into the physical body via the *chakra system*. The word *chakra* means 'wheel' in Sanskrit and while they are more commonly associated with the Indian medicine tradition, every living thing has chakras. Much is known about chakras by the general public these days, so I will not labor the point too much here as there are excellent books on the topic, but essentially chakras are spinning wheels or vortices of energy which emanate from the spinal column, expanding out to the surface of the energy body, around four inches in diameter, rather like a little whirlpool. Ancient medicine traditions make mention of up to 88,000 chakras within the body! However, most therapists focus on the seven main chakras, which can be found:

- At the crown of the head
- Between the eyebrows
- At the throat
- At the center of the chest
- At the solar plexus
- An inch or so below the navel, called the sacral chakra

- At the very base of the spine, emanating in the area between the genitals and the anus.

The upper three chakras (crown, third eye, and throat) are aligned with our spiritual selves, and the lower four are aligned with our Earthly selves. Each chakra has its own unique vibration and is responsible for the health of the organs around it, and also works in connection with other chakras – for example, problems in the sacral or 2nd chakra can also cause the throat chakra to be affected.

Healthy, clean, clear and quickly spinning chakras are essential for the health of the energy body and therefore the health of the physical body. Each chakra informs not only our organs but also our endocrine system and our emotions. Imagine them as satellite dishes if you like – receiving information from the world outside of us and feeding that information into our consciousness, and also transmitting information to the outside world about our state of being. Chakras connect us via 'luminous filaments' to *everything* in our world.

It is common for certain chakras to be 'out,' depending on the issues the client is concerned with. For example, imagine the chakras of someone who has been sexually abused. I would expect this person to have blocks in the following chakras:

- The base/root chakra (lack of security, fear, poor relationship with the body and therefore the Earth)
- The sacral chakra (wounded Inner Child, sexual trauma, loss of personal power, sexual issues)
- The solar plexus chakra (loss of sense of self, identifying with victimhood, low self-esteem)
- The heart chakra (lack of self-love and betrayal if the abuser is a family member, which sadly is most often the case)
- The throat chakra (unable to speak out against the abuser for fear of retribution or rejection or direct threat; hence all

unsaid words remain stuck in the throat). Anger will also be stuck here if the person does speak out but is not believed. Interestingly most of the people who suffer from being sexually abused are most traumatized by not being heard by their parents rather than from the abuse itself.

- The crown chakra (cut off from Source energy – they often feel that they do not deserve to receive it or alternatively they believe the Divine has abandoned them).

Someone who is struggling to get a book written will probably have blocks in:

- The sacral chakra (lack of creativity, inability to manifest their desires)
- The third-eye chakra (lack of vision or clarity)
- The base chakra (fear and security); this may be affected, depending on what they are writing about!

So it is important that the chakras are clear and balanced not only for health but also for emotional wellbeing and for the *achievement of our goals in life.*

As you will have read in the Practice Notes, our energy fields can harbor a huge amount of information. Past-life memory is not only held in the cells, but also in the energy body, *along with* energetic remnants of objects which resulted in our death in the former life or lives, such as axes, daggers, lances – once I even had to remove a bear-trap from a client's side! I have also removed numerous pieces of armor over the years, some of it medieval, and some of it highly advanced. Often, as soon as I mention what I have found, clients exclaim that they often sensed something in the area, but could not figure out what it was. After removal, any pains or feelings of congestion fade away, and the energy field in that area is clearer and lighter.

It is important to also understand that our energy bodies and chakras also contain 'imprints' of information. These are like little computer programs which, when triggered, create a behavioral pattern in us, or automatic responses to certain stimuli. A typical example is when we go home to visit Mum, and find ourselves behaving like petulant teenagers again, or despite our best efforts, we allow her to wind us up! Imprints are quite difficult to get your head around, but try to imagine them this way: imagine a person is covered in little iPod shuffles. *All* the iPods have information downloaded into their memories. Some iPod shuffles are turned on and are playing the information that has been downloaded onto them – whether we like that information or not. Others are inactive, but can be activated at any time, should the right conditions arise. So, when we say that someone 'really pushes our buttons' we are really referring to the fact that they trigger our imprints!

Sadly though, imprints aren't iPod shuffles with lovely songs on them. The imprint itself could be of a disease, a personality trait, or a vibration that attracts certain circumstances to the person – this in fact is why we constantly seem faced with 'pattern repeats,' because an imprint is in operation. Alternatively the imprint could hold information about a phobia, a personal circumstance, a positive aspect such as the release of an artistic ability, a genetic condition, past-life trauma, or ability (which can loop into this lifetime causing repeating patterns) – pretty much anything actually, positive or negative! Imprints can even contain behaviors and traumas experienced by our *ancestors*! *Do not* underestimate the power of imprints; they can govern our lives so that we are reduced to being nothing more than puppets on a string. We can be totally controlled by their effects on our health, wellbeing, happiness, relationships, luck or abundance – anything at all.

You may find the existence of imprints hard to believe but they do exist. One of the easiest ways to see an imprint at work is when we go to visit our mothers! Mothers seem to have an inbuilt sense of where our imprints' trigger points or 'hot buttons' are. It is as if they purposely poke them and activate a preformed response within us. How interesting it is to stand back and observe how we react when our mothers rub us up the wrong way! Normally we behave like moody teenagers or little children! This is our imprints at work. We may be calm, assured, kind people with our friends and colleagues, but five minutes with Mum can turn us into spitting harridans! Our heart rate increases, our adrenal response kicks in, our shoulders shoot up around our ears, and our self-esteem can fly out the window, all because this is the *programmed response* within the imprint. We are like automatons being fed a computer program, and unless they are cleared, we are slaves to them.

Much of spiritual progression and enlightenment works towards *breaking out* of pre-programmed responses to people or certain events (like the chicken salad approach – *we* decide how we react to events as opposed to being informed by our imprints). Events can also be brought about and governed by imprints. The most commonly triggered, particularly at the moment, are those to do with financial security. We can be fine and dandy until we are faced with the thought of losing our job, home or our fortune, and we can be reduced to a gibbering, anxious wreck in seconds. Often, this is because a *past life or ancestral* imprint of poverty or loss is triggered, bringing up abject fears and past memories, which prevent us from dealing with the situation at hand in a calm, logical and focused way.

So, what happens to the energy body when we die? My sense is that the energy body, which includes all our chakras and all the information and imprinting contained within it, leaves our physical body through the crown of our heads. Many people who have witnessed the death of a loved one claim to see a string of colored lights – the chakras – of the deceased person rise up above their heads for a little while. This then forms into an orb. This 'orb' of our beingness then ascends to the higher dimensions of light, taking with it all that is you. The *real* you, *not* the body, which really is not the real you at all. The body can be likened to a suitcase which the spirit inhabits for a few, short years. My sense is that after death the spirit leaves the suitcase it has inhabited and then resides in the upper dimensions for a good few years. While it is in this upper dimension, the spirit 'you' reviews your last lifetime, taking the learning from it and deciding what it would like to experience as part of its soul's journey in the next lifetime.

When it is time to incarnate again, the orb, containing all the chakras and all the programming of the being which is you, enters the body of a baby in the womb. Nothing remains of the 'us' that we used to be, other than our energy body. (Some say that the only physical aspects carried over from lifetime to lifetime are the eyes – not the actual eyeballs themselves but the irises. I am not so sure about this, but it would explain why we can often totally recognize complete strangers – as if we have known them forever – just by looking into their eyes.)

So, our 'story,' which is held within our imprints and our chakras in our energy body, can follow us around from lifetime to lifetime – until we finally seek to heal it, once and for all.

As you know, one of the reasons I love shamanic healing is that it really gets to the *core* of the issue as far as the client is concerned; and the core issue, in most cases, is emotional. I work on the emotions whether the client is coming to me with physical problems or not. If, for example, the client has cancer, initially I *totally* ignore the cancer, because I see it as a *by-product*, a *symptom* of a deeper emotional problem. After all, the body's natural preferred state is health – if it goes wrong in some way, it is demanding our attention and it wants something healed! At some point in the healing sessions I will address the cancer itself, and actually 'ask' it why it has manifested. The most common answers (via the client who is in a very deep state of relaxation at the time) are that it is there...

- As a 'wake up call,' as some aspect of life needs to be changed
- In order to force certain lifestyle changes (for example, less stress or better diet)
- On 'request' from the client (he or she was looking for an 'exit' route out of life for some reason)
- In order to force certain emotional issues to be healed, whether those issues arose in this lifetime or a former lifetime. (Perhaps the person has been abused in some way and not mentioned it to anyone before or sought to heal the effects of it.)
- As a result of stored up and previously unexpressed emotions – anger, grief and guilt seem to be the main culprits.

To me (and in most shamanic traditions), it is generally accepted that *all* physical problems have an emotional root; as mentioned earlier, if we can get to the root of the problem and clear it, truly heal it, the body then has no *need* for the physical problem and it is fully capable of healing itself, even when that is seemingly impossible.

In working with clients I have seen a perfect correlation between people's past history and their health. One of the first things I always ask clients is, 'How is your health?' If the client then reels off a list of complaints, and surgeries, then I automatically know that that person is going to also provide me with a list of events which caused them severe emotional trauma. On *very* rare occasions I have seen clients suffering health issues despite very happy lives and good childhoods. I have then found that trauma was very much evident in their past lives (which do affect us whether we believe in them or not!).

It is my desire to sow the seeds in people's consciousness and provide a deeper understanding of the physical form and the variety of things that affect it. I see *so many* clients that *in my view* have suffered dangerous, unnecessary and expensive operations.

I once heard that the Indian mystic Sai Baba called the human body a 'walking temple' – and I have to agree with his analogy. We are indeed walking temples, for we have within us a spark of the Divine; therefore we are, in actual fact, holy. My work has taught me that the human body is just about the biggest miracle there is on this planet. Now I know that from a purely *biological* point of view, the body is quite amazing when you think about all the millions of functions it carries out each and every second. However, through working with clients over the years, I have been honored, and humbled, to witness that the body has an intelligence that is quite staggering. It has far exceeded my previous understanding – which was restricted to basic biology – and instead has regularly led me into a whole new world – one I could not even have dreamt of.

It is my greatest hope that this information about the relationship between the energy body and the physical body may be taken on board by the medical professions, rather than being pooh-poohed as 'New Agey' or viewed as threatening in some way. Members of the medical profession do a truly wonderful job and work under terrific pressure. However, when I have put my judgments aside and followed the direction the *client's body* has led me in, great healing has taken place, *without* the need for medication or surgery – and it has happened very quickly indeed. The other point to bear in mind is that frequently, clients have exhausted standard medical routes to no avail, before coming to see me.

My greatest hope is that in the future, the medical profession and the shamanic / 'alternative therapy' traditions, such as acupuncture, homeopathy, naturopathy and herbal medicine, will be able to work in closer relationship to one another for the benefit of all. Surgery itself is terribly traumatic for all aspects of the human body – not only the physical body, but the energy/subtle bodies and the spiritual aspect, the soul. We are far more 'finely tuned' than we realize.

I am not of course saying that we should avoid medication and surgery – I would not be here today if it were not for surgery – but I would prefer surgery to be reserved for a time when all other avenues have been exhausted, and the body has been given every opportunity to heal itself. The greatest benefit in doing this for the medical profession is that millions of pounds could be saved on unnecessary medication and operations. Of course the biggest challenge facing the medical profession is that a radical change would be required in the way the body – and its awesome intelligence – is perceived. But my view is that it would be worth it, in the long run, and we could all benefit.

I would just like to reiterate a few points here. A body is like a baby. A baby draws attention to the fact that something is not quite right by crying. A body draws attention to the fact that something is not quite right by going wrong in some way. It has to be remembered that a body's natural and preferred state is *always health*. If there is disease (dis-ease), disorder or pain, it is the body's way of drawing attention to that area and saying, 'You need to work on some stuff here.' But, more often than not, it is NOT the disease, disorder or pain itself that needs to be healed – after all, this has been manufactured by the body; it is the *emotional or energetic trauma* which is at the root of the symptom which needs to be addressed. When this is cleared, when the body no longer has a need for it, the body can then fix the disease, disorder or pain by itself. Remember, if the body has created something, *it can un-create it*.

I am going to mention this next point briefly, at the risk of being deemed a lunatic and carted off to the asylum: *We have to talk to our bodies.* I know this sounds crazy but it is really important. Having dealt with bodies on this level, I can only liken them to small, frightened children who are unsure and don't understand what is going on. We tend to think that because our mind knows (or thinks it knows) what is going on, our body also knows what is going on, but this is not the case. Our body has its *own* consciousness and it needs *love and reassurance* – and it needs it fairly consistently, regardless of whether the body is healthy or not. It serves us to have happy, informed and contented bodies; we need them on our side! Bodies that are angry with us, or ones that feel unloved, tend to go wrong. Like a fractious baby, they are crying in order to get some love and attention from us.

Tell your body it is doing a great job and that you are very happy with it and thankful. You may then notice after a short while that your healing response is faster than it was before. For example, if you cut your finger, you may notice that the wound heals very swiftly indeed, or you may notice you have fewer colds. When the body feels that it is being heard, it is less likely to manifest illness in order to get your attention.

Your body is a gift from the Divine, and a gift it surely is, for *everything* you need to know is within your physical being. So please try to ensure that you give attention to developing and nurturing your physical body as well as your spiritual being, *regardless* of whether you are on a spiritual path or not.

Overview

I hope this chapter has widened your eyes a little to the brilliance of the body. Here are the main points to consider:

1   Physical symptoms usually have an emotional root. If you heal what is at the root of the matter, the body can normally clear up the physical problem, no matter how severe the physical problem is.
2   A person will normally be affected *physically* by *emotional* trauma within *ten years* of the emotional event occurring.
3   A 'pain body' can be established if a person has suffered trauma and has not dealt with it.

4   If the body is going wrong in a particular area, normally it is trying to draw your attention to that area in order for an emotional, energetic or spiritual/soul issue to be cleared up there. The related chakra will also give you some clues.

5   Past-life memories are stored in the energy body and in each cell of the physical body.

6   Items that were on a person when they died (e.g. armor) or items that *killed* a person (e.g. bullets, axes, lances, swords, daggers, rope nooses) in a past life can still be present energetically and affect the physical body. Again, the body will normally trigger off some physical ailment in order to draw your attention to the affected area in the hope that you will get this removed.

7   The body will often create 'diversion tactics.' It will purposefully manifest a condition in order to divert you away from an emotion (e.g. anger or rage) that your subconscious deems to be unacceptable. There will often be no medical explanation for your condition in such instances.

8   The body will obey the subconscious beliefs or subconscious needs of the mind, *or* obey the needs of a person. For example, if you need to stay safe, it will manifest a condition where you perhaps need to stay indoors a lot.

9   The body will cause pain, or inflammation, as a warning, and a request for that area to be rested while it fixes a problem.

10 If the body feels unloved in some way, or an aspect of the person is not integrated properly, then again, the body will manifest a problem. I have seen a link between girls who have terminated pregnancies and then in later years manifested cancerous or pre-cancerous cells in the cervical area. This is because that area of the body is rejected or ignored due to feelings of guilt and shame

(even if the person says they have dealt with the termination mentally). The body picks up on those negative thoughts and the negative energy directed at it, and cellular changes ensue. Again, this is why it is important to heal any issues you have properly, on all levels of your being. Very often, talking about things does not cure problems on energetic and physical levels, and on some occasions it can drive issues further into the body.

11 Remember to talk to your body nicely, *even if it goes wrong*, and keep it 'in the loop' as to what is going on. Your body has its own consciousness and it likes to be informed, particularly if you are about to do something that will cause it stress or concern.

My Tips for Tip-Top Health

1 *Do your personal healing work* – address any emotional issues that you may have pushed away.

2 *As far as possible, align yourself with joy and positivity.*

3 *Be in nature as much as you can.* The Earth vibrates at a rate of 7.83 Hertz (cycles per second), which is a very low C# sound wave. This is a very healing vibration for the body, which is why we feel better, mentally, physically and emotionally, when we have a day out in nature. If you are ill, put a blanket down and lie on the Earth and it should help bring you back into balance. Just remember to keep warm.

4 *Exercise! Move that body.*

5 *Eat well!* Good digestion = good health, so get plenty of fiber and make sure you 'go' regularly! It is always beneficial to have a session with a well-qualified nutritionist. Some studies suggest aiming for 80% raw food a day for optimum health. There is a brilliant film called *Food Matters*, available on DVD, which I think everyone

should see. It is an amazing film, a real eye-opener and highly informative, and really provides the motivation to eat better.

6   *Limit toxins and chemicals* – not only in foods, but also in cosmetics, shower gels, shampoos, body creams, deodorants, household cleaners, air fresheners etc. Natural is *always* best. I highly recommend Janey Lee Grace's latest book published by Hay House, *Look Great Naturally – Without Ditching the Lipstick*. This is a treasure trove of information on this topic and is useful for everyone, despite being focused on women. Janey has written other marvelous books about the natural self, the home, and baby and toddler care, all available on Amazon or via her website, www.imperfectlynatural.com, where many chemical-free products are also available.

7   *Limit stresses in your life* – if they are hard to avoid then find a way of releasing them such as exercise, or meditation. Meditation is *unbelievably* good for health. Do try to ensure that you have a good life/work balance and try to find some 'me time'!

8   *Love yourself!!!*

9   *Have fun* – laugh as much as possible! A happy you = a happy body. I have heard stories of people that have cured themselves of cancer by watching funny films and having a good old laugh!

10 *Love your body* – it does amazing work for you. We all have bits that we would like to be different, but they are our bits and they need to be loved. If you have a big nose, love it. A new nose or a boob job *will not* magically bring you the self-esteem and worthiness you are looking for. Good health to you, and remember: *Listen to your body!*

6. Soul Loss and Soul Retrieval

Memories 6.1

I sit and wait with my mother in the consultant's office. She is white-faced and rigid, but trying to smile at me reassuringly. The consultant opens her file. She reads, frowns, and reads some more. I realize that I am not breathing. She looks at me kindly, takes a deep breath, and tells me that the operation failed. They did their best but things have progressed too far and cannot be turned back. I hear the words but they do not make sense.

'I am sorry to tell you this but it appears that you have gone through puberty *and* the menopause at the same time, which is why you have felt so ill for so long. At 17, you are very young to have gone through the menopause; it is very rare indeed, but our tests have confirmed it. I know this has been a source of great suffering for you, and I am sure you are feeling very angry that this has not been discovered before, but it is unlikely your doctor would have ever considered you were going through menopause.'

I swallow back tears, dreading what is coming next, even though I know in my heart what is coming next. I feel faint, and also like a part of me is trying to escape, trying to do anything to get out of that room and away from the words that I am soon to hear.

'Sadly, this means that you will never be able to have children of your own. You will need to be put on hormone tablets straight away, which you will need to take until you are 45. Here is a prescription; please take it downstairs to the pharmacy. Take care.'

I stand up, and the world tilts around me unsteadily. I feel a very, very long way away from my body and am having problems co-ordinating myself. My mother shoves her hand under my armpit and I feel myself being propelled out of the room by her.

I am not going to be able to have children! My every thought has been about my children, since I was tiny. And now my dreams have been shattered. Feeling faint and unable to speak, I lean against the wall for support.

I have been back and forth to the doctors for *years*, convinced I was dying, sometimes fainting up to eight times a day – once nearly passing out in the middle of a busy road. I have been unable to concentrate on anything for longer than a minute; my schooling and exams have been ruined. The doctors did nothing, other than tell me to eat more fruit! My head spins, and my heart feels like it is going to burst out of my chest. Tears rage in my throat but don't seem to be able to come out.

By the time I arrive home an hour later, I feel completely empty.

Practice Notes 6.2

I relax into the rhythmic sound of my rattle and drift into altered consciousness. When I feel the familiar jolt in my stomach, I know that it is time to start my journey and I descend into the Lower World. I am met by my power animal, which guides me to the chambers of the soul.

I find the chamber which contains the lost soul part – the part my client needs to have returned to them. I open the door and look around. I look again. The chamber is completely empty! I take a breath to calm myself and raise my eyebrows questioningly at my power animal. He looks at me and then turns his head slowly, so I follow his gaze. He is staring intently into the left-hand corner of the chamber. It is dark and I cannot see anything there. What is he looking at? I squint into the gloom – suddenly I see it. Sheltered among the shadows of the chamber is a tiny doorway. One thing I have learned in my work is to expect the unexpected, but I can't help wondering what I will find behind this door. I turn the doorknob.

Suddenly – WHOOOOOOSH!!! I am being pulled at an unbelievable speed through the Universe – scintillating stars streak by in brilliant white lines, and I am being drawn away from Earth at a terrifying speed towards a distant planet, which looms closer by the second. Eventually I find myself standing in a strange and misty world. I look around, but see nothing. I call out for the soul part, tell it that it is much needed, that it needs to come back to itself, to my client, who needs it, and that I am here to collect it. My voice carries away from me into the silence.

The mist before me shifts and swirls, coalesces and becomes more dense, until I see standing before me a young child, a child that I know was once part of my client, part of her soul.

'Would you be willing to come back with me?' I ask the child. She nods once, solemnly, and holds up her arms so that I can gather her up in mine…

I make the homeward journey and return to the Middle World and my client. The energy in my hands is almost too much to contain, but I position myself over my client and blow the soul part back into her energy body. As I do this, my client cries out and folds her hands over her belly, as if to keep her soul part from escaping again. She weeps – a keening sound that touches my heart. That which she had lost has been returned to her. She is a step closer towards wholeness.

Notes 6.3

How does one explain the soul? Let me try. There is a huge, magnificent part of us which is spirit, pure energy. This 'oversoul,' or Higher Self, largely resides outside of us, in the Upper Realms.

But a part of it also resides within us. While the body itself is weak and can be destroyed, our soul is eternal. It is energy, and as we know, energy cannot be destroyed; it can only be transformed or moved. Lifetime after lifetime this soul enters a physical body, and at death, it leaves the body behind, like an empty suitcase.

So then – what is *soul loss*? The best way for me to describe this process is to use the analogy of an orange. Imagine that the physical body is represented by the orange peel; this, like the body, houses the soul. The soul is represented by the orange segments, which are the most vital and important parts of the orange. The segments also contain juicy sweetness and calories – units of *energy*. Our soul also contains our vital energies. The orange peel serves to protect the segments, which are soft and squishy, just as the physical body serves to protect the soul, which is fragile, delicate and *very precious*. The presence of the soul within the body provides vital energies, which go some way to energizing and also *protecting* the physical body, as they increase the vibration of the energy body.

In an ideal world, the segments reside and remain safe within the peel. But life, as we know, is often not ideal. Therefore, there is a protection mechanism by which segments of the soul can leave the body, in order to prevent themselves from being irreversibly damaged or destroyed. The segments, or soul parts, along with their vital energy units and particular characteristics, flee from the body upon suffering emotional, mental, physical or spiritual trauma of some kind. This process most often occurs before a person reaches ten years of age. However, it is important to remember that soul loss can occur at any age. I have seen examples of soul loss occurring prior to incarnation (as in Memories 1.1) or *in utero* – particularly if the child senses it is not wanted in some way – and more frequently as a result of difficulties in past lifetimes.

Here are some common causes of soul loss:

- Feeling scared or unsafe as a child
- Loss of a parent, through death, divorce or separation
- Physical injury or accident
- Surgery

- Death of a loved one
- Witnessing a horrible accident or violence
- Shock – perhaps upon hearing some very bad news
- Living in a state of constant hardship and difficulty
- Losing a job
- Losing a partner through infidelity or divorce
- Traumatic birth experience (either for the baby or the mother)
- Deep fear
- Threat of death, e.g. being held at gunpoint
- Survival issues, e.g. being lost, being injured in a remote location, nearly drowning in a river or at sea, fearing for one's life generally
- Great disappointment, e.g. failing an important exam and not being able to attend university, loss of dreams, loss of a business
- Loss of security, e.g. a home, job or partner
- Abuse, whether that be sexual, physical, emotional or mental
- Becoming greatly overwhelmed in a negative way (as a child, perhaps at a fairground or large gathering)
- As a child, witnessing a parent becoming disabled or injured (which causes the realization of lack of safety even for grown-ups)

The soul parts themselves flee to their home. For most people this will be the Earth. For others, such as Starchildren, it will be the place their soul was originally sourced from. I have often retrieved soul parts from other planets, simply because this was the place from which the soul was *seeded – where its journey began* – as with the client detailed in the Practice Notes to this chapter. I have also been taken on a shamanic journey to the Sun to retrieve a soul part for one very special young man, and recently I was taken to a place beneath the sea! But most often, the soul parts return home to the Great Mother, the Earth.

Often, when people first hear about soul parts returning to the Earth, they fear that their soul part is trapped in some type of hellish place, but this is not the case at all. It is simply another dimension, a Lower World within this world, accessed through the subconscious realm.

There are many problems which occur as a result of soul loss. The first is that a *pattern* of soul loss is established. If soul loss first occurs at the age of eight, it is as if the characteristics of the child from the ages of 0–8 are lost. He may 'forget' how to play, lose his childish curiosity, and appear to grow up very quickly. Once a pattern is established, at each subsequent traumatic event, even more segments leave the orange peel, or the body, leaving the person further weakened, until the peel is virtually empty and the person has become an 'empty shell person.'

The effects of soul loss are:

- Depression
- Reduced protection, leading to increased psychic attack
- Weakened immune system
- Low levels of physical energy
- ME/Chronic fatigue symptoms
- Difficulty feeling any type of emotion
- Inability to relate to, or play with, children
- Problems finding one's place in the world
- Problems finding one's purpose in life
- Problems with motivation
- Problems manifesting dreams or wishes
- Low levels of creativity (either ideas-wise or artistically)
- Lack of interest – in anything
- A feeling that something is constantly missing
- Failure to succeed in life
- Failure to find peace in life
- Always seeming to be on some big search – whether it is to

find purpose in life, a spiritual path, a mate, the perfect job, biological parents, the right house etc
- An inability to find joy in life
- An all-pervasive feeling of being lost
- An inability to 'take part' in life, always feeling on the outskirts of life
- The loss of a particular character trait
- Feeling 'zombie-like'

These factors of course are very damaging, not only to the person but also to their health and their quality of life. Therefore in my work, it is important to firstly heal the *effects* of the trauma, i.e. clear up any emotional and energetic baggage, and then carry out a *soul retrieval* to bring the person back to wholeness.

Soul loss may seem like a terrible and confusing thing to get your head around, but it really is quite a clever protection mechanism and an important and necessary function. We have all heard descriptions of soul loss without perhaps realizing it:

- 'A part of me died when she left me.'
- 'I have never been the same since the car accident.'
- 'XYZ affected me deeply.'

People who have been sexually abused will often describe leaving their bodies or floating away in some way. This is because they *do leave their bodies*. The soul comes out of their body, for it does not want to be in the physical body while it is being abused. The clever part is that after the event is over, not *all* the soul segments go back into the body. Think about it: how would a person cope after something like that has happened? Less of 'them' goes back in, leaving them 'dumbed down' effectively. This is purposeful; it happens so they can survive the event.

Very occasionally, a person can experience *spontaneous soul retrieval*. If the person works hard to address their personal healing, faces their fears and traumas, gains understanding and moves on in life with a positive attitude, then very occasionally the soul part will emerge from the safety of the womb of the Mother and automatically return home itself, back to the physical body. Most often, however, it is necessary for a shamanic healer to carry out a retrieval to find the lost soul part(s).

Most shaman 'journey' by accessing an altered state of consciousness halfway between wakefulness and sleep. Shamans are assisted in reaching this state by the rhythmic sound of their rattles or drums, which also have the added benefit of making their client sleepy. (Ever wondered why babies are given rattles?) When the client is sleepy it is easier for the shaman to access the person's realms of consciousness (for the shaman journeys into the *client's* subconscious realm, not their own).

Each shaman has an entry point to the Lower World, the subconscious realm; commonly this can be tree roots, a cave, a lake or a natural opening in the earth such as a spring.

When I journey, I first of all look to find the source of the wounding, i.e. why the soul part left in the first place. This information comes in one of two ways. For example, I may enter a room and hear loud arguing and sense violence around me and this may indicate the actual conditions of a person's childhood. Or, I will be shown a scene which will invoke in me a certain feeling – for example, a deserted street in a ghost town will give me a sense of desolation.

If the soul loss occurred in a former lifetime, then I will be shown a present-day grown-up version of the client. However, they will often be shown wearing the dress of the era so I can place them more easily – although sometimes I wish I were better at history!

While I was in Peru I heard a story about a shaman there. She was once visited by the parents of a young local boy who had nearly drowned in a river. The boy had become very weak and ill after the incident and despite seeing many healers he had become bedridden, leaving his parents to fear he was dying. The shaman used her tracking/divination abilities to find out what had happened to the boy and told the boy's parents she had seen that the Spirit of the River had 'stolen' the boy's soul. She then carried out a ceremony in order to bargain with the Spirit of the River in return for the boy's soul. Then she made a doll out of bread dough, baked it, and dressed it in some of the boy's clothing. She gave the doll to the boy's mother and asked her to take it to the part of the river where the accident had occurred. After a struggle, the river gave up the soul part and this went into the bread doll. The doll was then placed next to the boy while he slept. In the morning he woke up, fully recovered. It's quite a story, isn't it?

In my tradition, during the soul retrieval process, as well as retrieving the soul part we also find gifts for our clients which are held in other dimensions. These gifts are usually items which help a person to move forward in life. These gifts vary widely, and can range from the sublime to the ridiculous. The gifts often make no sense to me, but they always have relevance to the client. For example, sometimes I will be given a compass, which is intended to help people either find where they are or find a new direction forward. Or a bow and arrow – this can be used to help a person decide where they wish to go or what they wish to achieve and then they fire their arrows in that direction. Often swords are brought back for people, and these are used for protection and for cutting ties to the things that do not serve them.

I also bring back 'power animals' for my clients. The Native American Indians maintain that we obtain our main power animal at birth. These act as our protectors and guides throughout life and they also bring with them the qualities of the animals they represent. Legend has it that if our main power animal dies, we die. Through soul retrieval practices we can also be gifted with power animals to help us with particular areas or times in our life, which work alongside our main animal. I have known my main power animal since I was about four. On very rare occasions I have seen it leap out of me, which is always startling!

When I journey to find a power animal for a client, I bring back whatever I am given without question. Of course it's nice to bring back a majestic power animal – such as a tiger – for a client, rather than a rabbit, but I have seen that the animal gifted always matches the needs of the client. I remember once doing a run of soul retrievals for clients and every time I went to collect a power animal, a horse would appear. I think I brought back five that week at least!

During the next soul retrieval I did for a female client, I went down and was stunned to see there was yet another horse waiting for me. I noticed that it had very unusual markings on it, but still, it was another horse! The image persisted strongly so I brought it back with me. When I later described the horse to the client she sobbed for an age. When eventually she stopped, she told me that this sounded exactly like the horse she had when she was a child which she had always felt a strong bond with. She was delighted to have him with her again as her power animal.

Soul retrieval is highly beneficial and essential for true healing. The effects can be very subtle; after all, it is part of the *self* that is being returned to the individual. Occasionally though, it can have a dramatic effect. I remember bringing back a joyful soul part for a female client a few months ago. My client had been quite repressed and unsure of herself and she had been off work for some time with anxiety and depression. Her soul part showed itself as a little girl, full of energy, containing all the love of the self that the client had been lacking.

The client called me a few days after her session, sounding completely different. She told me, 'I just had to share this with you, even though you'll probably think I'm completely mad. Yesterday evening I was walking my dog as usual in the park. It was a lovely evening, quite warm for once. Suddenly an overwhelming feeling overtook me! I ripped off my trainers and socks, and started running around barefoot on the grass, with my arms in the air, shouting at the top of my voice, "I LOVE MEEEEEEEEEEEEE! I LOVE MEEEEEEEEEEEE!" Everyone looked at me as if I was nuts, but you know, I just felt so happy to have myself back again, the old me, that I just couldn't contain it anymore. Thanks so much – I feel *fantastic*!'

7. The Exorcist

Memories 7.1

I sit at my desk at the bank, trying to avoid the enquiring gaze of my friend and personal assistant, Mia, but as usual she does not miss a trick. 'Shall we go out for lunch?' she asks, as if I have a choice. We drive to the nearest café and before I can take a sip of my tea, she starts.

'OK!' she says. 'I know something's the matter – you've been preoccupied this morning. So what's up?'

I roll my eyes heavenwards in defeat. 'Oh, nothing really, Mia. I just had a *really* weird dream last night and it's really freaking me out. It was one of those lucid dreams, very real, and truly bizarre. But there is something about it that's bugging me, something I'm not getting, and it's playing on my mind, that's all.'

Mia tucks in to her jacket potato and I vaguely wonder whether I should have had that instead of the stir-fry. 'What was the dream about?' she enquires.

I consider keeping the details to myself in case she thinks I am crazy, but then I reconsider. We are very close friends and she has always been very supportive of my 'spiritual struggles' over the years so I figure she will be OK with it.

I take a deep breath. 'OK, you asked for it so don't complain if you don't like it! Tell me what you make of this. In my dream, I see myself in a large room; there is a bearded man with me and we seem to be working together in some way. There are perhaps twenty people lying on massage couches laid out in rows across the room. They are all deeply relaxed, but they are not asleep. I am walking around, sort of *releasing* things from them. I can't remember the actual process, but I know I am healing them in some way.

'Suddenly I look up and this huge, demon-like entity is trying to push its way through the wall of the room, on the far side. It is as if the wall is made of rubber and I can see the outline of the demon clearly – you know, like you see in the horror films.'

Mia's eyes are wider than I have ever seen them and her potato is growing cold on its plate. 'What did you do?' she asks.

'That's the funniest thing really – I just sigh and casually walk towards the wall *completely nonplussed*. I stand in front of the demon thing and yell at it, "Leave NOW!" and then I throw some sort of energy at it; then I get back to what I was doing.'

'Spooky or what!' says Mia.

And all of a sudden I get it, the thing that had been bothering me all day. 'Well, that's just the thing you see, Mia; the spookiest thing about the whole dream is that I was doing this work *as if it was the most natural thing in the world,* as if it was an everyday occurrence, as if the demon-like thing was a *slight inconvenience*. I wasn't scared at all! Why wasn't I scared though? Why was I so calm?'

Mia leans back in her seat and regards me over her cup of tea, thoughtful and wise as always. I appreciate how lucky I am to have her as my assistant and my friend, how great it is for me to have someone at the bank I can actually talk to. I think I would go insane without her friendship and support.

'What do *you* think it means?' she enquires cleverly.

'I'm not sure. It was so clear though. I have a feeling it's important in some way, but I don't understand it. I mean, I work as a corporate pensions consultant and a financial advisor in a *bank*! Why would I have a dream like that? But, I tell you, the weirdest thing is, that work – whatever I was doing for those people – seemed so familiar, so ordinary, like I was doing my everyday job.'

Mia throws her head back and laughs. 'Hmmm, that would make an interesting CV entry, wouldn't it? "Financial consultant," then "Exorcist." Bit of an unusual career change, isn't it? That would certainly raise a few eyebrows!' She makes me laugh about it as she always does, supportive as ever. 'Don't worry about it, honey; it's just a dream.'

'I know, I know,' I say and tuck into my by now lukewarm stir-fry. 'I'll have forgotten all about it by tomorrow.'

But deep within me, I have the strangest feeling that I will never forget the dream, and that within the dream lies a clue. A clue about my future and my true spiritual path, my true calling.

Practice Notes 7.2

I look at the family squashed onto my sofa – I had expected one of Andrew's parents to accompany him, but not both. Andrew has such a sweet face: upturned nose, freckles, and spiky hair in the current fashion, yet he looks much younger than his 12 years.

Andrew's parents are concerned for their son as he has been a victim of bullying at school. He is an easy target: short, slightly built, polite, and very sensitive and studious. They tell me he used to be at the top of his class in most subjects. Since the bullying started he has fallen behind in his studies to the extent that he has to have special lessons after school. He is also showing signs of anxiety and in addition is displaying some slightly odd behavior. I ask Andrew how things are at school now.

'Well, the boys got into lots of trouble, so they don't bother me too much now, and my arm has healed. But since then I can't seem to concentrate in class anymore. Sometimes it's like I just can't hear what the teacher is saying. Even though I can hear his voice, it… just doesn't go into my head… it's like the teacher is foreign and I can't understand the language. I've been getting really bad marks – I used to be quite good, but now I have to have a special tutor as I've fallen behind so much – and I even find that hard. I just don't seem to get it anymore; nothing makes sense to me.'

'I see,' I say. 'Do you find it hard to concentrate because there's a lot going on in your head, a lot of confusion, lots of thoughts and lots of noise?'

Andrew nods solemnly.

His mum looks very concerned. 'We've been very worried about him – he used to be such a happy little boy, but now he's so insular and quiet… and… well…' She looks to her husband and he nods for her to continue. 'Well, this sounds a bit odd, but when he's at home, the only thing he wants to do is to go outside and sweep the patio! Sweep up the leaves. Sweep! Sweep! Sweep! *He's always sweeping!* A couple of times a day – more than that recently – even if there's not much to sweep up. And while he's doing it he has a very, very funny look on his face, sort of grumpy, miserable and contorted. And he mutters to himself all the time; he really concentrates on it – he has to get every leaf up!'

'No I don't!' cries Andrew, who is now visibly flushed.

'Yes, you do, you do,' says his father gently. 'I can't explain it, but there's something about it that just isn't right. He doesn't want to play anymore; he just wants to sweep!'

I turn my attention back to Andrew. 'What are you thinking when you're sweeping up, Andrew? What's going through your head?'

Andrew looks at his feet, a little sullen. 'Don't know,' he shrugs.

Confident with my diagnosis, I press ahead.

'OK, Andrew, I think that I might be able to help you with the confusion *and* the sweeping, would you like that? Mum and Dad can stay in the room with you; they can read some magazines over there at the table, and you can lie on this comfortable couch for me and I'll put a nice blanket over you to keep you warm – is that OK?'

He nods and as he lies on the couch he tells me he just wants to feel happy again. I cover him with a blanket to make him feel more secure. He looks tiny, vulnerable and very cute. Sunshine shines in through the window and bathes him in a golden light. I whisper to him very quietly, and teach him how to breathe away his memories of the bullying, his sadness and pain. He whispers to me about the images he sees in his mind, and I keep reassuring him that everything is OK. Even though there are four of us in close proximity, my work with Andrew feels very private and sacred. I sense he has gone very deeply into the work. I know it is now time.

I ask Andrew to look for energy within him that is not his. I know he will find something; I am ready for it.

'My chest,' he whispers calmly. 'There is something in my chest. It isn't part of me. It came to me in class when I was feeling very sad and afraid... and angry.'

'OK, Andrew, well done. Just check for me: is the energy sad and afraid too?'

He nods slightly. 'It's a very sad man – he's old too.'

'Does this energy like to make you sweep the patio?'

He nods. 'I remember now what I'm thinking when I'm sweeping! It's bad things, very bad things. Bad things about the boys who bullied me.'

I know we have found the cause of the problem and I speak to the spirit of the old man within Andrew's energy field so he knows what is going on and what is going to happen. The old man's pain and sadness are tangible so I do not want to frighten him. He co-operates as I knew he would, and I gently remove him from Andrew's energy field. The old man tells Andrew he is sorry before he leaves him.

Andrew looks beatific, peaceful and tranquil. I can already see that his energy field is brighter. I finish up the process with Andrew, teach him some protection methods, and explain to his father that he will now have to take over the patio sweeping responsibilities!

A few days later, Andrew's mother calls to tell me that he has just come top in a math test! She tells me that his teacher can hardly believe it. 'He's so happy,' she said, 'and so am I. I've got my little boy back.'

Notes 7.3

The dream detailed in the Memories section of this chapter happened in 2001, when I was still working in corporate finance. It seems strange thinking back to that time because my working life is so very different now: it is now quite common for me to perform up to three 'exorcisms' a day – although I now tend to refer to them as 'extractions' or 'spirit releases.' And the funny thing is, doing what I am doing now seems far more 'normal' and comfortable than working at the bank ever did!

Sometimes I do wonder if I would have been better off *not* knowing some of the things I know now. I have had conversations with several shaman friends who have stated that if they had known what they were getting into at the outset, they would never have gotten into this work, because it *really does* open your eyes to things that knock your understanding of life – of physical existence, of death, and of the 'afterlife,' for want of a better word. But then, as I pointed out to my friends, we would not have seen the miracles of the workings of the Universe, or witnessed the amazing intelligence of the body, had we not followed this path!

As you know, I chose the title *A Healer of Souls* for this book as this phrase has particular relevance to me, for I now understand that these words reflect the identity of *my* soul, and describe my core purpose in life. At the time though, being a pensions consultant in a bank, I was confused. A healer of *souls* – how did anybody heal souls? It was only many years later, when I started doing spirit release work and soul retrieval, that I realized the relevance. I was indeed 'A Healer of *Souls*,' because not only do I assist souls *with* bodies, i.e. people, but those *without* bodies as well – the many discarnate spirits who are all around us, whether we like to believe it or not!

To be honest with you, I used to think that death was pretty simple, an automatic process. Admittedly, the run-up to it may not be particularly easy, especially if there is illness, disease or injury involved, but I always thought that when you took your last breath, that was it. GAME OVER. One minute, you are alive; the next you are dead. But I have come to realize that the death process may not be so straightforward, so automatic at all. Due to the dream I mentioned previously, I was aware that there were such things as 'entities,' 'spirits,' 'spirit attachments' or 'discarnate energies' – call them what you will – but it was only when I started my shamanic training that this was made an everyday reality for me.

Shamanism advocates respect for ALL of nature – and a spirit *is* part of the natural world, no matter how much we would like to disagree with that. We *are* energy, spirits *are* energy – the only difference between us is that spirits don't have physical bodies. Therefore, there is nothing 'supernatural' about a spirit! We were told during our early training that spirit attachment is an *extremely common* phenomenon, and our job as shamanic healers is to release such unhelpful and misplaced energies from our clients' energy fields. This is necessary because spirit attachments are parasitical in nature; they actually feed off our vital energies, therefore they need to be dispatched, pronto!

Mention the word 'entity' and the majority of people will immediately think of the 'scariest film of all time,' the 1973 film *The Exorcist* – which remains, at the time of writing, the thirteenth largest grossing film *of all time*. Adapted from a book written in 1971 by William Peter Blatty, the film shows a graphic representation of *demonic* possession. Blatty is said to have gained inspiration for the book from newspaper reports of a drawn-out exorcism of an American boy in 1949. Some say that the story itself is an actual amalgamation of exorcisms carried out on different people – or maybe it is just pure fiction from the writer's imagination. However, the most important thing to bear in mind is that this story illustrates the very *worst case scenario*, which is *demonic* possession. I have on occasion worked with people with demonic possession and they were nothing at all like the person shown in the film, and of all the people I have seen in my healing practice, I have come across demonic possession very few times, maybe as little as 2–3% overall.

In the vast majority of cases, the spirit attachments are 'earthbound,' which means that at some point they were people, and then they died, but they did not *move on* for some reason; they stayed in this realm. So, the majority of attachments (around 90%) are like the one that little Andrew had managed to attract in the first part of this chapter – simply an old man who had died and who for some reason got lost or stuck between the dimensions.

I appreciate that this concept may be very difficult to accept and I am sure that many of you will want to put this book away and try to forget you ever read about this stuff, but it is *important* that you understand that spirit attachment *can* happen, because actually, *it is very, very common*, so please read on and let me put your mind at rest. Remember the old adage: knowledge is power!

Very little research has been carried out on this subject. It is, after all, a very difficult area to carry out research in, not only because most people would not want to admit to it, but also because most of them are not even aware they have a spirit attachment in the first place. But to give you an idea of how common this is, it is usual for me to see three people a day and if we assume they are all new clients then I can pretty much guarantee that one of them at least will have some form of spirit attachment. Further, I would like to add that I do NOT have clients coming to see me who believe they are 'possessed' – 90% of the clients I see have no idea that I work in this area, and the same percentage have *no idea* that they can even be affected by such energies.

Having a spirit attachment can certainly cause problems for you in your life and stop you moving forward, although of course this is not always the reason people fail to move forward in life. Bear in mind as well that very few people have any idea that they have an attachment, *because the energy shift is normally*

very subtle. The affected person will certainly feel out of sorts
for a while; they may feel light-headed and jittery, or even
be shorter tempered. Over time they may start to display other
uncharacteristic behavior such as addictive tendencies and
strange likes and dislikes.

People who already work in the spiritual arena, or people
who have a very good understanding of themselves, *do* visit me
and explain casually that they feel they may have 'picked
something up,' but most people don't have a clue. Picking up a
spirit attachment – or getting one removed – does *not* need to be
a big, dramatic, scary thing at all, so it is nothing to worry about.
It is important to remove it though, as spirit attachments are
parasitical in nature. They feed off our vital energies by linking
into our nervous system via a chakra and they use *our* life force
to live on, so the sooner we get rid of them, the better.

As previously stated, such energies are all part of the natural
world, like it or not. When I first started out on this path, it was
very easy to think of such energies as 'bad,' 'evil,' or 'nasty,' but
I soon learned that a true shaman knows there are only two types
of energy in the world: light energy and heavy energy (*sami* and
hucha, as we call them).

To illustrate this, I will tell you a wonderful story I heard
recently about the late great shaman and Q'ero elder Don
Manuel Quispe. He was once in ceremony at Machu Picchu with
one of his students in order that they might both release their
heavy energy into the sacred earth at that place. Don Manuel
told his student to sit below him in a cave. He would then send
down his hucha – his heavy energy.

His student replied, 'Why would I want you to drop your
hucha onto me?'

Don Manuel laughed and said, 'To you, my hucha [heavy]
energy is sami [light] energy, so don't complain!'

Does this make sense to you? Don Manuel had such a high
rate of vibration that even his lowest vibrating energy (his

hucha) vibrated at a much higher rate than his student's sami energy, so therefore it was actually beneficial to the student to carry out this exercise. So it is all relative, and it is all *just energy.*

So, an entity or spirit attachment is classed as 'heavy' energy – just heavy energy and nothing else, just something in the wrong place which needs to be taken to the right place. Such entities need to be dealt with in a compassionate way where possible, *even if* they are demonic in nature. I once worked with a demonic-sourced entity and it was so pitiful, so full of pain and suffering, that it was almost unbearable, and I ended up feeling huge compassion for it.

How do I ascertain that my client has 'picked something up'? I always sit and talk with clients over a cup of tea before we start any intervention method and while the client is talking I pick up on their energy. Normally, if they 'are not alone' then I get a tingling at the top of my head, a pressure in my solar plexus, or I just feel dizzy, as if plates are spinning within my energy field. I find it hard to concentrate on what I am saying and often it will seem that I cannot *see* the client very well, as if there is a dark cloud over them.

In addition, I can tell by the conversation if it is likely – clients will say things like, 'I was involved in a fight in a nightclub and I haven't been the same since,' or 'I haven't felt the same since my dad died.' Sometimes clients will notice something that is out of character for them, such as, 'I can't stop collecting stamps / crocheting for some reason, and I don't know why,' or 'I feel myself being much more angry about the smaller things than I used to be.' Some will comment that they have a 'pain which seems to move around.' The most common comment is, 'I have this negative and nasty chatter going on in my head all the time.'

Now, before you all make a grab for a crucifix or a Holy Book and fly into a panic, please bear in mind that these comments DO NOT NECESSARILY point to the fact that you have a spirit attachment. We *all* have chatter going on in our heads; (sadly) this is our **ego** mind talking, which is responsible for keeping us safe, but tends to take its work rather too seriously. So please do not worry. But there are certain 'chatters' that DO point to something not being quite right.

The most important point to remember is to NOT go into fear; if you do this, you are directly feeding the spirit what it wants, plus you are attracting more heavy energies and negativity towards you!

Releasing any type of heavy energy or spirit comes with inherent risks to the practitioner, for it is possible for the energy to attach itself to the person carrying out the 'extraction.' Therefore care needs to be exercised. I am very aware of such energies and know instantly what it feels like to pick one up. Now, you may think that you have to go skulking around a graveyard at midnight in order to obtain an attachment, but this is not the case at all! I once picked one up in a coffee shop, when a friend touched me on the hand to emphasize a point. I felt the spirit attachment hop onto me. I was annoyed about it, but I had cleared it by the end of the day. *There is no need to freak out about it; it just happens.*

There are many methods which can be utilized to remove a spirit attachment. I was taught to use large amounts of energy to dislodge the spirit from a person's spine and then use an optically perfect, multifaceted crystal with which to entice it and trap it until it can be released. I have seen another shaman remove one using fire and a large flower. Another shaman I know uses swords. I have even heard of a powerful shaman in Peru who 'shoots' at spirits with an imaginary gun! (Don't knock it – it works!) Other shamanic traditions use different methods, and organizations such as the Catholic Church use a set ritual and exorcism prayer.

It is very important to bear in mind that it is rarely sufficient to simply remove the spirit. They are usually linked in to an 'affinity' within us which is often a negative emotion, or a memory. In Andrew's case it was anger; it can also be guilt, or fear, sadness or loneliness, but whatever it is tends to be *negative* in nature. Here is *yet another* good reason to be a chicken salad person! This negative energy has to be removed before the spirit can be cleared, or else the client can be prone to reattachment.

The most important thing to remember is the need to raise the vibration of the client's energy field, as such energies come in on a 'like attracts like' basis, i.e. there is some resonance between the client and the spirit emotionally and vibrationally. For example, a lonely spirit will be attracted to a lonely person, not a wild party-goer! Therefore I always carry out procedures to clear the client's energy field as much as possible before the extraction.

If a spirit has attached itself to a person it *does not* have an affinity with, then that person's body will be able to clear the spirit itself – often it will appear that the person has developed cold or flu-like symptoms. But if there is an affinity there, then the body cannot clear the spirit and it will remain in the energy field of the person. It is particularly important to clear out the chakra in which the spirit has been residing. This is a bit like going in to clean a house when someone has moved out. After the extraction, refined *sami* energy is brought into the energy body to raise its frequency and to protect the client from further reattachment.

Often, the client can feel a little weak or strange immediately after the extraction process, but after a drink and a protein-based snack to ground them, they normally feel well enough to drive home. They can often also remark about having the feeling that they have forgotten something, or they feel they have left something behind, and often this can last a few days!

During my shamanic training I was taught a method of extraction which I used for a while. Eventually though, I found this to be unpleasant and difficult for myself, the client, *and the spirit*! I also felt that an opportunity had been lost. The spirit could have been with the person for 20, 30, or 40 years, or much,

much longer, and then suddenly it is gone? So many questions are left unanswered: Why was it there? What did it want?

I have had some entities who say they have been with clients for 500 years, or 'since 1610.' In fact I remember one process which revealed that the client's entity was in fact his young son from a past life. The son had left home and joined in a battle in order to be with his father and as a result he became severely wounded. (As memory serves, I think we were told that the battle took place in France in 1762.) The son died in his father's (my client's) arms, *but then stayed with him,* instead of moving on. So please remember, spirit attachments are not necessarily anything to be scared about; they could, after all, be someone's nice cuddly granny, and they are normally just very confused, lost and scared.

So, I asked my spirit guides to help me find another method, an easier and more compassionate way to do this work. Gradually, through trial and error, I started to develop my own ways. Many spirits are terribly frightened and need major reassurance about what is going to happen to them should they leave the host. When all their questions are answered and the spirit is reassured, they normally co-operate without a fuss. Often, these spirits do not understand that they have died. The M. Night Shyamalan film *The Sixth Sense* therefore has more truth to it than is immediately apparent!

From these conversations with spirits, it seems that – true to the Hollywood interpretation – at death, friends, relatives or angels come to collect the newly deceased and take them to the Light. It sounds fairly straightforward, doesn't it? But the death experience can be very frightening to the newly discarnate spirit and often they try to run away.

When I ask these spirits why they were attracted to my client, they often say, 'Because I felt safe with her.' I have noticed that they do seem to be drawn to highly sensitive people, more often than not. Maybe they think they will get fairer treatment!

Many spirit attachments seem to happen during childhood, particularly if the person had a difficult or lonely childhood. Perhaps these are the 'invisible friends' that children can become involved with? I have heard some spirits say that they went to the client as a child to help them and protect them in some way, although sometimes I think this is a ruse so that we will act more kindly towards them.

Alternatively, the spirit *can* be aware of what has happened to them, but is terrified to go to the Light and refuses the assistance they are offered at the point of death. Sometimes this can be because they feel they have done something bad or have 'sinned' in their lives. Perhaps they have done something they believe God will not forgive them for and therefore going to the Light will result in severe punishment; or even worse, they fear they will be sent straight to hell. One of my clients had a female spirit attached to her that was highly traumatized. She had died, as had many other thousands of women, as a result of the brutal torture that had been inflicted upon her during the witch trials as an aid to obtaining her 'confession.'

I tried to remove her to go to the Light, but she flatly refused to go. I tried to get to the bottom of her issue, rather than forcibly extracting her using another method. Eventually she said, *'I can't go to the Light because God hates women. I don't want to be totally destroyed, so I am going to stay where I am.'* Her sadness and grief were palpable; her host, my client, had been plagued by issues involving anger toward men and a deep depression and grief as a direct result of picking up on the thought-forms of this spirit. Eventually I managed to persuade her that to the very best of my knowledge, this was not the case – God loved all His children unconditionally – and eventually, she left my client and was free for the first time in many, many years.

Many clients often feel huge sympathy for the spirit which has been lodging with them and often cry or feel sad as it is being released. Once the spirit has been taken to the Light, they then have the opportunity to continue to evolve as a soul – and evolution of course is the purpose of all life. *Evolution*, not *revolution*, and definitely *not* stagnation, which is what the spirits are doing with their hosts: just stagnating. It does not serve these spirits to be sitting in someone else's energy field for eons!

So, what do you do when you are dead? Remember this! Look around you; if you see a deceased relative, a friend, or someone with a fine pair of feathered wings attached to his back, go with them! Do not be afraid; be calm and just 'go towards the Light'!

8. As Above, So Below, As Within, So Without

Memories 8.1

I run through the dark streets of London, wrapping myself up against the chill wind. It's hard to believe an hour ago I was lying on my sofa, warm and cuddled up with a mug of tea, watching my favorite film. But then my new investment banker boyfriend rang and asked me to visit him. I said no, but he whined and told me he was making a lovely meal for me, so I relented, hauled myself onto the train and the Tube, and here I am. I was displeased to see that he wasn't waiting for me at the Tube station, but I imagine he must be rushing about preparing the lovely dinner. In fact, he is probably wondering where I am, as I am running late. I increase my pace as visions of overcooked mushy vegetables and burned-down candles come to mind. I start to feel excited. What a romantic gesture!

Eventually, a little out of breath, I arrive at his door and ring the bell. Happily, he does not look annoyed that I am late. I sniff the air, and then sniff again. I can't smell anything at all.

'Come through,' he beckons, as he walks into his large study at the end of the hallway. 'I'm just finishing up some day-trading on my computer. Take a seat; I won't be long.'

I sit speechless in the chair behind him, looking at the back of his head and his broad, rugby player shoulders as he clicks away on his mouse, buying and selling stocks. Is he *kidding* me? In the end, I find my tongue. 'So, where's the lovely dinner you promised me?' I say with an edge to my voice.

He continues to stare at the screen. 'Oh yes, silly me. Could you be a love and get it started while I finish this? I got us two spaghetti bolognese microwave meals for half price as the sell-by date is today! Could you just chuck them in for a couple of minutes and I'll come through when I'm done?'

I hold my breath and walk into the kitchen on automatic pilot. I am livid. *Microwavable spaghetti bolognese?* Firstly, I don't eat things that have been microwaved and I am pretty sure I told him that. Moreover, I am a VEGETARIAN and have been for over 20 years! I grab my handbag and walk out the door in tears. So much for visions of good food, romance and candles! How *could* he!

Practice Notes 8.2

Emily arranges herself elegantly against the cushions. She is in her mid fifties, slim, attractive and well groomed. She looks around the room as if wondering how to start, then she seems to pluck up some courage.

'I'm here because I think I'm cursed, blocked in some way from having a long-term relationship. I have never been married, not even for a short while. I've had longish relationships with men – a couple of years here or there, sometimes as much as three or four years – but as soon as it gets to the point where they would normally make a commitment and propose, the men dump me for some reason. The normal pattern is that they say, "Thanks for everything. You've really helped me a lot, but I think we've come to the end of the road now. I think you want something that I just can't give; I'm simply *not* the marrying type, I'm afraid." 'And *then*, only a few months later, I find out they've had a whirlwind romance and have *gotten married*! They don't want to marry *me*, but they *always* marry the very next girl, and reasonably quickly too. And it hasn't just happened once; it's happened lots of times.'

'How many times?' I ask.

'At least ten, maybe more. As I say, I think I'm cursed!'

'And you *really* want to get married – are you very clear on that?'

'Oh *yes*! More than anything in the world. I'm devastated it hasn't happened before now and that I've now lost my chance to be a mother. I've dreamed about my wedding for *so long*! I want to share my life with someone, grow old with someone.

'I'm a good woman, I'm caring and kind – why does no one, *no one,* want to marry me? Is there something wrong with me? I make huge efforts with my appearance; for God's sake I get up at 5am every day to do my hair! I've kept my figure; I'm a great cook and housekeeper. I'm cultured and can have an interesting conversation with anyone, I appreciate many things in life, I've traveled... what *more* do I need to do?

'My friends are all amazed by it; they can hardly believe it, but the same thing happens again and again: men leave me, and then they marry the *very next girl.* Even the men that I'm not actually that keen on say goodbye to me, and before you know it they're saying, "I do."'

* * *

Inge looks flushed in the cheeks, and I can tell that she is trying not to cry. 'I mean, what *is* his problem? I just don't get it. I work hard, I'm responsible, I'm a team player. What does he want, *blood*? Nothing is ever good enough for him! He's constantly dragging me into his office, because I haven't done this right, or that right. I do my best, you know? It's a tough work environment. But my boss, I tell you, he's something else.

'And do you want to know what's weird about this? He's just like the boss I had at my old firm. He was nasty to me too – he stabbed me in the back whenever he could, didn't promote me when he promised he would; I never forgave him for that. So what am I going to do? Leave *another* job? Try again?'

I think for a moment and then ask, 'How exactly does he treat you?'

She thinks. 'Like I'm never good enough, whatever I do. Like I'm substandard in some way. He makes me feel small and insecure; I can't even speak straight when he's getting on to me.

It's very upsetting.'

'Think back for me. Has anyone else ever treated you like this?'

'What – other than the last boss, and the one before that? I don't think I can think of anyone. Unless you count my mum, of course. She made me feel terrible about myself. She still does, actually. You're *not* saying that these bosses are treating me badly because my mum does, are you? That's *crazy*!'

Notes 8.3

'As above, so below.' This sentence or 'axiom' (i.e. a universally recognized truth, established law, astute observation, or general truth) forms the basis of much spiritual thought and literature. The full saying, 'As above, so below, as within, so without,' is attributed to Hermes Trismegistus, who is said to have been an ancient Egyptian sage/priest/philosopher, most famed for his writings entitled 'The Emerald Tablet.' An understanding of Hermetic philosophy is not necessary for the purposes of this book. What I do want to share with you is the great power, importance and significance of these words, which are frequently found in magical, occult and spiritual circles – and for good reason.

What could it mean – 'As above, so below, as within, so without'? You may ask yourself, 'What is meant by "above"?' and that question cannot be easily answered. My sense is that 'above' and 'below' are all-encompassing; it can mean whatever you want it to mean. It can mean, for example, that if the Divine is above you, He is also here, within you. It can mean that if the Universe is above you, then it is also within you. If the stars are above you, they are also within you – who knows, perhaps they are represented by the chakras? But then the meaning is multi-layered and actually does not end in any particular place; rather it loops back around upon itself.

The 'Microcosm/Macrocosm' theories come into play here.

The microcosm can be seen as the self, the macrocosm as the Universe; *within each is the other.* More simply put, the greater can be found represented in the smaller. A simple example of this can be seen in the body. It is commonly held by reflexologists that the entire physical system (the *macrocosm* in this example) is reflected by the reflexes in the soles of the feet (in this example the soles of the feet are the *microcosm*) and by manipulating and releasing tensions in these areas, benefits are reflected in the physical body. Similarly, in iridology, the entire physical being is believed to be reflected within the irises of the eyes, and symptoms can be spotted at the microcosm level, treated at this level, and the healed state is then reflected in the macrocosm, the physical body.

Gandhi's famous quote, 'Be the change you wish to see in the world,' rings more true with an understanding of the 'As above, so below' principle – *that which is outside of you is also within you*; if you want to see peace on the *outside*, you need to *be peaceful within*. The outside is *always* a reflection of the inner. So, it follows that if there is hatred and violence in the world then there *must* be hatred and violence within us – and our world is just reflecting that back at us. It is no good fighting against the hatred and violence; it is no good trying to effect change on the outside, because it is simply a *reflection* of the inside. It's rather like a film being projected onto a screen in a cinema: if you don't like what you see on the screen, it is no good trying to remove the image from the screen with a big eraser. The source of the image is the film within the projector; in order to change what is on the outside (the screen) the film needs to be completely re-edited.

This then is what we have to do within ourselves: edit our movies, and know – really know – that if we don't like what is going on outside, it is *not* because of our boss, or our lover, or the Universe; it is because of what is going on *within ourselves*. This can be very hard for us to get our heads around, because we are so caught up in 'what is going on *out there*.' As if it is separate from us in some way! But it really isn't separate from us; it is a *projection of our internal reality*. Accepting this, however, involves taking a whole lot of responsibility. When we accept responsibility for our lives, totally and completely, then we have to come to the very painful, yet truthful admission that *we are the Creators of our own reality*. And that leaves us no one to blame. Not the horrible boyfriend, or the nasty boss... or even God Himself.

You may well be reading this, nodding to yourself, saying, 'Yes, Dawn, I know this!' and trust me, many clients say the same thing. But they really *don't* get it, because the next time something happens, they wail, 'Why did X/Y/Z happen to me?!' It is one thing to read the Gandhi quote and say, 'Yes, what a wise man. We need to *be* peace.' But many of us completely miss the point and it is SUCH an important point! If I am totally honest, even I forget about it sometimes. This weekend something crappy happened and I immediately switched into my old conditioning of 'Why me?' but fortunately it was not very long before I righted myself, and asked, 'What is it *within me* that has created this reality?' Painful stuff, but fantastically beneficial.

Think of it like this: imagine that there is only YOU in the world. That's it. Nothing and no one else. And *everything* in this world, good or bad, everything and every person, is a reflection of an aspect of you – of your beliefs, your conditioning, and the way you treat yourself. Everyone else is like a blank screen, and you are the projector from which all the images and experiences are sent out. Think of yourself as the director of the film of your life. You create the film, you choose the actors, and you write *all* the scripts. Scary, isn't it? What a responsibility! It is so much easier to have external circumstances to blame!

My sense is that this is exactly what life is. A reflection of the self. Pure and simple. Take for example my experiences in the Memories section of this chapter. It happened a long time ago, when I had significantly less understanding than I do now (now, there is no way I would have ever got off the comfy sofa in the first place!), but at the time I was *livid*! And very, very upset at the thoughtlessness of my boyfriend – who quickly became an ex-boyfriend after that! I told the story at dinner parties and all my friends were very sympathetic. 'How horrible of him to do that!' they cried. 'Poor you!' But it was years before I *got it*, before I applied the concept of 'As above, so below, as within, so without.' And it happened quite by chance one day. I was standing in my kitchen, on the cold stone floor late at night, eating toast. I was eating toast because, once again, I hadn't had time to go the shops to buy food and I had nothing in the fridge. And I hate to admit it, but this was a regular occurrence. It was not even the fact I was eating toast – I was *standing up*, in the kitchen, eating toast. The toast wasn't cut up all nicely on a plate, and I wasn't sitting at the dining table, or even on the sofa eating toast comfortably. I was *eating toast, uncomfortably.*

All of a sudden I had a 'ping' moment. The light bulb got switched on over my head and the memory of that evening popped to mind. And all of a sudden, *I got it.* I had gone to Sebastian's for dinner, expecting the full works. A properly set table, with candles and a tablecloth. A well thought-out, well cooked and nicely presented meal, prepared with love. But, had I *ever* done that *for myself*? Set a table, planned a meal, *nurtured and loved myself*? A big resounding NO followed. No, I have an empty fridge most of the time and I normally eat standing up in my tiny kitchen or sitting on the sofa in front of the TV. Even today, I eat out most of the time. So then, WHY did I expect Sebastian to do for me something that *I wasn't prepared to do for myself*? Why indeed? He was simply treating me as badly as I treated myself. *He was just an outward manifestation of my poor treatment of myself.*

I appreciate that this isn't a terribly good example, and that it may also be better suited to the 'Relationships' chapter, but the realization struck me so hard in the kitchen that day that I just had to include it. Instead of continuing to fume about horrid

Sebastian, I should have been looking more closely at horrid *me*. So, sorry about that, Sebastian, wherever you are.

I remember reading a quote once which read, 'Show me your garden and I will show you your life!' At the time I didn't get it. But later, as I came to understand the power of the words 'As above, so below,' I *really* got it. And I walked into my garden and looked hard and dispassionately at it. I noticed that there was very little color in it. It was pretty overgrown and unloved. Hmmmmm. Feng shui works on a similar principle to the 'As above' axiom. For example, my feng shui lady told me that I had chosen my house absolutely as a result of where I was personally at the time of purchase, even though I had no understanding of feng shui at the time. I bought a house which is entered by the 'Spiritual Development' area, and most surprisingly, due to the layout of the house and the garden, there was a huge chunk missing out of my 'Relationship' area! How interesting is that?

If we refer back to the Practice Notes, what do you think was going on with the clients mentioned? Emily *consciously* wanted to marry, but *subconsciously* really didn't want to marry at all! She had a good life and she also liked her independence. So that was why *she attracted* men who would not marry her. Then this pattern created a belief: *Men always leave me and marry others,* so this was being reflected back to her constantly; and seriously, this had happened to her over and over again.

After a very difficult childhood, Inge had created the belief that she needed to be treated badly, and also had problems with honoring and respecting her own power; hence her bosses continually misused theirs.

I have a client in America who continually fails to see the connection between the way she treats herself and the way others treat her. Recently, she told me that she had a new boyfriend and he was 'amazing and marvelous and I am madly in love.' I just thought, *Oh no!* I knew that he would be reflecting her treatment of herself back to her. A couple of months later the cracks started to appear in the relationship and he started to be abusive towards her. 'Why would he be like this?' she wailed. 'Why do men treat me *so badly*?' Try as I might, I just cannot get her to understand that these men are simply reflecting her poor treatment of herself. Clearly she has a need to continue to beat herself up; after all, it is all she has known all her life – in a way, it's her Known Zone. She is a work in progress, but I hope that she will finally 'get it' one day!

Truly, if we have someone who is causing us problems in our life, *we should thank them*! Why? Because they are unwittingly enabling us to see 'our stuff' – what we need to work on and the aspects of ourselves that are in 'shadow.' *Shadow* is the word commonly used to describe aspects of ourselves that we disown, but it is not a brilliant word really, as it implies that those aspects of ourselves are 'dark' in some way. But this is not the case. For example, we may be forced to disown our happiness, our peace, our ability to relax, our joy, indeed a whole number of things that are positive, as well as the aspects that are darker, such as fear, hatred, rage etc. Through necessity, I have devised a method of identifying and healing those disowned aspects of self in my healing practice, and my sense is that this method, which I call 'power retrieval' (note: not 'power animal retrieval') is as important as soul retrieval. Often our greatest source of energy, power and 'beingness' is held in those disowned parts, which, like the soul parts, retreat angrily to the Lower World once they have been banished from us.

Many people, particularly 'spiritual' people, pay a dear price for being 'nice.' They try to love only the parts of themselves which are light and love, and they hate and banish their darkness. But the *whole self* must be loved in order to prevent the creation of unruly shadow aspects. If we are to become enlightened, the *whole self* becomes enlightened, not just the nice bits of us. But many people fear their own shadow, the bits of themselves they have locked away behind bars. And these parts become angrier every day they are separated from us, resulting in them popping up unbidden in our dreams and in those difficult people around us. And unchecked, they can be the cause of much violence and destruction. Sadly, we have all heard stories about what happens when a priest is forced to put his sexuality into shadow, or when a man refuses to acknowledge his rage.

Additionally, we need to come into a place of integrity with ourselves. That means saying what we mean. If a friend phones up and suggests that you go out and do something, and you don't *want* to do that thing, *don't do it*! If you say 'yes' by accident or habit then phone them straight back. Be honest. Stop being nice and just promise yourself that you will be in integrity with your heart and speak your truth. You can speak it nicely, kindly, but *speak it*. You will find life becomes a lot easier when you do this.

We all accumulate limiting or negative beliefs. We need to challenge them and heal them and recognize that our world is a reflection of our innermost being, and our experiences are created by ourselves, to prove our beliefs about ourselves right. But they can be healed, and habits of a lifetime can be changed. But for now I would like you to think about being the only person in the world, and the Creator of your own reality. Look around you: what have you created? Does it serve you? If not, you may like to consider addressing your relationship with yourself and your deeply held beliefs. The journey may not be an easy one, but it will be worthwhile and you *can change that script*.

9. Relationships

Memories 9.1

While I am listening to the wedding speeches, a man catches my eye. He is dark and handsome and is wearing a beautifully cut charcoal-gray suit. He catches me looking at him, and smiles, which lights up his fabulous chocolate brown eyes. I do not know what it is about this man but I feel like I have been hit by a train. After the speeches, the seat beside me becomes free and the beautiful stranger lowers himself into the available chair. We spend the next few minutes chatting pleasantly, although I have no clue what I am talking about – his eyes are locked on to mine and it is almost as if I am hypnotized. He looks deep into my eyes, into my soul, and politely asks me what I am doing after the reception, which is soon coming to an end. I tell him I have no plans, and he says he would be honored if I would consider spending some time with him. I am elated and tell him I would like that very much.

When the reception ends we step into the sunlit streets of London, and as we cross the busy roads he grabs my hand and keeps hold of it as he leads me to an area full of busy bars, cafés and restaurants. His hand feels familiar in mine; it is as if I have always held it, known it, and there is an unbelievable energy between us. I know he feels it too, by the way he keeps looking at me. As we wait at a busy pedestrian crossing he takes my face in his hands and kisses me, and the outside world slips away; everything recedes, and all that remains is the softness of his lips, the taste and scent of him. And I know I know this man, that this is not the first time I have kissed him. I do not want it to end. The lights on the crossing change from red to amber to green to red again and again but we remain glued to the spot, afraid to move in case we break the spell.

Eventually we part and he smiles at me and leads me to a

seating area outside a trendy bar. I am lost for words, elated, riding high as a kite on the thrill of his kiss. I struggle for words, and try to bring myself back to reality. I can't think straight, and rummage around in my head for something to say, finally coming up with an uninspiring, 'So, where do you live?'

When he replies, 'LA,' I feel like I have been clubbed over the head. *America?* AGAIN? You have GOT to be kidding me!

* * *

Some months earlier...
'So, where do you live?'
'Montana.'
Some months later...
'So, where do you live?'
'Washington DC.'
Etc, etc.

* * *

'The thing is, Dawn, I'm kind of a "lone wolf" kind of guy. I like to be free – like the wind. And after my last relationship I decided that I would have a two-year period in which I would be completely on my own, before I went into another relationship.'

'When does that two-year period end?'

'In September.'

'But haven't you been going out with me for the last year?'

'Ah yes, yes, I guess I have, haven't I? Hahahahaha... But do you get what I'm saying?'

Practice Notes 9.2

The international telephone line is crackling badly but I can hear Helene's kind, soft voice clearly. She tells me:

'I just want to be loved. I want someone to love me. I *need* someone to love me. I want it with all my heart, *all* my heart. I cannot tell you how much I want it. Tell me what I need to do; I'll do anything, anything at all. I will change any aspect of myself, go anywhere, and do anything. I have to have this; I cannot die without it. I cannot die alone.

'I'm 74 now, but I take very good care of myself. I'm fit, I hike, I try to always look my best and wear pretty clothes. I've recently had six hours of facial surgery to lift and strengthen my chin and smooth out my neck, and my friends say it looks really great. Next month I'm booked into the hospital again to have my knees lifted, so they look better. If I'm as pretty as can be, someone will love me, won't they? Won't they? Oh, *please* say that they will!'

* * *

Lucinda flicks back her blonde bob and looks out from under her fringe with wide baby-blue eyes. She is trendily dressed, poised, and has a lovely figure. She has a highly successful and exciting career as a fashion journalist, yet, like so many of my professional female clients, her romantic life is a complete mess. Her biological clock is ticking so loud it's almost deafening; she desperately wants to find Mr Right and settle down to a life of married bliss, yet the right relationship eludes her. Even if it appears her men have it all, cracks soon start to appear in the relationship and everything comes crashing down around her. And very often, she finds that the men are simply not *manly* enough for her. They are either in awe of her and are too weak, or alternatively appear to be in direct competition with her, causing the relationship to turn into a battlefield about who can outdo the other.

She is not attracted to the men who are clearly attracted to her, and it seems the men she finds attractive do not want her, or cannot give her the attention she desires. Some men appear lovely, but she could only see herself being friends with them as there is zero sexual attraction. Yet, in relationships with the men she *is* attracted to, the sexual side seems less than satisfying or not as frequent as she would like, for some unknown reason. She tells me she is well educated, well traveled and is a great conversationalist, with a good sense of humor – so where is she going wrong? What has happened to the fairytale relationship she grew up to expect?

* * *

Margo charges through the door with a baby stuffed precariously underneath one arm and a large bag underneath the other. She plonks herself down on the sofa and looks exhausted. Her coarse brown hair is scraped back haphazardly from her unmade-up, pale face in an off-center ponytail, tied with a rubber band. She is wearing a baggy grey sweatshirt which is spattered with baby vomit. Her jeans are straining at the seams over her thighs, and on her feet are a pair of old grey trainers.

I make her a cup of tea as she looks like she needs that – and about a month's worth of sleep. I ask her how I can help and she tells me she is fed up and that her husband is 'crap.' I ask her what makes him so crap, and she spits out that he is just rubbish.

I ask her how she would like him to be and she tells me, 'Strong, manly, attentive, loving, efficient, in charge, and dynamic.' She tells me she *yearns* for the day when he strides into the room with two tickets for a long weekend in Paris. He will have organized everything, including babysitters, in order to whisk her away for a weekend of romance and luuurrrrrvvve, but she tells me there is 'fat chance of that happening!'

I ask about him, and she tells me that he has turned into some simpering weakling, who asks her what he should do almost all the time. If, on some rare occasion, they get to go out, she is the one that has to organize everything, including choosing and booking the restaurant, and *she* has to drive him to the restaurant so *he* can have a drink. They sit facing each other with very little to say.

He has also let himself go, and she feels like she has one extra child with him around. She has taken complete control of the house, the garden and the finances as she is now at home while he works full-time. I ask about their sex life, and she snorts so loudly she nearly inhales her tea, and tells me that their sex life has been rubbish for years – he is even failing at that.

* * *

Miranda tells me that she runs her own successful business but this involves very long hours and an incredible amount of stress and responsibility, along with increasing problems with staff as her company grows in size. Arriving home from a hard day's work, she is immediately besieged by her three boisterous boys, two dogs, her useless and hysterical nanny, and her increasingly difficult husband. She rushes upstairs to get changed into something comfortable, then comes down and starts to make the evening meal. By the time she has cleared up and the boys have settled down and gone to bed, there is just enough time to watch half an hour of TV before craving her bed and some sleep. In bed her husband will frequently request sex, which she often declines as she is so exhausted.

She tells me she feels like a zombie, constantly overwhelmed by the pressures of work, family and responsibility, and the increasing stresses within her relationship. She is now the main earner in the family as her husband came out of investment banking to do something more 'socially and environmentally responsible.' He works hard, but for a small fraction of his previous salary. Yet he seems to resent his wife's success and often tries to belittle or criticize her personally, professionally or as a mother, either to her face or more often in front of their friends.

She feels generally unloved, unsupported and unheard, and is crumbling under the strain of carrying everything on her own shoulders. She starts to cry as she tells me that she wants to die, that she is so tired and she simply cannot keep going anymore.

* * *

The plain, overweight housewife tells me that if she was slim, she would feel much better about herself.

The slim interior designer tells me that if she was clever and worked in the City, she would feel much better about herself.

The pretty lady who is a partner in a City law firm tells me that if she were more creative, like say, an interior designer, she would feel much better about herself.

The curvy businesswoman tells me that if she was more successful, she would feel much better about herself.

The beautiful single lady tells me that if she was married, she would feel much better about herself.

The stunning married lady tells me that if she were single and independent, she would feel much better about herself.

The slim, beautiful, fit, clever, kind, generous, funny, creative, successful, rich and independent woman tells me that if she were different somehow, she would feel much better about herself.

Notes 9.3

I just have to share this with you! My mum just called me and asked what I was up to. I told her I had just made a cup of tea and was going back upstairs to write the next chapter of this book. She asked about the subject of the chapter and I told her it was about relationships. By the time she stopped laughing, my tea was cold. But I have to be honest, I can see her point. As you will have seen from the Memories section, my relationship history has not been particularly successful to date (depending on how you define success, of course). For many years, for some reason I seemed to only attract American men. Or commitment-phobes. Or commitment-phobes who lived in America. And I had no idea why this happened again and again. So for the last couple of years, I have stayed out of relationships and instead worked hard on my *relationship with myself.* Our relationship with ourselves is the blueprint for *all* our relationships, not just with lovers but with *everyone* – friends, family, colleagues, our bosses – and even with our bodies.

When I was young, my mother always used to say to me, 'You have to love yourself, Dawn, before anyone else will love you.' I would roll my eyes in typical teenage fashion, mutter, sigh, and groan, 'I DO love myself, Muuuuuuuum!' I reasoned that as I didn't *hate* myself, I must therefore love myself – right? *Wrong.*

So, even though my relationship history hasn't been much to write about (although admittedly it has been a constant source of entertainment and hilarity for my friends), I have learned a *lot* along the way.

You may have read elsewhere in this book – particularly in the 'As Above, So Below' chapter, that *everything is a mirror and reflects back to us our internal state and beliefs.* Nothing really exists outside of us, rather like in the *Matrix* films, where everyone lives in a kind of computer program. *We* have to take responsibility for the quality of our lives, *regardless* of the circumstances of our childhood, regardless of how good or bad Mum and Dad were.

Let's look at the client issues in the Practice Notes, starting with Helene, the more mature lady who lived in the US. Helene was, as you can tell, *desperate* to be loved. Every cell of her being longed for it, and as you read, she told me she would do *anything for it.* So I asked her to do something to attract to her the love she so desperately wanted – I asked her to love herself. I asked her to be kind to herself, to speak kindly to herself – both out loud and in her thoughts. I asked her to do some activities that she enjoyed, to pamper herself, and to get to the point where she could look in the mirror and say, 'I love you, Helene!'

Well! You would think that I had asked her to saw off her legs and arms! She cried, 'I can't do that! No! No! Anything but that!' I pointed out to her that she said she wanted a man to love her, so therefore, if she couldn't love herself, wasn't she wanting a man to do something that she couldn't bring herself to do?

She told me that the *only* way that she could even *think* about loving herself was if a man loved her *first*, then that would give her the confirmation that she was, in fact, lovable. What do you think the chances are of her finding that man? That's right, *zero*. Because a relationship with a man (or a woman) will mirror your relationship with you. If Helene *did* manage to attract someone, he would in time behave in a way that would prove her beliefs about herself were true – that actually, she was undeserving of love.

And why did Helene have this belief that she was unlovable? Because her father had left the family home when she was three years old. At that time, in her little child's mind, she had decided it was *her fault* her father had left, because she was totally unlovable. And what's more, she had held on to this belief for over 70 *years*! She had never *once* looked at the situation with an adult brain and reasoned that her father might have left because his marriage was failing, or he was having an affair / had realized he was gay / was a commitment-phobe / felt trapped / had a life purpose that needed fulfilling elsewhere / had gambling debts / wanted to join the Foreign Legion, or a million other reasons. How likely is it that he left because his three-year-old child was so utterly unlovable? Unlikely! But she did not want to see this.

Why? *Why was she holding on to this excuse for dear life?* She was blaming her lack of relationships on her father, when in actual fact, what emerged after a few sessions was that in truth, she did not actually *want* a relationship – because she was terrified of being hurt again. So it was actually easier for her to remain single and *dream* of a perfect, fantasy man, instead of forming a better relationship with herself, getting out there, and dating a *real* man.

Can you see how deeply we wish to believe in certain things? How hard we try to *fool* ourselves? Eventually, after many sessions of going round in circles, Helene admitted to me that she *didn't* actually want the thing that she was asking me for (i.e. a relationship) after all, as she was too frightened of being hurt again, so we stopped her sessions. But not before she had blamed her lack of a relationship on all sorts of reasons: her father, her appearance, where she lived, her age, her weight, a mean school teacher who upset her in childhood, numerous other people, God, the fact she couldn't use a computer, the fact she wasn't enlightened, the fact she wasn't very confident... so she was blaming pretty much everything else in her life, but the actual truth was that she *did not want* a relationship.

I am so grateful that Helene allowed me to share her story with you, because it is a perfect example of what taking *responsibility for your life means*. It means being truly, deeply honest with yourself, and not blaming other people, events, situations, childhood memories, geography, appearances, levels of spiritual development, or a million other excuses for our current situation. If something isn't happening in your life, then at the *deepest* levels it means that *we don't want it to*!

You would not believe the amount of fabulous, gorgeous, hugely intelligent and successful women I see who in all seriousness tell me that they haven't got a boyfriend because they are a (UK) size 14, and someone will only go out with them if they are a size 10. *Rubbish!* Look at this yourself, and tell me: Is this true? Do men only go out with or marry women who are size 10 or below? Clearly not! Many of the men I know actually prefer women a little more curvy! Now, let us look at that another way, and imagine that men DO only date size-10 women or below. If that situation was true, and you *really, really, really* wanted a boyfriend, wouldn't you go on a *diet*, instead of steadily eating more and not exercising? Of course you would!

So, once again, this is a prime example of someone saying one thing, yet meaning something else altogether. The client's mouth may be telling me that she desperately wants a relationship, but her blaming of x and y and z, along with her *actions* (or lack of them), tell me something else altogether. When we stop blaming, then we can get down to the real crux of the matter and live more truthfully.

I have many women coming to see me who moan about their failed marriages, their horrible husbands, etc. Then, later on in the conversation they admit, 'Of course I knew as I was walking down the aisle that I was making a huge mistake!' It is much better for you to say, 'I take full responsibility for my current situation; I knew he was not the right man for me, but I married him anyway, so now I am dealing with the fallout from that.' It's cleaner and more honest, isn't it? When we blame, we expend so much valuable energy and we *never* move forward.

Ask yourself now, in a gentle and loving way, 'Who am I blaming for my current situation in life?' And 'What would the advantages be of taking full responsibility for finding myself in this position? How did I arrive here, really? And if I take responsibility for getting myself out of this situation, what would that look like?'

If *subconsciously* we are scared of being in a relationship, for whatever reason, then we will *purposefully* attract a string of Mr Wrongs to ourselves, because *deep down, in truth, the thought of marriage or relationships frightens us and it can also make us feel trapped*. Remember that our energy fields are vast and intelligent and they will *assist* us in attracting the wrong man, because we *want* to attract the wrong man – despite what we say and think on a conscious level. Remember, please, that this is *subconscious* behavior; we do not know we are selecting the wrong guys. Well, actually when you look at it objectively, and because we know that the Universe always works, we are actually attracting the perfect guys – guys who are not available, don't live in the same country as us, or ones that won't marry us! But we really need to take a very hard look at ourselves, particularly our *actions* – not our words or our thoughts but our actions; they reveal an awful lot.

So, this is how it has been possible for me to attract the one American in a crowd of a few hundred, again and again, because that situation – a long-distance relationship – served me well. Who was the real commitment-phobe in this story? Yes, that is right – ME! And it actually took me sooooo long to work that one out, *despite* my understanding about subconscious projections and mirroring! When I did eventually work it out, I was *completely horrified and shocked*! Because if you had asked me what I wanted, like Helene, I would have told you, *truly*, that I wanted the whole shebang. That I wanted to meet my soul mate, share my life, my hopes and dreams with him, to love and be loved, to share my life's journey with him, to support him on his journey, to get married, to grow old together and have deep, deep intimacy with him (and of course have great sex). And I meant it! I really, really thought I meant it, as do so many other women who come to see me.

But there is that part of us inside our heads, that subconscious part of us which goes, *Yeah? That's want you want, is it? Like HELL! There is no way I am letting that happen! Look how you got hurt last time!* And it is this naughty subconscious aspect of us that actually creates our reality. All the Law of Attraction books and films tell us that our *thoughts* create our realities; and they do, certainly. But, as I have mentioned previously, it is the thoughts and beliefs of our *subconscious minds*, NOT our *conscious* minds, which create our reality. Do you see my point? I do appreciate that this is quite difficult to understand. But truly, if you had said to me, 'Dawn, if you truthfully answer this question, I will give you ten million pounds: "Do you really want to be in a relationship?"' I would have answered, 'Yes, most definitely!' And I would have *lost* the money!

Now, I bet you are thinking, *Is she NUTS? I definitely want a man and a great relationship!* And, like you, I would have read this and thought exactly the same thing, to be fair. But do look at this carefully and really, really, *really* question yourself, and once again look at your *actions*, because therein lies the truth.

If I am very honest with myself, looking back I can see that my *behavior and actions* actually went *against* the thing that I said I wanted, i.e. a man. For a start, I made no real effort to meet someone, despite all my friends encouraging me to go on internet dating sites, or speed-dating events, which had worked for them. I would say, 'That just doesn't feel right to me; I'd prefer to meet someone naturally.' Now, from what I gather, meeting someone on the internet *is* now the normal way to meet someone! So there is the first clue. Also, if I was going out somewhere where there was a possibility of meeting someone, let's say at a friend's party or a trendy bar, for some reason I could not quite understand, I would not present my best self. I would often only give myself ten minutes to get ready!

So let's be straight here: if you are *really* intent on doing something, whatever it may be, you should notice that *all your efforts* are following that direction, and if all parts of you are in alignment with your desires, you should start to see *results*!

OK, so now let's assume you *do* actually want a boyfriend and all the parts of yourself are behind that want. And we shall also assume that you do make the effort to get out and about and you do meet someone. If you do not love or care for yourself, or if you have negative beliefs about yourself (or men), how is that relationship going to go? Correct, it is going to go badly, as my client Yasmin found out. When I asked the beautiful Yasmin how well she looked after herself, she said she didn't – she just couldn't be bothered. She told me that when it was about herself, anything went and she didn't make any effort at all, but if she had guests, she would be a great hostess and make sure they had lovely food and everything they needed. She wouldn't make nice meals for herself, or pamper herself in any way. She judged herself harshly, and therefore so did other people.

So, here are a few questions for you. Write them down on a piece of paper, and then note your answers underneath.

Question: How do you treat yourself?

- Like someone you love?
- Like someone you tolerate?
- Or like someone you hate – or even loathe?

Question: What actions do you take to nurture and pamper yourself?

Question: Do you love yourself? Can you look at yourself in the mirror and say 'I love you' to yourself without any problem?

How do you *really* feel about yourself? Here are some more questions which will hopefully get you thinking:

1   How well do you physically nurture yourself? Do you cook nutritious and tasty meals for yourself? Do you eat at the table? Do you arrange the food nicely on the plate, or do you just throw it on?

2   Do you get the exercise that you need, and are *you* happy with your weight? (No one else needs to be happy with your weight, only you.)

3   Are you physically well? (Illness can often be a sign of lack of self-love.)

4   Are you 'present' with your body – do you care about it, pamper it and treat it to such things as nice candlelit baths and regular massages (or whatever your thing is)?

5   What things do you do for the happiness of your soul? (Souls like things like dance, music, art, beauty, creativity and nature.)

6   What needs do you have and how do you ensure those needs are met? For example, do you ensure you get enough rest, and have a good work/life balance? Do you

put yourself first or do you put everybody else first? If you have always wanted to learn to do something, do you make sure that you make the time to do that thing, or do your needs get shoved to the bottom of the pile?

7   How tidy, clean and well organized is your bedroom? This may seem an odd question but many people keep the 'public' areas of their house nice, and sleep in a tip. This indicates you might be putting other people before yourself. How many times do you say, 'It's only me that is going to see it, therefore it doesn't matter'? (It does matter! You deserve a nice space to sleep in!)

8   How many times do you say 'Yes' when you really mean 'No'? How often are you out of integrity with yourself, and go along with others so you are not seen to 'rock the boat'? How well do you stand up for yourself? Like Miranda, how much do you push yourself to be perfect, to keep going, to keep everything together, when really what you need is a good scream and a year spent in a health spa?

9   How much *fun* do you have in your life? How many exciting or lovely things do you have booked into your diary right now? (Always try to have at least three things booked in to look forward to: shows, day trips, visiting friends, exhibitions, concerts etc.)

10   How do you *allow* other people to treat you?

11   Are you your *best* self? Have you achieved your fullest potential? Are you happy and fulfilled where you are? Or could you be more, do more, have more than you currently have? (Remember, it's all about *you* being happy with *you; no one else's opinion matters.*)

12   Are you doing what you want to be doing? Or are you working in a certain job to make someone else happy? (You would be amazed at the amount of people I see working as accountants, lawyers, solicitors or doctors just

because it's what their parents wanted them to do, but not what they wanted to do.)

13　And here is the best question: *Why* do you want a partner? What do you want from them that you are not giving to yourself? We have to give ourselves all the things we need first – *we* have to meet our own needs! (If you are unhappy outside of a relationship you will be unhappy inside a relationship. It is **not** your partner's job to make you happy, contrary to popular thinking. **It's your job.**)

These may seem like silly questions, but really take your time in answering them and be honest. Most of the time, we treat ourselves *horribly*!

Is this ringing any bells for you?

What do *you* do for fun? Seriously, what constitutes fun for you? We spend so much time thinking about negative stuff that happened in our past and getting caught up in life, most of us don't even know what *constitutes* fun for us, never mind actually getting around to *having* the fun! When I ask clients this question, I am pretty much always met with a blank stare and a shrug. Many reply, 'Fun? What's that?'

Do you remember the guy I mentioned in Memories 9.1? I have a lot to thank him for. As you may have guessed, I was crazy about him; whatever it was between us was hugely powerful. After our first meeting, he arranged to come back to visit me in the UK the following month. I went completely mad! I decorated the house, cleaned it to within an inch of its life, had a huge throw-out, replanted the garden, sorted out the shed, bought some new bedding, crockery, glasses, clothes and jewelry, got myself waxed, plucked, manicured, pedicured, highlighted and tooth-whitened, and filled the fridge with lots of tasty delicacies. I was devastated when two days before he was due to visit he *emailed* to say he wasn't coming as he had 'met someone else.' I was heartbroken, and very angry. I had done all those things *for him*! I had made such a huge effort! And now he *wasn't coming*? And then, slowly, gradually, the horrible realization crept in: *Dawn, all this stuff should have been done ANYWAY.* Because someone very special lives in my house – ME! And then I got it – I got what my mother had been saying all these years. I realized I didn't love myself!!! I had 'made do.' I had allowed things to slide, because 'no one else is going to see it; it's only me, and it doesn't matter.' It *does* matter! YOU do matter! And despite my upset, that was a very, very valuable lesson for me. We need to treat ourselves as *our most beloved lover*. If you were your best lover, what would *you* do for you? I know it can be hard to keep looking at yourself; sometimes it is easier to answer such questions by focusing on someone else, as we are *so* unused to thinking nice things about ourselves. Here is a little exercise which will help you:

1   Think of a celebrity that you lurrrrrve. (Try to be more original than George Clooney – he's mine anyway!)
2   Imagine that you have met that celebrity somehow and they have fallen madly in love with you. In one month's time, they are coming to stay with you in your home for one week. OK, now ask yourself:
i) Would I change anything about myself (appearance-wise)?
ii) Would I make any changes to my home?
iii) Would I buy anything new, either for myself or for my home?
iv) Would I wish to look any different, e.g. lose weight?
v) When he or she comes to stay with me, what things would I do for him or her?
vi) If he or she offered to take me out for a treat, what would that treat be?

If you can honestly say, 'I wouldn't change anything or do

anything differently to what I am doing now,' then TOP MARKS to you. You love yourself as you would your best lover. If you have a long list of things to do, like I had, then perhaps there is some room for improvement! If we were *really* nurturing ourselves, there should not be any jobs to do at all, apart from buying some tasty food perhaps. Now don't get me wrong, I am not asking you how well you would look after a celebrity, nor am I telling you how to get ready for a lover; the point is that you should be doing these things for *yourself*, already, with you in mind, not anyone else. Your home should be as *you* want it, you should be at your best (to suit *you*, no one else) and you should do all the things that you would do for a lover, for *yourself*. Run a lovely bath with rose petals and oils in it for *yourself*. Enjoy a glass of chilled champagne while you are soaking away the trials of your day, if that is what you like. One of the biggest questions to ask yourself, along with 'What constitutes *fun* for me?' is 'What constitutes a *treat* for me?'

Maybe you hate champagne or even baths. So what *do* you love to do? This sounds simple, but just try asking a few friends; the common response is, 'I don't know; I've never really thought about it. I don't have time for all that stuff anyway!' It is about doing for yourself all the things you would do for your lover. If you are single, it's about making a lovely tray of food for yourself, cutting a flower, making your favorite coffee, then running back up to bed with it all, cuddling up in your duvet with a new novel, and enjoying the food along with the pleasure of pampering yourself. Treat yourself like a prince or princess. *Always question yourself, 'Am I treating myself like I would my best lover?'*

Nowadays, if something annoys me, like a dripping tap for example, I get it sorted out straight away, whereas in the past I used to try to ignore it – until I just couldn't bear it anymore. With any change we wish to make in our lives, if we keep doing something regularly enough it will eventually become a habit. Just take small steps, every day, and you will get there!

So then, what about those of us who are actually *in* a relationship? How does that work for you? If it's a bit of a minefield, here are some little gems which have helped my clients in the past.

You don't need to be a genius to realize that men and women are very different creatures! Ladies, your man is *not* like you, does *not* think the same way that you do, and yes, he does have his funny ways. *Do not* make the mistake of trying to turn him into one of your girlfriends. Trust me, if you do succeed in this (and sadly, many women do), afterwards you will not find him attractive sexually! And remember, you are his *lover*, not his mother! (Mother him and you will find you have a kid on your hands – and they are not sexy either!)

And men, sorry, but we girls *are* pretty emotional beings. That is the way we are made; there is not much we can do about it really. When we rant and rave we don't really need you to do anything other than make reassuring noises and tell us every-thing will be alright.

There are many books on the differences between men and women; if you haven't already read them then I suggest you do so. It does need to be remembered that we *all* are made of a mixture of both masculine and feminine energies and therefore we have both within us. For example, if a man *or* woman is dealing with a child, then the female energy will be utilized by both of them; or if a man *or* woman is co-ordinating a massive business deal, then the masculine energies will be prevalent. We switch between states as circumstances dictate. Both male and female professional executives need the masculine energies and characteristics of determination, single focus, forward thinking, and 'going in for the kill' in order to succeed. But it is these masculine qualities that have led us to treating each other, and the Earth, with disrespect. The masculine energy – in both men and women – has focused on material gain at the expense of humanity and nature, and even on building financial systems on less than solid foundations.

What I wish to look at is the *dominant* energy within us – look at the position on the masculine/feminine scale where we reside most of the time, as this *is* going to affect our personal relationships. In Andean shamanism we have something called *Yanantin, Masintin*: 'the harmonious relationship between equal yet opposite things.' What I find most helpful with clients is to look at the *archetypes* of the male and female, because understanding these archetypes helps you to understand what is going on in a relationship, or what is required to get things working really nicely – for both of you. It's quite hard to describe what an archetype is, but in the context I am referring to, an archetype is a very powerful living embodiment of a character which lives within us and influences us, sometimes negatively, sometimes positively. You may not know this but the Major Arcana of the Tarot cards actually depict the main human archetypes. For now, we will stick with the masculine and the feminine.

(Note: This can get a bit tricky in same-sex relationships, but generally the masculine archetype will govern the most masculine partner etc.)

The Male Archetype – The Story of Parsifal

The male archetype is based on the character of Parsifal from the Holy Grail legend, which has deep spiritual meaning. There are many variations of this 12th-century legend but here is a précis for you.

Young Parsifal is brought up very simply and innocently by his mother, his father having been killed along with his elder brothers in battle. One day, Parsifal meets some knights (Templars) and goes against his mother's wishes in order to follow them. He trains as a knight, and one day finds himself in the wondrous, magical, mystical castle of a wounded King. Within the castle itself is the *Holy Grail*, that wondrous, mythical vessel of Christ, which can cure all – but for some reason, the

King himself is forbidden to drink from it. Parsifal, of course, is not aware of this. Prophecy has foretold his coming and requires him to ask a certain question which is, 'Whom does the Grail serve?' Sadly, Parsifal fails to ask the question. Thus the King remains wounded and his kingdom negatively affected.

The next morning the magical castle disappears in a poof and Parsifal finds himself back in the real world. He goes off with his men again, his mother dies of grief, and many years go by, full of knightly adventures. He vows to find the castle and the Grail, and along the way he grows as an individual. Despite the fact that he continues to make mistakes, his errors assist him in his development. He conquers knights, comforts distressed damsels, falls in love, helps the poor and, of course, slays some dragons, becoming in the process a famous and valiant knight.

One day, *finally*, he has earned enough merit for the magical, mystical castle of the wounded King to reveal itself to him once more. This time, he asks the magical question, 'Whom does the Grail serve?' and the King is healed from his wounds, and one can assume that harmony and balance are brought to the kingdom once more.

So, girls, what does this tell us about men? For me, this story shows that a man firstly needs to find his own way, to follow his own heart and not that of his mother. Those apron strings need to be cut! He then needs to go on his *external journey* and slay some 'dragons' until he experiences a feeling of connectedness. Therefore, he needs to feel *free* enough to go on his own hero's journey, find his own way, make his own mistakes and learn from them. *Only then will he grow.* I think women have too often seen the difficulties which appear when a man's much-needed freedom is threatened! A man, like it or not, is all about freedom, adventure, excitement *and a quest* – which is usually for success or recognition of some kind. Then in mid-life, a man often starts to question everything he has done as it seems worthless and futile. This is the point when *hopefully* he should realize the false worth of the external, material things he has acquired and start his *inner* journey, realizing that the things he is seeking have been within him all along. Sadly, many times, men experience these classic 'mid-life crisis' symptoms and will try and push the feeling of failure away with a new wife/career/car, never quite managing to fill that gap – and *never really realizing why*.

Outside of the Grail legend and the archetypical male, then, what else defines a man?

The thing that strikes me most is that single-focused concentration which nothing, but nothing, can move him away from. If ladies recognized this fact then they would save themselves a lot of heartbreak! Men are SINGLE FOCUSED and directional. Full stop. Nothing is going to change that. Let's look at that for a moment. Imagine, ladies, that you have just met a great guy, you are completely smitten with him, and you have had a few dates. Now, he will be on your mind all the time. But your guy will be focused on his stuff – and a man will usually put work before relationships. It's just the way they are; they are programmed this way. It does not mean that he does not like you; he is just *wired differently* to you. The biggest problem most women have is the belief that a man thinks about things the same way that they do. *He doesn't*.

I saw something very interesting on TV recently, which I thought was very telling regarding relationships. It was an episode of *Miami Ink*, which is a program about the daily goings-on in a tattoo parlor based in Miami. A very hairy, muscular, bald man came into the shop asking the owner for a tattoo of a particular fish. While he was being tattooed, his tattooer asked him why he wanted a tattoo of this particular fish – what was so special about it? The big hairy man explained that this type of fish is special because it can change sex whenever that may be required. When the tattoo artist asked why that was relevant, he replied, 'Because I was born a woman!' Now, obviously there is nothing wrong with this, but what fascinated me was what he said next.

He explained that he believed the differences between the sexes were all down to hormones, nothing else. When he was a woman, he said he didn't know where he was, couldn't tell left from right, and everything was kind of confused and fuzzy. But when he started to take the male hormones, everything became crystal clear, actions became apparent, and he could find his way through life much easier and everything shifted. Isn't it interesting?

So direction is very, very important to a man and we need to be careful about questioning this ability as it is actually very hurtful to him when we do this. Someone once told me that if a woman asks a man, 'Are we lost? Can't you ask for directions?' it is as bad as a man saying to a woman that she is fat and ugly!

Now, I am not exactly diplomatic at times – I speak first and then often think later – but I can remember learning about this fact and vowing I would try to apply it. I was on holiday in Tenerife once with an (American) boyfriend and we were in the car, chatting away, when I realized that we were going the wrong way back to our apartment. Normally I would have immediately opened my mouth and said, 'Are you sure you're going in the right direction? Are we lost?' but I caught myself just in time and tried to apply what I had learned. We went past a huge billboard with a poster of a lady carrying oranges on it. I seized the moment and said, 'Isn't it funny – all the times we've been down this road to the apartment and I've never noticed that huge billboard over there!'

'Yes, very funny!' he said, but out of the corner of my eye I could see him start to look around. I didn't say a thing at all. In a very short while, he said, 'You know, I seem to have taken the wrong turning; I'm going to turn the car around.' How cool was that? I still got my message across, but in a way that was not hurtful or emasculating to him. So think on, the next time you criticize a man's sense of direction!

When I was young, my father (who maintained that women should be chained to the kitchen sink!) once told me I could 'emasculate a man at thirty paces.' I was deeply offended by this as I had always prided myself on being independent, able to look after myself and not being a 'weak helpless *girl*.' He told me that if a light bulb blew in the house, I should sit in the dark until my husband came home, then he could come in and fix it and he would then feel like a hero! I went MAD! After that I picked up the chainsaw and trimmed the hedges, hung the wallpaper in the spare bedroom and painted all the gloss work, operated a rotivator on the garden, washed and sorted out the cars...

Now I know this is going to hurt, girls, but here I am many years later, with the wisdom of hindsight... and I have to say that, to a *degree*, I can see that my father *was right*. Remember – the man needs to be the hero, right? So, where can he fit that in, if we are constantly super-efficient? How can he feel good about himself when we have taken a break running the world to quickly renovate the house and landscape the garden on top of looking after the kids and looking fantastic? Well, what happens most of the time in these circumstances is that the man will do one of two things.

Firstly, he will move imperceptibly but most definitely into the 'feminine mode.' He will become helpless, girly and pretty useless. He will certainly *not* be ravishing you up against the stairs and bringing home tickets for Paris! Ladies, if you are going to wear the trousers, he has *no option* but to start wearing the skirts! Here is a question for you.

Question: If your man has settled into the feminine, how do you get him back into the masculine?

Is the correct answer:

1   By criticizing him, yelling at him, throwing meals at him, and doing everything yourself?
2   By shifting yourself back into a more feminine energy?

Correct, you move back into the feminine – *somehow*. Just for a second, think about how you were when you were dating, how you dressed, the effort you went to, how you treated him. How much has that behavior changed today? Margo, as you can imagine, was spectacularly unimpressed by my suggestions at stepping back into the feminine. But she promised to try. She (really) went down with the flu, leaving her husband to do everything. But he really stepped up to the plate, looked after her well and took charge. And that is the crux of it: a man is only going to turn up with tickets to Paris when he feels like a man. Many clients have tried this out and it has worked like a dream. Mention the words 'You're my hero' and he will be yours forever. Remember, if you are wearing the trousers, guess what he will be mincing around in?

This brings me then to the second thing men do when women wear the trousers: they will fight to take them back off her in some way. Miranda's husband tried this by a) belittling every-thing she did, b) trying to get her to wear more feminine/sexy clothes, c) wanting sex to stamp his masculinity on her, and d) generally disempowering her and knocking her confidence.

The polarity between the masculine and feminine is shifting as our roles become more similar. This does not bode well for relationships, as we need polarity in order to have great sex! Remember the heart-throbs of the 'olden days' – Clark Gable, Rock Hudson (yes, I am aware that he was actually gay), Steve McQueen, Robert Redford; they were all 'manly' men. These days, that polarity is being neutralized, therefore heart-throbs such as Jude Law, Orlando Bloom and Johnny Depp all have a feminine quality about them and lean more towards being beautiful, rather than handsome.

One of the things that female clients struggle with the most is what I call the 'shattering of the fairytale' – all those childhood promises of strong, brave princes on horseback. Some women cling to this. They say to me, 'What? You're telling me that there isn't a brave prince, that he actually is a little bit insecure, needs an ego boost and is maybe *threatened by me*? That isn't what my mother told me!' And I gently remind them that their mother, in all likelihood, also told them about Santa Claus, but they let that go as they got older and now they have to let this fairytale dream go too. Men are *human*, and are not necessarily confident, with great self-esteem, just because they are men! They have their self-doubts, and their issues, just as we do. We have to live in reality, not in Wonderland, and sometimes that can be a bit disappointing. (In my case, it was a LOT disappointing, as my parents had the fairytale marriage and I grew up thinking that it would be the same for me!) But the princes ARE out there, and are more likely to find us, the more we behave like princesses.

I know it sounds crazy, but it helps to imagine that in any relationship there is only one pair of trousers and one dress – nothing else. The outfit you wear determines what your partner gets left with.

The Feminine Archetype – Psyche (a Greek and Roman myth)

Myth tells us that Psyche, daughter of the King, was incredibly beautiful, which represented a great threat to the Goddess Venus (Aphrodite). Venus plots to get Psyche to fall in love with a vile creature, and persuades her son Cupid to help her. Cupid fails in his task and instead falls in love with Psyche himself, although he is invisible to her. Venus flies into a rage, and puts a curse on Psyche which prevents anyone from marrying her. This angers Cupid, who withdraws his arrows of love, and no one marries or mates so the Earth starts to wither. Venus has to eventually rescind and Cupid starts to fire his arrows again.

The King, mystified as to why no one will marry his daughter, visits an oracle who tells him to chain his daughter to a mountain as she is too beautiful for mortal men. The King does this but the winds rescue her and take her to a paradise valley. At nightfall, her God Cupid comes to make love to her, on two conditions: 1) that she never asks questions, and 2) that she promises never to look at him. Of course, Psyche is eventually persuaded to look at her lover one night. Shocked at his beauty and at the realization that he is a God, she pricks her finger and instantly falls in love with him. Cupid wakes and, angered at the breaking of her promises to him, flees away from her back to his mother.

Psyche goes on a great mission to find out how to get Cupid back, and eventually is told that she has to deal directly with Venus, the cause of all her problems in the first place. Venus gives Psyche some very difficult tasks to complete, which are so tough Psyche contemplates killing herself before each of the tasks. But she is aided in succeeding in these tasks by the help of some ants, a river, and an eagle. Finally she has to visit the Goddess of the Underworld – Persephone – in order to obtain some of her precious beauty ointment. She manages this task but, being too curious, looks into the cask of ointment only to find it empty. A sleep overcomes her and she collapses in the Lower World. Cupid, however, comes to her rescue. He then flies to see Zeus and asks to be allowed to marry her. Zeus agrees, so Venus has to welcome Psyche as her daughter-in-law, and the lovers marry. Psyche is given a cup of ambrosia to drink which turns her into an immortal Goddess.

What does this myth tell us about the feminine archetype? To me, it refers mainly to our need to see God in our man, which is why we sometimes refuse to see a man for who he truly is. For many of us, rose-colored spectacles abound in the first few months of a relationship. This is the 'in love' part of a relationship, where we will most often blind ourselves to what is really in front of us so that we can live in that Paradise place for as long as possible. That Paradise place is not a real place, which shows that we sometimes do not want to live in the harshness of reality. This is one of the reasons why we hold on so ferociously to the fairytale stories we were told as children.

As for the chaining to the mountain, this represents to me, firstly, the sacrifice we will make of ourselves for the sake of relationship, for relationships are far more important to a woman than to a man. Secondly, the mountain refers to our need for space and a quiet place to reflect and be with our *innermost* selves. This is why pampering retreats and spas are so popular with us girls, as this is how we recharge ourselves. A man generally recharges himself by going *outside of himself* and slaying a few dragons.

The feminine energies, then, are mainly *internally focused* and the male energies are more *externally focused*. The breaking of the promise not to look at Cupid refers to our curiosity, our need to know, and also to the fact that we will often push at the boundaries of relationships. When we truly 'look' at a man in the harsh reality of daylight, we then see him for who he really is, warts and all! This indicates to me that it is often the woman who will want to push further into a relationship; she will want it to evolve and to see what is really there, where it is all heading.

Of course, when our man is revealed in the lamplight this can come as a bit of a shock for us – it can push us firmly out of the illusion of Paradise and into reality. This stage, I feel, is when we step out of the illusion of 'being in love' and take off the rose-colored spectacles. This can again be cause for much death – the death of the illusion of our mate and the first glimpse at reality. It is at this stage of course where most relationships fall apart. When we are less mature, we can 'fall out of love' at this point, because many of us can be caught up and addicted to the *illusion* of the fantasy, of being 'in love.' But as we mature, we can see that the shattering of the illusion (commonly called the honeymoon period, which tends to last about 6–18 months) is a normal part of a relationship and when it is over we can get to the *real* task of loving. It may be more human and ordinary than the Paradise version, but it is also more *real*, and true bonding can occur at this stage.

When Psyche is given the four tasks, it is interesting that she contemplates taking her own life before attempting each one. This perhaps points to our over-dramatic nature at times. We have a good cry, throw a tantrum or a fit, but afterwards we feel sooo much better! Also I think that this part of the myth represents the dying of certain parts of ourselves as we grow and mature into women on our life's journey. For example, when we marry we step into a new archetype as a wife; this is of course cause for celebration, but the maidenly part of us has to die before we can make that leap, which can cause some sadness and feelings of loss. When we have children, again we step into another archetype, and yet another part of ourselves has to die in order for us to step into the role as mother, and again many sacrifices have to be made. (And often there can be many problems with our mothers-in-law but we won't say too much about that!)

It is also interesting to see that unlike Parsifal, who was assisted in his quest by knights and fair maidens, it is nature – ants, rivers, and eagles – that help Psyche achieve her tasks. This is probably why girls like puppies and 'fluffy bunnies' way more than a man does. The feminine principle has a greater affinity to nature and the qualities of the Earth, while *also* having the connection to the spiritual qualities of Heaven, or Paradise. This then brings us our instinctual nature and our intuition – 'women's intuition'!

Given the differences detailed above, it's a wonder that men and women manage to have relationships at all! But although there are some primary differences – and it would be a good idea to bear these in mind if you are in a relationship – essentially most of us want the same thing. We want to be loved and accepted for who we are, and we want to be seen, heard and appreciated.

The rules of dating are many and confusing and I am not going to go into detail here, other than to say I have noticed something very interesting about men. If you run towards them with open arms (i.e. if you are really into them and let that be known) then they tend to run in the opposite direction – away from you. If you move away from men, however, then they tend to chase after you! It is not about playing games, but when dealing with men, remember the archetypical story, ladies: *they like* to go out to slay the dragon and rescue the princess, *they like* to do the chasing, and *they like* to feel that they have something that needs fighting for, and something that is worth fighting for. In short, they *want* to fight for the prize – you. They want to *win* you, to grab you out of the arms of other suitors and prevent other men from having you. Additionally, they need *freedom*. They need time alone or with the boys, and if we try to curtail this we can very soon find ourselves on dodgy ground. These needs are deeply programmed within men.

I remember that many years ago I worked with a very handsome and charming man. Every Monday we would all hear about his sexual escapades over the weekend – he certainly was a player; he had a whale of a time and could quickly charm a woman into bed. One Monday he talked a lot about a particular woman – how stunning she was, how amazingly well they got on, how passionate they were together – and I made some typical girly comment as to whether he thought she might be 'The One.' He looked at me as if I was mad, and said, 'Of course not! She slept with me the first evening we met! I wouldn't marry any woman who did that.' When I pointed out that I was sure she would have been charmed into bed by him, that she didn't just grab him by the tie and drag him upstairs, he retorted that it made no difference. The woman he would marry would be the one who refused his charms – and for a considerable time. He wanted a *prize*, like most men.

A woman often wants to be liked and loved and will perhaps sleep with a man far too early on because she is fearful of his judgments and of losing him. This is why you have to be solid in your love of yourself and in your self-worth. The vast majority of men want and love sex, and will try hard to get it. They will assure you that of course they will still respect you in the morning, as they gaze lustfully into your eyes. The truth is, in the vast majority of cases *they won't*. Know your own worth, take your time, and really get to know each other; let the passion increase slowly, and be a lady. If he is worth his salt, he will respect you for it. And he *will* wait.

This information is not intended to encourage manipulation of the opposite sex in any way. I am not suggesting that you play games, but if you bear in mind how a man or woman operates on an *archetypical* basis, then you should see that your relationships become more successful, which of course is what we all want.

The most important thing to bear in mind as far as relationships are concerned, whether you are male or female, is to try to organize your life so *that you are as happy and fulfilled as possible*. This goes for everything – life in general, spiritual development, as well as dating and relationships. This then brings me to a good question.

Why Do You Want a Relationship?

If your answer is anything other than, 'Because it would be nice to have someone to share the special moments with,' then you, my friend, have some work to do. Make a promise to obtain the things you want *for yourself*, even, as we have stated before, the love. Remember – we *do not actually truly HAVE ANYTHING that exists outside of ourselves*. It is so important to remember this. We need to find love, happiness, security, joy, passion and self-worth inside of ourselves; only then do we truly have those things. And only then can they never be taken away from us. Everything else is illusion. But so many of us do not take the time or make the significant effort to generate within ourselves the resources that we need and instead look *outside of ourselves* for fulfillment.

This is one of the greatest problems with relationships. The vast majority are *dysfunctional*, because *we* are dysfunctional. Just listen to the lyrics of love songs on the radio: 'If you leave me I will die' and 'You are my everything.' We have come to view this kind of romantic love as normal, but it is not – it's horrific! 'If you leave me I will die'? *Are you kidding me?* Is your total worth caught up in a relationship? Do you not have a life of your own?

I remember being in the cinema somewhere around 1996, watching the Tom Cruise film, *Jerry Maguire*. In it, there is a famous scene when Tom says to Renée Zellweger, 'I love you; you complete me.' And I clearly remember that the entire female audience exhaled 'Ahhhhhhhhhh!' If someone said to me, 'You complete me,' I would run a mile! What they are telling me is that they are an *incomplete* person – is that supposed to make me want them? Sadly, I have to say that if we look at the majority of Hollywood films, there is, more often than not, an element of dysfunctional love in them, a little like in the fairytales.

I am a big fan of the philosophy of the Indian mystic and spiritual teacher Osho. Osho maintained that 'true love can only happen between a king and a queen,' and I think this is very true. Osho is trying to refer to two people who are whole and complete in themselves, people who are with each other because it brings them pleasure, in a relationship where there is no actual *need* of the other, just great mutual enjoyment.

Here is my main relationship theory and I think I should get a Nobel Peace Prize for it! One of my teachers once said to me, 'A relationship should be like the icing on a cake.' For ease of explanation, I am going to transform that cake into a chocolate chip muffin. Let us equate the muffin to you and your life, and your partner to the icing. We can see that the muffin, with the addition of the icing, would be a little bit sweeter than it was before, but ultimately, without the icing, it is still whole, complete and yummy in itself. If your partner (i.e. the icing) leaves you, you are just as good as you were before, and just as tasty. But the biggest problem we all face is that, more often than not, we are *not* a whole chocolate chip muffin at all; we are just a poor little chocolate *chip*, all alone in that big paper case, not feeling very good about ourselves! We are of course conscious that we are not the whole muffin, that there is a lot of us missing, but instead of going out and doing our personal work and developing those internal qualities we have already talked about, we look for them *externally*. We want a relationship and a partner to come along and give us the *illusion* of being the whole muffin!

Let's now assume that in this situation a partner comes along – is that truly going to make us happy? Well, maybe it will, for a short while, but then what is going to happen? Perhaps we will start to become terrified that that person will leave us, and take away the illusion of our wholeness, leaving us to revert to our former chocolate chip selves. We can become jealous and possessive, and start checking each other's texts and worrying if our partner goes away for any length of time, rather than trusting them.

Here is something else to think about: If everything is a mirror to *you* and you are just a chocolate chip... Right again, you will *only* attract a person who is also not whole and also just a chocolate chip. And then you will find yourself in a two-way dysfunctional, co-dependent relationship. So there we have it in a nutshell. If you want the perfect man or woman – the whole muffin – guess what YOU have to be? It's simple really, isn't it? And when we are whole and complete in ourselves, then we can love as we are meant to – unconditionally.

I have a couple of questions for you:

1   Are you a chocolate chip person, or a whole muffin person?
2   If you are less than a whole muffin, what do you need to do, learn, address, heal, achieve or be, in order to become whole?

I am sure you have had enough muffin-ness now, so I will leave it with you, but I really do think that this is the way to true happiness in relationships, because you are responsible for your own happiness, and when you have that internal happiness, *no one can take it away from you.* Remember, nothing *external* to you can make you truly happy and nothing *external* to you can take your happiness away, either.

I often hear clients moan, 'Marriage is boring!' Or they moan that their long-term relationships are boring, and they are becoming attracted to other people and craving some excitement. Remember, the relationship is the *sum total of the people within it.* I always ask these people, 'What are YOU doing to make it interesting? What do *you* have to talk about? What passions are you pursuing? How are you growing?' The common answer is, of course, that they are doing nothing. They are expecting their partner to do something they are not prepared to do themselves. Marriages or long-term relationships need work – from both parties – to keep them alive. I often think that couples can be too close. If someone is with you all the time, day in, day out, what *are* you going to have to talk about? I think the secret is to have joint activities, something you both love as equally as possible, and then you both have your own activities or hobbies to do as well, and your own groups of friends. People need space in a relationship – no matter how much they love each other.

Everyone should ideally be growing, evolving, pushing themselves just that little bit, trying new things; yet so many people enter into relationships and then everything seems to just stop – so no wonder that things start to stagnate! You have to work hard to keep things fresh! Particularly as far as sex is concerned! It's just isn't going to be that exciting after 17 years, unless you work at it, and that may mean getting out of your comfy PJs every now and then!

I remember that when I was a child, about 15 minutes before my father came home from work (he was like clockwork), my mother used to go and refresh her make-up. She would brush her teeth and hair and reapply her lipstick and eye shadow, so she looked pretty for my father. It is nice to make an effort for someone; it makes them feel appreciated and it makes you feel good about yourself. So many people come in from work, take off their smart suit, and throw on their jogging bottoms and a sweatshirt for the evening. Although we do need to be comfortable when we are relaxing, we can still give our appearance a thought and make sure we look nice for our partner. In longer-term relationships we can let ourselves go somewhat!

Maybe you have friends who are divorcing; I bet they end up slimmer and trendier than they were when they were married! The first thing a woman normally does after a separation is to change her hair, lose weight, and get a restyle – well, this should have been done already; there should not be any changes necessary. Again I am not advocating that we are continually trussed up like chickens to suit our partners, but as I have said before, it is about *self-love*, about looking your best – for you. If we are not happy with ourselves before we are in a relationship, then we are unlikely to be happy in a relationship.

About 18 months ago I attended a workshop which was run by a lovely man who was a Sufi sheikh. He talked a lot about relationships during this workshop, and one of the things he said which was very interesting was that women make the mistake of 'crowning their man.' In the early stages of a relationship, a woman turns her man into a prince, and because of this, the man feels on the top of the world. After a while though, the 'polish' gradually wears off. Perhaps he starts eating crisps in bed, admits to his mortal fear of spiders, or fails to stand up to his mother when necessary. We then rush to remove the crown from his head! We snatch it away and tell him he can't have it back, until he changes… *something*. The first point is that he can't change 'something.' He can't actually *make* that Hollywood feeling come back, because it is based in fantasy, not reality, and like it or not, we exist in reality. Secondly, the removal of his crown makes him feel very angry and hurt. Most importantly, we need to understand that the crown was *never* ours to gift in the first place! The Sufi sheikh said that only our God can crown us!

This was a massive realization to me – all the time I had been looking for that ecstasy in relationships and feeling bereft when it naturally died away... but all the time what I had really been looking for was that ecstatic connection to the Divine, which never goes away! Think about it! How does it feel to be in love? We feel on a high and feel that everything is good, that we are One with... well, *everything*. We are joyful inside, brimming with light; everything around us is colorful and all our problems seem to disappear. How does it feel to be connected to the Divine? We feel high and feel that everything is good, that we are One with... well, *everything*... is this making sense? It certainly made sense to me.

And now I understand the real value of relationships. It is not about living in that wonderful bliss state, which is pure fantasy and actually in no way connected to real love... it's about finding someone we can grow with, someone who is going to support us on our journey, someone we can respect and who can respect us, someone to nurture who will nurture us, someone *to help us heal ourselves, know ourselves, and help us to naturally become closer to our true selves and to our God*. Which kind of sheds a whole new light on things, doesn't it? They say that we only really learn to drive after we have passed our driving test, and we only really learn to love after the 'in love' feeling has died. Opening yourself to love, to real love, can be very scary indeed, but the rewards are immense.

10. The God Spot

Please consider reading this chapter, even if you are a non-believer, or have fallen out with God in some way. I am not writing from a 'religious' point of view. I am not trying to get you to go to church or start believing; rather I think there is a great principle that we all need to be aware of, which is part of all things. I feel it is important that we connect to that principle. I have used the word 'God' here for ease but please feel free to use your own name for the Divine/Source Energy.

Memories 10.1

The alarm clock goes off, shocking me out of a hectic sleep. Immediately the same old feelings creep up on me – the feeling that I am trapped in the wrong life, that I am isolated, empty and *separate*. There is a hollowness within me, gaping and endless, which feels like it can never be filled. In trying to reach the source of my emptiness, I realize that Source *is* my emptiness. *I miss God.* I miss His love. A panic, ancient and fierce, rises within me; it snatches the breath from me and explodes within my heart, my head. The tears run freely now and I feel as fragile as a lost infant searching for her parents.

'Where is He?' my heart cries out in anguish. 'Where is He? How can I find Him?' The pain is searing, the loss tremendous. I feel, once again, trapped in an alien world, a world of harshness, of *conditional* love. I miss feeling truly connected, truly loved. As wonderful as this world can be, *nothing* can match the exquisite feeling of being in His presence, which for some reason I seem to remember. And I realize that *this* is why I have spent so many years on my spiritual search; *this* is why I have spent so many years meditating. *All* of my efforts have been about getting back to Him.

I am now very late for work, so I force myself out of bed and into the shower. I look terrible, so I do my best to cover up the carnage with make-up. Distracted, I run out of the house and speed-walk to the office. All the time my heart is shouting, aching, 'Where is He? Is He here? How do I find Him?' I try to quieten my heart and focus on the day before me, but I can feel the panic rise again. The words repeat themselves within me like a scratched record.

Blinded by tears, I cross roads and junctions until I see my office rising tall and black in the distance, like a big gaping mouth ready to swallow up all who enter it. I wonder if I should actually go in at all, I am in such a terrible state! Then suddenly, as if a brake handle has been pulled, my body stops dead in its tracks. It is so abrupt it startles me for a moment. I try to move forward but I am paralyzed, as if my feet are glued onto the pavement. I start to panic, and then I hear a voice both in my head and in my heart, a deep and loving voice: *'Look up.'*

I hold my breath, still unable to move. I hear the voice again. *'Look up, my child.'* And I lift up my chin, tilt back my head and gasp in delight.

Instantly, my heart fills with joy. For I am looking straight up into an endless vision of beauty, into a vast and perfect cloud of shell-pink cherry blossoms which completely fill my vision. There are thousands upon thousands of delicate petals, each one perfect, complete, a fragile masterpiece. Perfect little pink faces of love, made by my Father, looking down at me. And I realize that *He is here*, in each blossom. Each blossom is a representation of His love. And then I realize: He is not just here; He is everywhere, in each plant, each tree, each blade of grass. In the rivers, in the rocks and stones. In each animal and in every child. In each man and in each woman. He is in me. I am in Him. He is not *outside* of me; He is within me, part of me. And a smile breaks out over my upturned face, the tears cease, and a deep and restful peace descends over me.

I stay there bathing in the pink glow of the tree while each blossom smiles down at me, each reveling in its own glory, in its own transient beauty. And it is quite glorious, holy even. I breathe in the memory of the blossom, so that I never forget it. My heart lifts and becomes filled with love. The gaping hole within me gradually closes up and becomes healed. And I know that now I am going to be *really* late for work, but somehow, it doesn't matter that much anymore.

Practice Notes 10.2

Alexandra tells me she has come to see me for a session as she is having marital difficulties. She confesses she is experiencing regular and quite enormous explosions of anger and rage and feels constantly stressed and agitated. This is her second marriage, and she tells me that she dearly loves her husband. She left her first husband and two daughters after 20 years of marriage in order to be with her current husband. She tells me that since leaving her first husband, she has fought against the crushing guilt she felt at hurting her children, as she left them with their father when she left home.

Since then, she has tried hard to be the best wife she can be, and has made huge efforts to integrate with her husband's large social circle. In return for her efforts, however, her husband has seemingly continued to behave like a diehard bachelor. She tells me that she regularly lies awake until 2 or 3am, waiting for him to come home from his increasingly frequent 'nights out with the boys.' Arguments about his inconsiderate behavior are increasing as the years pass and she has found herself nagging him constantly.

She confesses that she now feels at breaking point: her temper has become unmanageable, and she is stressed and unable to sleep. She says she wants to save her marriage, but she needs help with her emotions and is desperate to find some peace.

I asked her if she remembered a time when she had slept well, and she comments that before she left her first husband, she used to have a fantastic quality of sleep. She tells me she would say her prayers and then, the next thing she knew, it would be morning and she would wake up feeling refreshed.

She then adds flippantly, 'Of course, I can't pray now.'

'Why not?' I enquire. 'Your relationship with God and your faith has always been very important to you, hasn't it? You're a good person, Alexandra; you're kind, and you try your best, so why can't you pray?'

Tears pour from her pretty green eyes. 'I can't pray because God won't want to hear from me now. I'm a bad person. I left my husband and children to be with another man. I'm divorced, therefore I've sinned. I'm a sinner, and He won't want to know me. He won't love me now.'

* * *

Pierce is in his early thirties. He is very broad and fit, and could easily be described as a 'rough diamond.' He tells me that he has been imprisoned six times, once for manslaughter.

I ask him about his childhood, and the story of abuse he tells me and the treatment he received at the hands of his parents appalls and horrifies me. He goes on to say that he went on to seek the only security that was available to him – neighborhood gangs. Over the years, he worked his way up the 'ranks' and gradually became the gang leader, although he had to work hard to 'keep face' – but all the time he got deeper and deeper into trouble.

By the time I saw him, he was desperate to turn his life around. While in prison he had experienced a spiritual awakening, and had started reading spiritual and self-help books. He had realized that he had much, much more to offer the world than his current state of being. I could see that despite his awful experiences, his aura was absolutely radiant, full of light – in fact to this day I have never come across anyone with a more 'holy' aura and presence. Looking at him, I was reminded of the saying that sometimes we can find angels in the strangest of places.

He told me that it was his dearest wish to use all he had learned – the good and the bad – in a positive way by helping children who were in the same situation he himself had been in as a child, and who were headed in a similar direction. He explained that he would be perfect for this role as such children would not listen to the police or people of a similar nature. He had worked towards his goal by qualifying as a counselor and dearly wanted to give talks to children about the hazards of drugs and of being involved in gang culture.

Sadly, due to Pierce's police record, he was finding it impossible to obtain the necessary documentation required to enable him to do this work. Pierce desperately needed to make some good come out of the darkness he had lived with all his life; however, he told me he was barred at every turn and he had nothing to fall back on. I could already hear his stomach rumbling loudly from hunger and when I asked him if he would like something to eat he sheepishly told me he had no money at all until his social security benefits came in, but that he would rather starve than go back to stealing food as that way of life was behind him.

I asked him, 'Why did you not try to go straight before now? Why did you let things get *so* bad before trying to turn your life around?'

He looked me straight in the eye and said, 'When you cross that line, when you first do something bad, you know in your heart that you've gone too far. You know that God will never forgive you. You're a sinner, and there's nothing you can do to change that. Even if you wanted to turn the clock back, you can't.

'I have taken life. I didn't mean to; it wasn't intentional. But something went wrong and a man is dead because of me. Nothing will change that. I've committed the biggest sin there is. I got caught up in something I simply couldn't get out of. And once you get to that place, then you might as well just carry on doing stuff because there's no going back. You think it can't get better so it might as well get worse.

'God knows what I have done. I've served my time for the crimes, but God won't forgive me. I know that.'

* * *

Amanda sits opposite me. She is in her mid to late twenties and is very pretty and fresh-faced. She tells me she is excellent at self-sabotage and holding herself back from potentially excellent opportunities for happiness and success. She also appears to be determined to be unhappy – no matter what life brings her. There appears to be no reason for her to be like this, so I question her further.

Eventually, casually, she confesses to terminating a pregnancy when she was in her late teens. She reassures me that she has dealt with it, and that no other option was available at that time.

When we start work clearing up Amanda's energy body, she starts to sob uncontrollably and wails, 'I'm a bad person! I killed an innocent baby! God will punish me for it. I didn't even give it much thought at the time. *How could I have done that?* Was I crazy? I didn't know how badly getting rid of the baby would affect me. It haunts me. I don't deserve to be happy; I can't allow myself to be happy ever again. I have to pay for what I've done. I must not enjoy my life.'

Notes 10.3

I have a lovely friend who is terribly color blind. He will look at a flower and tell you in all truth, in all seriousness, that it is grey, which is his truth. I can quite clearly see that it is a pale red color, which is my truth. A butterfly, however, may tell you that the flower is ultraviolet, which is its truth. A bee will not be able to see the color red at all; to him that color simply does not exist. So, what is the truth about the color of the flower? And is my friend *wrong* when he tells me that it is grey?

I wonder perhaps if truth 'moves' in line with our levels of perception and the *degrees of consciousness* we have attained, and, as that is always changing, so are our truths. This is why I make it clear that the things I have written about in this book are *my* own truths, and by that I mean my 'current truths' – they are the truth as far as my current level of understanding and consciousness is concerned. As mentioned previously, it must be remembered that we are (or should be!) constantly evolving. Evolution is the nature of all things – even God Himself is constantly evolving.

So, what is your truth? What is your relationship to the Divine?

Personally, I guess that I felt very close to God as a child. Then I had a *massive* falling out with Him at 17. When I was 25, badly hurt, all alone and struggling to survive in a horrid bedsit, I remember denying Him *completely*. I withdrew my love along with my connection and told Him I hated Him and was never, ever, going to speak to Him again. However, what I realized later is that He never left *me*, even though I hurled significant abuse at Him! In fact, I can see now that I denied Him *because I did not understand His ways*. Again, everything is about *perception*, and this is where I think most people have an issue with God. They misperceive His role. They blame Him whenever things go 'wrong.' Today, I have a great connection and I enjoy it. I do firmly believe that a belief in *something* out there is *vitally essential to our good health*, as those Divine energies, which enter into us through our crown chakra, actually feed the physical form and the energy body itself.

About 18 months ago, while working with another shaman, I carried out an exercise in order to find not only my healed state, but also my 'fulfilled state.' I wanted to understand what it was that I was here to do in this lifetime, what my 'destiny' was, if you like. What I saw surprised me very much.

I had perhaps expected to see myself healing, teaching or speaking, but instead, what I actually saw was a vision of myself sitting on a chair, as if viewed from the side. Above my head sat an archetypical image of God (a big man with white hair and beard) and He was sending His energy and love down through my crown chakra into my heart chakra. I was then bringing that Divine energy through me in a kind of fountain, to remind people of their connection to Him, and then guiding them back, reconnecting them, to His light and His love. I saw myself bringing Him to those that were lost to Him – or *perceived* that they were lost to Him.

And in another way I saw I was to help individuals to find their own Divinity, to connect them to that spark that is *already* within them, and align them with it. I then heard these words resound deeply within me: *'Bring humanity back to Divinity and Divinity back to humanity.'* It shocked me to realize that this is what I had actually been doing in my healing practice, without really being aware of it. For I spend a lot of time helping people uncover that Divine light within them – *their light, which never dies and is **never taken away, no matter what they do.***

This seemed like a huge task for me to take on, but despite this I felt the truth of it within myself. Regardless of a person's religion or belief system – even if their belief is to have *no* belief – they *need* to be connected to the highest *light* and to hold this frequency within them. And most importantly, they need to understand that they are worthy of it. I will tell you here and now, throughout the years I have heard the most terrible stories of abuse and sorcery. But by far, the worst abuse is *that which we do to ourselves.*

For example, if a person has been sexually abused, then that abuse may have happened once, or for a period of months, or even over a few years. I often ask people that have been abused, sexually or otherwise, 'Who has been the biggest abuser in your life, i.e. for the longest time?' They look at me quizzically, as if it is a stupid question. It takes a while but eventually they say, 'Oh… it's me! I am my worst abuser. I treat myself terribly.' And while this is not true of all abuse cases thankfully, sadly it is the case with the majority.

Yes, it is hard helping someone to heal from sexual abuse, but the biggest challenge is not getting them over the abuse itself but in helping them to *love themselves*. To us, worthiness is very important when it comes to matters of the Divine. But *my* deepest truth, the thing I believe with all my heart, is this: Whatever we may have done or not done, whatever may have been done to us in the past, we are ALL worthy. *No matter what.* My strongest belief is that we are all loved – unconditionally. We also need to love ourselves the way that God loves us, which is *unconditionally*.

I am fortunate in that I have many spirit guides and teachers. One in particular is the absolute embodiment of love. He often reminds me, when I am about to get upset or angry, that it is 'all about love.' He reminds me that a spiritual master is a person who is in control of his or her emotions. A true Master aligns themselves with love and joy and remains heart-centered, *no matter what chaos and upset is going on around them*. 'Be love,' he simply tells me. 'Be joy.' And indeed these are wise words, as the Law of Attraction states that we receive back that which we are, and that we get what we think about or focus on. He is right to make me shift my state if I go off-center, *so that I do not create more of that which I do not desire*. This is most important, for all of us.

Often, people will contact me for an appointment and ask if they can ask a couple of questions first. One of the questions is always, 'Do you believe in God?' and my answer to that is yes, always, but I don't believe I have to attend church regularly to connect to Him. I don't actually believe that it is a *Him*, actually, but it is just easier to refer to the Divine that way. In my work I often journey up to the Divine, to ask for healing or for other information or assistance. I always perceive Him as an extremely bright, bluish-white light/energy, which is massively powerful – I have never seen a great man with a white beard and long hair. I just wanted to make that clear before we go on.

Although I do not attend church services, I regularly visit my local cathedral, which is beautiful, peaceful and powerful and has been a place of worship since 429 CE. I sit in peace in a small room away from the busy-ness of life to say my own prayers. The medicine people of the Andes believe that prayers should always be said from our hearts, using our own words – and they should be said out loud. I always have more of a chat rather than say a set prayer. Simply giving thanks for the things we have is quite sufficient.

As a child I had a deep interest in religion, and a near obsession with Jesus. I had a book about Jesus which showed a picture of Him on the front cover, and I used to stare at it for hours. As you have probably figured out by now, I asked my parents a *lot* of questions – I must have driven them quite mad. Bored of my questions, they eventually sent me to Sunday school, so I could learn about the Bible. I clearly remember attending the class and being told on the first day that I had been born a sinner, and that sin was in my very blood. I can remember thinking, *How can I have sinned? I'm only nine! I haven't done anything yet!* Needless to say, I told my parents that I didn't want to go back.

I have read the Bible and tried – and failed – to make sense of it. I found that it provided me with more questions than answers. I am a very logical person, I'm afraid, and I need things to make sense to me. How come, for example, in the Bible some people seemed to be about 800 years old? Who did Adam and Eve's children marry if Adam and Eve were the first humans on the planet? *Why* are we all born in sin? If Adam was the first man, born around 6,000 years ago, what about the Neanderthals? Weren't they an earlier version of man? Or shall we just conveniently forget about them?

So, as you can tell, I got into quite a pickle trying to make sense of it all. A thirst for truth is just that, and in my case, it needed quenching. This led to me developing my own philosophy, and I am happy that this works for me and it answers all my questions. I am not asking you to believe what I believe in, and please note this is not the shamanic viewpoint (although I will mention it where required). I am simply sharing my beliefs with you and you can decide if they make sense to you or not.

I believe that we are all God's children, that we are beloved as such, and that we are free to do as we wish with *our free will*. I believe that God hopes we will find our own way back home to Him, in order that *He* can evolve, and come to know Himself, truly. For evolution is the goal of ALL life forms, for all creation and even for God Himself.

I also deeply believe that God loves us beyond measure. I'll say that again. *I believe that we are loved by God, regardless of what we have or have not done, even if we reject Him or simply do not believe in Him.* And I also firmly believe that He did give us free will. Now, if you give a child free will, if you tell your child it can do ANYTHING it wants to and it then goes and does something 'wrong' – how could you as a parent condemn or punish that child? How could you cast it away from you and disown it? You could not. You could not give someone free will and then turn your back on them for wrongdoing. So my firm belief is that we are LOVED and we are FORGIVEN, full stop.

Do I believe Hitler is in Heaven? Yes, I do. He has to be. Because he was given free will and he used it to do what he thought was right. Do I condone or agree with what he did? Of course not! But I firmly believe that he is in Heaven along with *everyone* else. Now you may be thinking that is a terrible thing to say as it implies that anybody can do anything and get away with it. Not at all. Do I think Hitler will be punished by God? No. Do I think he will be accountable for his actions? Oh yes, most certainly, as will we all.

I have mentioned the shamanic viewpoint of God already, but I want to stress it again, as I feel it is very important. And please bear in mind that I already held a certain view of God before I came to shamanism, and was delighted to find that the shamanic philosophy matched my own. Across many different shamanic lineages there is a belief in a 'Great Spirit,' which is similar to our version of a great God in the sky. This God is not masculine, but carries both essences, more like 'Eternal Mother and Father, Source of All That Is.' Rather like the yin and yang symbol, Great Spirit is whole and complete, combining both polarities, a state rather like a hermaphrodite. (A hermaphrodite is a person who is anatomically both male and female; throughout history such individuals have been much revered in spiritual circles due to their *wholeness and their likeness to what is believed to be the True God*.) Of course I do not mean that God is perceived to have both sets of genitals, or indeed to have any kind of form. Rather She/He/It is more like energy, a *force, which can be found in all things*. As everything has Divinity in it, it is the shamanic way to treat everything with reverence and respect, and acknowledge that thus all natural things have an aspect of consciousness within them. It is this aspect of Divine consciousness which the shaman or medicine person communicates with.

I recently saw a YouTube video clip of a Richard Dawkins program entitled *Enemies of Reason*. Richard is a very intelligent scientist who is also an atheist and author of the 2006 bestseller *The God Delusion*, which essentially seeks to disprove the existence of God. I am currently reading and enjoying this book and actually agree with Richard on many points, just not his main theory! In the YouTube clip, Richard interviews the editor of *Resurgence* magazine, Satish Kumar. Satish speaks of the world consisting of the seen and the unseen, the visible and the invisible, and states that, to him, a tree has 'tree-ness' – to which Richard rather unkindly asks if a rock has 'rock-ness.' Satish agrees: yes, a rock has rock-ness, meaning of course that a rock has a consciousness.

Who is right and who is wrong here? Richard Dawkins, with his rigid scientific stance that if something cannot be proved scientifically then it simply does not exist? Or Satish, with his more shamanic viewpoint? In my view, they are both right, yet Satish has attained a higher degree of consciousness and perception and is therefore able to perceive *a greater degree of truth.*

To give you an example of this I will share with you a story I heard. The story is about the late great elder and *Kuraq Akulleq,* Don Manuel Quispe, who was deemed to be one of the greatest and most powerful of the Q'ero medicine people. Don Manuel was an absolute embodiment of love and joy, yet at the same time he had sufficient power to command lightning at will (remember, lightning was his teacher).

Many years ago now, Don Manuel was taken from his tiny hut in his mountain village of Chua Chua in the Peruvian Andes, to New York to carry out an important ceremony in a cathedral there. Can you imagine how that must have been for him? Going from a remote mountaintop village without running water or electricity to the excesses of New York City? A few hours before this important ceremony was due to take place, Don Manuel disappeared from a restaurant in the midst of the city. Eventually, after a long search, someone found him quietly sitting in a quiet back room in his hotel. They asked him, 'How on earth did you find your way back here?!' Don Manuel smiled and replied calmly, 'I asked the trees, and they showed me the way back here.' Isn't that amazing? Through a deep love and respect for nature and the Divinity which dwells within everything, Don Manuel was able to communicate with trees!

Writing this reminds me that recently I went to a talk given by a doctor friend of mine. She explained that scientists were currently very excited about their 'new' theory that the Universe was, in fact, 'holographic.' Now, I am not a science buff at all, but

I thought at the time, *Isn't this what shaman have been saying for thousands of years?* When we look at the 'ancient truths' such as 'As above, so below,' how can we think that the Universe is not holographic?

Do look up Google for a 'technical' description of a hologram. My (very basic) understanding of a hologram is that of an image – say of an orange for example – which is made up of many tiny images of an orange. The whole image, if you like, is made up of many tiny 'wholes.' The holographic Universe theory seems to have been triggered by the observation of the behavior of subatomic particles called *photons*. *Photon* is a Greek word for 'light,' and a photon, in its most basic sense, refers to the tiniest particle of light found within atoms. Quite amazingly, it seems that these tiny particles of light are able to communicate with each other – instantly – no matter how far apart they are.

There are many clues scattered through time which point out that the Universe is holographic. The Bible says in Genesis 1:26: 'Then God said, "Let Us make man in Our image, according to Our likeness."' In John 5:19 (King James Version): 'Then answered Jesus and said unto them, Verily, verily, I say unto you, The Son can do nothing of himself, but what he seeth the Father do: for what things soever he doeth, these also doeth the Son likewise.'

Are we not told in the Bible that we are ALL Creators? That we are all Gods? So is it fair to say that science is now 'discovering' that fact when it has been hinted at for so very long? What about the popular Law of Attraction? Doesn't that state that we need to *feel* what it is like to have the thing we want, to assume we have that thing already, in order to attract it to us? Didn't Gandhi say, 'Be the change you want to see in the world'? Doesn't that sound holographic to you? Where else can we see evidence of this? I haven't yet read the Koran but I will, and I am pretty sure that there will be references there too to a holographic world.

I had a quick look in one of my favorite and most highly

recommended books, the *Tao te Ching* (pronounced: 'Dow de Jeng'), attributed to the Chinese sage Lao Tzu. Written around the 6th century **BCE**, it contains remarkable philosophy which can be used to assist us in our journey through life. It teaches us how to live a life of harmony, love and compassion by letting go of a number of things. These include our desires, our attachments (to a loved one, our possessions or our *dreams*), our judgments (of ourselves, others and situations), and our conditioning. The book is set out in poem form, in 81 very short 'chapters' – some of which are only a few lines long – and it is easy to just open anywhere and read; in fact it can almost be used as a divination tool – simply ask a question and open a random page to get an answer! The *Tao* referred to in the book is also known as 'The Way,' which appears to be a form of *immensely powerful energy*. Admittedly, the work has had to be translated from Chinese (my favorite version of the book has been translated by Stephen Mitchell) so some distortions will have occurred, but to my *untrained* eye there seem to be a lot of references to quantum physics within it! Let me share a few snippets with you. (Please note that in the text below, 'It' refers to this great energy, the Tao.)

[Chapter 14]
… Seamless, unnamable,
it returns to the realm of nothing.
Form that includes all forms,
image without an image,
subtle, beyond all conception.
Approach it and there is no beginning;
follow it and there is no end …

[Chapter 25 (in entirety)]
There was something formless and perfect
before the universe was born.

It is serene. Empty.
Solitary. Unchanging.
Infinite. Eternally present.
It is the mother of the universe.
For lack of a better name, I call it the Tao.
It flows through all things,
inside and outside, and returns
to the origin of all things.
The Tao is great.
The universe is great.
Earth is great.
Man is great.
These are the four great powers.
Man follows the earth.
Earth follows the universe.
The universe follows the Tao.
The Tao follows only itself.

Just to be difficult, I picked up another favorite book of mine entitled *Hidden Music*, by the much-loved Sufi poet Rumi. This book, by the way, is 700 years old. Now this is not quite as clear, but just a few pages in, I found this:

He is back
The One who was never absent,
the water that never left the stream,
the essence of the musk
of which we are the scent.
Can the essence and the scent
be separate?

How about the William Blake poem, 'Auguries of Innocence'? It starts:

To see a world in a grain of sand,
And a heaven in a wild flower ...

Hmm, yes, it all sounds pretty holographic to me. Top marks to the scientists for 'discovering' this when it has been staring us in the face for hundreds of years!

The relevance of all this is that it confirms the shamanic understanding that God is in all things, and also in *us*, so there is no need for us to miss Him, or to search for Him; but we do need to remove all the dark and dusty layers that cover that bright, Divine spark within us all and let that light shine forth into the world.

My understanding of God's ways has been very hard won for me. I have looked at many other theories and nothing else makes sense. I *can* clearly see why people would think that there is not a God, given the terrible things that happen in the world. Indeed, this caused significant conflict for my father, who completely denied God for this very reason. I think that for him, the breaking point came when the atrocities committed by the serial murderer Fred West and his wife hit the headlines. My father cried, 'How could He have let this happen? Why didn't He strike Fred West dead, the minute he stepped out of line? How could He have stood back and watched those poor children suffer so much?' I remember clearly that my father was so upset by the Fred West case that he became very ill for a number of weeks.

I tried so hard over the years to explain the concept of free will and karma to my father, but he would get so upset that I just had to keep quiet. It pained me that he had this view, but I also recognized that he was on his own personal journey, and I could not interfere in that. But I feel that we have to remember that free will is *free* will. It cannot be given to some and not to others – everyone has it. God cannot give us free will with the proviso that we only use it for good deeds, because then it would not be free will! It is up to us and to our levels of consciousness as to what we do with it.

When I try to explain this, people generally have a common response of, 'That's all very well, but what about the poor starving people in Africa? Why doesn't He give them food?' Good question. *But is it God that lets people starve?* Or is it us, in the Western world? Many will tell you there are enough resources and 'food mountains' on the planet to feed *everyone.*

I am a firm believer in 'karma,' which is a philosophy that originates from the Indian religions. *Karma* means an 'action' or 'deed' which triggers a cycle of 'cause and effect,' e.g. if you sow goodness you will reap goodness. This principle makes us responsible for our *own lives* – it makes us think about our actions and the joy or pain that they may bring to ourselves or others (or to the Earth). The effects of karma extend through one's past, present and future lives.

You may have a view on karma, and think it is just used as a flippant means to explain away difficulty – but nothing else makes sense to me. We often hear of people who have done bad things, dishonest things, and yet had a great life, health, money and success. And we also know of people who are the most wonderful people we could ever wish to meet, and yet they seem to have lives beset by struggle, poverty, ill health and challenges of one type or another. Why? *Because we are not the sum total of this life only.* There is karmic deficit or excess from former lifetimes as we come into this lifetime for us to work out as necessary. I do not believe that God needs to come and strike down those who harm others, because the inescapable Laws of Karma will see to it that they do pay their dues.

The Laws of Karma are always in operation. However, the 'payback' for an action (good or bad) simply may not occur in this current lifetime, which is why some people can be perceived as 'getting away with it' or why others, alternatively, 'do so much good, yet seem to struggle so.' I have observed that the more highly evolved a person is (the closer to enlightenment they are), the more 'instant' karma can become; in fact payback can occur within the hour for some people! Also, I have noticed that the closer people are to coming off the life-and-death cycles, the more often they choose very difficult lifetimes for themselves, which appear to be used as 'karmic clean-ups' – as one cannot ascend until one's karmic bank balance is at zero.

The Laws of Karma are very complex; my aim here is to give you a simple understanding of karma and, if you wish, you can read up on it further as there are many good books available on the subject. I would like to make it clear that karmic 'debt' should not be judged as punishment, but as an opportunity to learn and redress any wrongs, so that we may work towards ascension and enlightenment. I have heard many people judging others – for whatever reason – and using karma as an excuse. I would like to stress that other people's situations should *never* be judged. We have *zero* understanding of where another person is on their soul's journey. Non-judgment is one of the greater spiritual principles for spiritual development; this also means that we should not judge *ourselves* as well as others.

Some people can be very eager to write off perceived difficulties as karmic payback, but it must be remembered that this is not always the case. Let me give you an example. I once had a lady contact me and ask me to heal her newly-born daughter, as she had been born blind. I told her that before I could consider this, I would have to ask the permission of the child's Higher Self / soul and also obtain the Creator's permission. She seemed stunned by this and told me, 'Of *course* she would want you to heal her! Who on *earth* would want to be *blind*?!' Who indeed?

So let us look at this example from a karmic viewpoint. We could say perhaps, 'Oh, the soul of that child may have perhaps blinded someone else in a former lifetime, and now she is getting her dues.' This is an extremely harsh way of looking at this example, and while it *is* possible of course, there can be many other scenarios being played out. Let's take a look at them.

1   The person born blind may have *wished to experience* blindness in this lifetime. Remember: the only reason we are here, and the only reason we have bodies, is to *experience* things – as many things as possible – before we ascend to the point of no longer needing to have bodies. You may ask, 'Why would someone choose this?' But why not? Maybe it was part of the spiritual development of the child's soul. Perhaps in this lifetime it wanted to look internally, rather than externally. Or to learn to rely on other senses such as touch and sound – as often many people with a disability are gifted with other amazing abilities. If we have many, many lifetimes in which to have different experiences, why not experience blindness in one of them?

2   Perhaps the soul had a hundred little bits of karma accumulated over many lifetimes, and chose to experience blindness in this lifetime to wipe their karmic slate clean in one go.

3   We often incarnate in soul groups from lifetime to lifetime and usually agree on our roles. Perhaps the *parents* of the child on a soul level wished to experience unconditional love and nurturing, so the soul manifesting as their child in this lifetime volunteered for the role so that the parents and others involved in the child's life could have this experience.

4   Maybe the child wished to be a teacher of unconditional love and compassion and inspiration in this lifetime to many others.

5   Maybe the child wished to be an inspiration to fully-sighted people, by teaching that one can have a disability but still function and be happy in the world. Or perhaps they wished to become an inspiration to other visually challenged people in some way.

I know this may be hard for you to swallow, so I did a Google search about blind people who have accomplished amazing things. Feel free to do this yourself so you know I am telling you the truth. The first site I came to was an ABC News clip about a young man who had been born with retinal cancer and had both of his eyes surgically removed at the tender age of three. His mother was a truly amazing lady who had deep faith in God and trusted that everything is *always* in Divine and perfect order. She reassured her child that despite the fact he could no longer see, he could still do anything he wanted and nothing need hold him back.

This amazing little boy quickly learned to develop something called 'echolocation,' by clicking his tongue frequently and listening to the sound the clicks made in his environment. (This is the same method bats use to navigate around objects.) News footage showed this young man *roller skating* down his street, and also walking along the sidewalk and suddenly navigating his way around a fallen trashcan lying in his path. More astonishingly, he could be seen beating his brother at a *video game*, all through the amazing use of his *hearing*! He went on to teach hundreds of blind people his clicking technique and completely transformed their lives.

Sadly, I went on to read that this courageous young man had died from cancer at 16 – but what an inspiration he had been in his short life! Apparently over 2,000 people turned up for his funeral!

What amazing teachers these people are to us all! We do not need to be blind in order to learn from them. Remember in earlier chapters when I said that life can be chicken **** or chicken salad, and we are the ones that choose? Well, here are two people that opted overwhelmingly for *salad*.

So I hope you can now see that things that can be perceived as 'bad' are not God's punishment, or always the effects of negative karma. (We can have good karma as well, by the way.)

This brings me to my most favorite and most regularly used quote:

EVERYTHING IS **ALWAYS** IN DIVINE AND PERFECT ORDER

You may be wondering, *How can bad things be in Divine and perfect order?* Let me share with you this example, which rather helpfully just popped into my head.

Imagine, if you will, a young Jesus, happily carving a lovely chair for His Mother in His carpentry workshop. The door of His workshop is wide open to let in the sunshine and the light breeze. Outside, a man walks by – but this is no ordinary man. This man is a seer, a mystic who has the ability to foresee the future. As the seer passes the open doorway to the workshop, he notices Jesus hard at work, and right at that moment his mind is flooded by visions of what challenges Jesus has ahead of Him. He sees it all: the betrayal, the torment, the torture and the crucifixion. This shocks the seer and saddens him, as he only sees the challenges and pain ahead for Jesus. He does not see that this is in fact Jesus' *soul purpose*, His whole reason for existing in this lifetime. Neither does he see the huge effects that Jesus' teachings will have on the world for *thousands of years to come*. The seer is, in fact, blind to all of this and only sees a fraction of the whole. But in wanting to help – and *having the best intention in the world* – he enters the workshop and tells Jesus that he has seen terrible things ahead for Him in His future. He urges Jesus to focus completely on His carpentry and never, ever even *contemplate* teaching or preaching in any way, shape or form. Does this make sense?

Think about it: if we are here to learn and grow – to evolve – are we going to achieve that via a very easy life? No, generally we learn through challenges in our life that help us progress along our spiritual paths. To quote the Dalai Lama: 'It is the enemy who can truly teach us to practice the virtues of compassion and tolerance.' This is one reason we should 'love our enemies' and 'find the gift within each challenge' – for these situations occur in order to *assist* us in our evolution. In many ways, therefore, it is our challenges which bring us our greatest gift – that of developing and evolving as a soul.

I won't go into it, but I have suffered a *lot* of conflict and challenge in my life. But this is the main way I have learned and obtained real knowledge. Deep inside I know that these challenges are here to teach me great things; they are not punishments inflicted upon me by God. This is just how I receive my spiritual teachings – not by some serene-faced teacher telling me everything I need to know, but by challenges, by *direct experiences*.

Essentially, for some time now, my ego has been going through a huge stripping-down process, which, I have to say, has been pretty painful. But trying to hold on to things, trying to control things, is only going to make my transition harder.

I remember a time when I was struggling with a few things and a friend asked me, 'What is it that you want? What have you been praying for?'

I replied that my prayers asked for assistance in achieving ascension/enlightenment, and that I be made a clear channel for Divine love and light.

My friend looked at me incredulously and said, 'You've been praying for those things and yet you're surprised you've been having a few challenges? Dur!'

And then I got it! Of course challenges would come if I was asking for spiritual progression – how else would I learn? Challenges are given to us to help us evolve, not as punishments from our God. *They are gifts!* It is to be remembered that we always have a *choice* – **** *or salad*. We can look at our current situation from a higher perspective – what a shaman would call the 'eagle' perspective – see the bigger picture and try to find what the lesson is in it for us. We have to learn to *let things go*.

We are taught in the Old Testament that God is vengeful, full of wrath, and that if we sin, we burn in hell for all eternity. I do not believe this at all. I think this is a way of keeping us in fear, of keeping us controllable, of keeping us away from the true light of our own being. Did God write the Bible? No, He did not. Man wrote the Bible, and there were various councils over an extended period of time which decided what should be included and what should be excluded from it. It is generally accepted that there is a gap of 400–600 years between the writings of the Old and New Testaments. I am by no way a specialist in this department, but there are many books out there that can provide you with information should you wish to learn more, and of course there is a wealth of information on the internet.

My own personal sense is that the Bible is a *guide* for life. Yes, we have been given free will, but if we follow the Ten Commandments our lives *will* be easier because we will not be attracting negative karma to ourselves.

Jesus told us that He was the Son of God, and I believe He IS the Son of God. I also believe that we are *all* God's children, and we *all* have within us that Divine spark.

But instead of treasuring that spark within, it seems we are all walking around being hard on ourselves, believing that we have sinned in some way and therefore we might as well give up now. Perhaps this is as a direct result of being born of Adam and Eve, or because we are divorced, have committed a crime, are gay, etc. But what is the nature of sin? My interpretation of sin is that it is anything which takes us away from finding that spark of Divinity within us, anything which lures us away from the pathway of Light. The word 'sin' comes from the Greek word *hermatia* which is related to archery and means to 'miss the mark' – to go 'off course,' if you like. Because we are taught that our primary nature is the fallen nature of Adam, that we are sinners from the get-go, and that any additional sin will result in judgment in hell, is there any wonder that we are so ready to beat ourselves up? And like Pierce in the Practice Notes, if we have committed a sin, and are therefore 'beyond redemption,' what is the point in even bothering to try to change our ways? What stops us from committing more and more sins? After all, we are going to burn in hell anyway! But not one part of me believes in this.

What makes more sense to me is that Adam, like Pierce, is an illustration of *separation*. He believed he had sinned because he ate the apple, so he lost his connection to the Divine. But the Divine is *always* there for us, whether we believe it or not. It is not a case of us being cast out of the Kingdom of Heaven, out of the Garden of Eden. We cast *ourselves* out because we believed we were no longer worthy of it. But all we have to do is to open our hearts to the Divine and know that we have always been loved and accepted. We all have Divinity within us, if only we would seek to find it.

We have to stop beating ourselves up. We need to start loving ourselves as God loves us, which is *unconditionally*. We have to forgive ourselves as God forgives us. Totally. Yes, we need to be conscious of our actions, we need to try our best to be good people, and we need to remember the natural laws of cause and effect, or karma. But if we have done something 'wrong,' then we need to acknowledge that, to learn from it, forgive ourselves, do our best to make up for what we have done, and then we need to let it go – and resolve to make different choices next time.

So many clients are very unhappy about things they have done in the past and do not understand how they could have made such choices or done such things. I always tell them that they made those decisions with the *consciousness* they had *at the time*. Not with the consciousness they have *now*. We cannot beat ourselves up for things we did in the past. In most cases, there is nothing we can do; we can't go back and do things differently. We HAVE to let it go. Of course if there is something we *can* do, any apologies we can make, then we should do our utmost to do this, but sometimes our only option is to forgive ourselves and start over.

We are spirits having a human experience. We have bodies to enable us to experience and feel things. We are here to learn, to grow, and most of all, to evolve. Each birth-and-death cycle is an opportunity for us to move closer towards enlightenment, to connect to the Divinity within, and to live from that place.

This brings us to the question: Where are we now in terms of religion? Certainly, people seem to be moving away from organized religions towards forms of spirituality that they find more agreeable. My understanding of this, and of the times we find ourselves in now, is the need for a time of *balance*. I feel that any 'new' religion going forward will have to have that sense of balance within it.

Throughout history, there have been many bases of religion. The ancient Egyptians, Mayans, Aztecs, Inca and many North American and European pagan cults worshipped the Sun (not a completely bad idea as we would be pretty stuck without it). Other civilizations worshipped the Earth, and the feminine principle. Christianity, as we now understand, initially found it hard to acquire converts, such was the pull towards the more pagan religions. These pagans were not 'devil worshippers,' as is popularly thought, but merely people who practiced a more nature-based form of worship. The Church therefore absorbed many pagan principles, celebrations, and places of worship.

To give a few examples, in ancient art there can be found many images of the ancient Egyptian Goddess Isis breastfeeding her baby son Horus, and there are also many similar images of Mother Mary nursing baby Jesus. Jesus' birth date was *chosen* as 25 December by the Church in 354 CE; it was a date that had been celebrated for the previous *80 years* by the Romans as the *Natalis Solis Invicti*, the 'Birthday of the Unconquerable Sun.' Huge festivities took place around this date, gifts were exchanged, and the pagan rituals of holly, mistletoe, trees and Yule logs were all used – and copied for our own Christmas celebrations. The date 25 December is also said to have marked the birth of Horus the Savior of the Egyptians, and Osiris, his father. The Greek Gods Adonis, Hercules and Bacchus were also said to have been born on this day, as was the Persian God Mithras. So 25 December is a very popular birthday!

For thousands of years people worshipped the feminine principle of the Earth and the Goddess. Then with the advent of the Christian Church, the masculine God ruled. Nowadays many are once more drawn to the gentler nature of the feminine religions. But my sense is that, as in all things, we need a religion which is balanced *between the masculine and feminine ways*. Because of the dominant male energy over the last 2,000 years, we have come along in huge strides as far as industry, technology and scientific knowledge are concerned. If you recall from the 'Relationships' chapter, masculine energy is determined, single focused, goal orientated, pushes ahead, is focused on freedom, and of course it is also the warrior energy.

However, there has been a significant downside to being purely aligned with the masculine energies. A quick scan on the internet found a table of democide (murder by government), apparently taken from the 1987 book *A Dictionary of War* by the author G. C. Kohn, showing that there had been 169,202,000 such deaths in the period dating from 1900 to 1987 alone – *in the 20th century alone, folks!* Pre-20th century, dating back as far as 221 BCE, records show a total of 133,471,000 deaths through war, and such lovely things as the witch hunts, the Spanish Inquisition, African slavery, and the Christian Crusades to name a few – although I guess those records are a little more shaky.

Now, I am spectacularly crap at math, but my calculator shows me that in the 87-year period starting in 1900, 3,573,100 *more* people were killed through war than in the *total* period from 221 BCE to the 19th century. Excuse me, but aren't we supposed to be more civilized now? And even more recently it has been estimated that between 50 and 70 million people died in World War II alone. FIFTY MILLION PEOPLE!

Sadly, we have progressed in some areas, but at the expense of the feminine principles of compassion, nurturing, wisdom, allowing, love and consideration, and of course, doing more than one thing at once (go on, I had to get that one in!). But what I want to make clear here is that I am not having a go at men, but at the *masculine energy*. We have, in effect, raped the Earth of her resources, and then polluted and damaged her in return for a quick buck and bottom-line results – all actions which could actually lead to *our* destruction.

Jesus Himself said that the only path to take is the middle path, the path of balance, and it is this now which we need to focus on. We are currently coming into a time of resurgence of the feminine, and this is very much needed. But we must take care and not go too much the other way, and turn into nations of tree huggers (although it is always good to hug trees and we must start loving them more!). The feminine energy has already found its way onto the faces, if not the hearts of men – the market for men's grooming products (Manscara and Guyliner, to name a few!) was expected to reach $14 billion in 2009. But what the world needs, going forward, is an honoring and appreciation of *both* the masculine and feminine principles – the yin and the yang, if you like – because this is where *wholeness is*.

If women simply do to men what men have done to women over the last couple of thousand years then we won't have gotten very far, and after another couple of thousand years the balance will shift again, like one great big pendulum. We need to break out of that cycle and embrace *both* qualities. YES, the feminine principles need to rise into awareness once more; if we do not volunteer to change our ways then we may be forced into it.

The current economic crisis is just part of this global movement, and by 'global' I mean *made by* the globe, the Earth. But once these principles have arisen, we need to balance them out with the masculine energy. So for example, we can use and appreciate the masculine qualities of determination and focus to build new economies, technologies, businesses, governments and societies, but at the same time, use the feminine qualities to ensure that such things are built on solid foundations, that those things which are highly precious to us – the PLANET, nature, animals and mankind – are treated with respect.

And to me, and many others, this is why the shamanic principles are so magical. They combine the masculine principles of Great Spirit (God) and the Sun, and the feminine principles of Great Spirit (God again, the eternal Mother and Father) and the Earth, and they work with respect and reverence for both. For example, if a road is required up the side of a mountain in Peru, the engineers and workers (directional = masculine) will take action, but not before a ceremony is carried out in order to ask permission of the Earth, the nature spirits and the spirits of the mountain (love, nurturing and compassion = feminine). And more than often, the building work then goes without a hitch, because everyone and everything is in harmony and balance. This may sound bizarre to us in the West, but cultures have worked this way for many centuries. For thousands of years in Eastern cultures, a feng shui priest would be employed to carry out a ceremony in order to ask permission of the land before a building project started, and this practice continues today in the Orient. This may sound old-fashioned or superstitious, but we do need to have the land on our side!

We are all a part of the Great Spirit. We all ARE the Great Spirit. We are being called upon now to harness and utilize the qualities of balance and start to build a New World. Are you ready?

11. Enlightenment

Memories 11.1

Arriving home from my course I feel unpicked, unraveled. I have done so much soul searching, so much inner work, that I feel tired to my bones. I look around my house; it seems different somehow. I don't feel at home and yet I am in my own house. The phone rings, and a friend tells me a few of the girls are out having a drink and they want me to join them. I go upstairs to get changed, and search for something suitable to wear, but it feels like I am going through someone else's things. Who bought these clothes? They seem so *old*, even though some of them were recently purchased. I can't find anything that seems right, anything that seems to reflect me, who I am now. I want to throw everything I own away, every last thing, and start again. If only! I throw on a dress, refresh my make-up and leave the house.

The bar is crowded and noisy; the energy of the people overwhelms me. I find my friends and sit with them. They are all dear to me, and I love them all. They want to hear all my news, but I find that I can't tell them about my course, so I talk about fairly neutral subjects. Then they start talking, about work, about husband and boyfriend problems, about the trials of motherhood, and the latest juicy gossip. And I sit there smiling and nodding, watching their pretty, animated faces. All of a sudden, I feel a horrible and sudden distance from them, as if I am being pulled back into another dimension. The words *What am I doing here?* resonate around in my head, coming as if from nowhere. No! These are my friends, I love them all, I want to be here! But the voice repeats, *What am I doing here?* I don't know why but I feel uncomfortable and part of me wants to leave, wants to run away, in fact, which is very distressing indeed.

* * *

Abundant jungle life is all around me; plants and trees are growing within and on top of each other, all competing for space and light. Dusk descends; the thick air quivers and falls, folds in upon itself. The Ayahuascero commences his ceremony, singing his haunting jungle enchantments to bring the powerful plant medicine to life. He kneels before me, offers me a dirty yellow plastic tumbler three quarters full with dark brown Ayahuasca brew.

'*Chocolata?*' he asks in jest, dark eyes dancing.

The night condenses around me as I take the tumbler from him and drink down the vile-tasting liquid before I change my mind. The taste is practically indescribable: a mixture of deeply condensed jungle, along with a large measure of battery acid. My stomach flips over and over as the liquid hits it.

Around me the chaotic sounds of the jungle seem to intensify... and then seem to fade away... as I sink deep, deep, deep into the core of the Earth. I sense that I am in an earth-cradle, and Pachamama, Mother Earth herself, is rocking me as if I am her baby. I have never felt so held, so safe, in all my life. Back and forth... back... forth... I am soooooo sleepy... lulled into a deeply peaceful state.

Suddenly – BANG!!! I am jolted out of my comfortable reverie to find myself standing in front of massive golden, diamond-encrusted gates – so tall they reach the velvet sky above me. The gates creak open to reveal the most amazing Cinderella-type carriage. It is enormous, white and decorated with sparkling stars and is being pulled by eight massive, muscular white stallions, their long manes flowing in the light breeze as they prance forward.

I glance up towards the top of the carriage and see the Goddess of the Vine herself, Mama Ayahuasca. She is stunning, an Amazonian mixture of Angelina Jolie and Tina Turner. A tight white, diamond-encrusted cat suit is stretched over her bodybuilder's physique and large proud bosom. Her long black silky hair is pulled away from her face in a high ponytail. She is supremely beautiful, feminine, sexual and sensual.

The carriage draws to a halt directly in front of me. Ayahuasca throws down her reins and stands proudly on top of the carriage. She smiles delightedly, flings back her head and throws her arms up to the sky expansively, as if in victory. 'All this…' she exclaims, indicating the sleepy starlit jungle below her, '… is *MINE!'*

I watch in wonder as she leaps like an animal from the carriage and, Tarzan-like, uses the vines to swing through the trees at speed. She somersaults above the canopy of trees, all the time laughing deeply in apparent delight as she swings from tree to tree.

My body longs to join her so I call out respectfully, 'May I be permitted to dance with you?' Suddenly she stops dead in the night sky, looks at me and then jets down towards me. She grabs me by the wrist and yanks me up with her. We whoosh high into the air, perform somersaults and laugh in ecstasy as we tear through the jungle at terrifying speeds.

I see a crystal-clear lake below me and as we fly over it I see my body reflected in the water. I am surprised to see that my body is the same shape as hers, but encased in a black diamond-encrusted cat suit. My hair, also caught up in a long high ponytail, flies out behind me in the wind rush. I feel unbelievably alive and powerful.

She lets me go, yet strangely I do not fall; I just keep on flying, faster and faster, like a rocket. We explode through the canopy of trees at breakneck speed, and as we pass by I notice that the trees themselves are glimmering with life. Sparks of white light emanate from them, and the sap is illuminated as it courses up the tree trunks like the lifeblood it truly is.

Ayahuasca and I come together and arc in front of the huge full moon, then somersault ourselves though the starry black night. We dance together like the most supreme, majestically acrobatic ballerinas. I feel her joy; her love for the jungle and all that dwells within it is tangible. She is its Queen and reigns supreme, and everything around us knows that.

Suddenly my vision shatters like glass cobwebs; I am shocked back to my body and the ceremonial hut as someone bumps against me in the darkness. Annoyed, I try to return to my vision, but it is over, fractured into a thousand pieces. I know that whatever else I may experience tonight, the memory of that dance with the Goddess Ayahuasca will be emblazoned in my mind forever.

And gradually I settle back down, until the lullaby of the *icaros*, the jungle enchantments, lulls me into further visions, and I go out into the jungle again, once more, on the magic of the song.

Practice Notes 11.2

Melanie looks brighter and fresher than I have seen her look for a long time. She tells me with pride that she has changed the way she relates to her children, no longer letting them get away with murder because of the guilt she felt at leaving their father. She can now see how her experience of childhood abuse had forced her to mistakenly believe she was a bad person, that she did not matter and therefore did not deserve love or respect. She tells me she now realizes that she is worthy of love, respect and self-worth.

'There's only one problem,' she says, looking sheepish.

'What's that?' I enquire.

She sighs and looks around the room, unseeing. I know she is searching for the right words.

'It's my partner. We just don't seem to *fit* anymore. He doesn't like the new me; he keeps trying to do things to knock my confidence. And he's SO negative. It's unbelievable! *How come I hadn't noticed that before?* It's as if he doesn't want me to improve, doesn't want me to heal, to move forward or challenge myself. I'm happier now than I've ever been – why isn't he more supportive? But in order for me to truly move forward, I'm going to have to leave him! I don't want to be with him anymore, I'm fed up with his crap, with his picking on me, and I certainly don't want him touching me. I have no option; I am *not* going to go back to how I was – that's for sure!'

Notes 11.3

Trying to write a chapter on enlightenment is like trying to fit the *Titanic* into a garden pond, but I wanted to include some detail on this topic as so many people come to see me because they are searching for enlightenment. When I ask them, 'Why?' they reply, 'Because when I'm enlightened I will live in peace and harmony forever and everything will be so easy!' And my answer to that is, 'No, no, no, no, NO!!!' Being enlightened *does not* mean that you will no longer have problems or difficulties – indeed many times it can test us to the limit and bring us *more* problems and difficulties.

So before we go much further, I should perhaps attempt the impossible and try to describe what the state of enlightenment means, or what it is like. Here goes. An enlightened person is…

One who has transcended the human life-and-death cycle. Therefore, once they leave their body in this life, they will not have any need to have another human incarnation, as they have reached the pinnacle, if you like, of human spiritual experience and the goal of humanity. So their evolution after death will further them along the path of spirit.

One who has evolved out of the human need to suffer. This DOES NOT mean that the person no longer suffers, i.e. only good things happen to him, but that he takes the chicken salad approach to all things. If I said to you now, 'You have six weeks to live,' or 'I am afraid that your child has died,' the normal human reaction is firstly, to *react* in the first place, and secondly to be sad, upset, devastated, angry, hysterical, negative, grief-stricken, etc, etc. If I said this same statement to an enlightened person, there would probably be no reaction at all, because an enlightened person has transcended their sense of self (i.e. they are not attached to their human identity) and their attachment to their body/humanness, and also they are master of their emotional state, rather than being a slave to it.

- One who has transcended human desires. So you will not find them lusting after an Aston Martin, a house in the Hamptons, the latest handbag, chocolate, sex, or recognition!
- One who has a deep knowledge, love and acceptance of Self, both the light and the shadow aspects. (This does not mean they are overly 'nice' but that they know and accept themselves wholly.)
- One who has complete control over their thoughts and their emotions.
- One who has attained a very clean and clear 'light body,' and a very high level of vibration.
- One who is at all times cognizant of their thoughts, words, actions and deeds, and the impact that these may have on another.
- One who is in alignment with both the Divine aspect within themselves and also outside of themselves.
- One who has perhaps undergone an amazing transformative spiritual experience or vision of some kind.
- One who perhaps has altered neurological brain function.
- One who resides in their heart and gut as opposed to their heads.
- One who lives in the present moment, not the past or the future.
- One who does not struggle against *what is*, but has acceptance, trust and faith in whatever they are faced with at the time.
- One who can access the Mind of God, or receive information from the Quantum Field / Void – i.e. they receive

knowledge direct from Source energy rather than by learning from others.

- One who is in alignment and connection with their Higher Self / soul aspect, rather than with their human/bodily aspect.
- One who has a deep understanding and love of life and humanity.
- One who perhaps has enhanced senses and psychic ability.
- One who devotes themselves to others.
- One who is empty inside. This does not refer to a person who is an 'empty shell,' but to a person who is a clear vessel for Divine light and who therefore becomes filled with it.

I do hope this makes sense; please appreciate that it is very hard to explain the state of an enlightened being using words! It is a state of being that is available to all, but achieved by very few over the centuries. It is not difficult or dangerous in itself, but it can be perceived as such, as the more attached we are to our human journey and to our human 'beingness,' the more difficult it is to achieve enlightenment.

But, let me reiterate, rather than suddenly becoming free from all problems, being enlightened means that you will simply be *present* enough to always be a chicken salad person. You will *choose to react to conflict or challenge in a chicken salad way*, and, like the story of the monk hanging off the cliff and only tasting the sweet juice of the berry, you *will always strive for the highest possible thought in each moment*.

In the 'Chicken Salad' chapter I mentioned how a caterpillar in the cocoon is completely pulverized, and how its previous identity and personality have to be destroyed before the beautiful butterfly can emerge from the cocoon and take flight. Our spiritual journeys can be likened to this process, for everything about us has to change, including letting go of our fears.

If we look at our friend the caterpillar, we see that it is connected to the Earth; it hungers for leaves and fears birds, hedgehogs and gardeners. Its fears are relevant to it – *in its current identity.*

But, as a butterfly, it knows the summer sky and the winds. It has a hunger for nectar and for the vibrant colors of flowers. It no longer fears the things it used to fear, because it is simply not necessary. Birds and hedgehogs are no threat to it, and gardeners appreciate its bright beauty. From its heights the butterfly can now see the bigger picture; it is free and a beautiful thing to behold.

Do you think that the butterfly resents or regrets its journey? Do you think it yearns for the taste of cabbage and misses its old caterpillar friends? Do you think it feared for the loss of its old self, its old identity, while it was in its cocoon? Or did it submit – willingly and joyfully – to the process, trusting that whatever happened was for its best, as a necessary part of its journey?

This brings us to an important question on your journey: How do *you* react to change and to the potential loss of your old identity? Do/Will you go into fear? Or will you surrender to the process? As I have mentioned before, the 'comfort' of the Known Zone is incredibly difficult to walk away from, even if our Known Zone is a very difficult and uncomfortable place for us to be.

One of the problems we have is that we cannot see into the future; we do not *know* that after being liquidized we are going to be beautiful butterflies, and of course those butterflies are unfamiliar to us. Additionally many people fear becoming butterflies and then doing something 'wrong' which will turn them back into a caterpillar! So we cling to our old caterpillar ways, and become stuck, because *stuck equals safe.* We focus on the hardships of our journey to date and very often we fight change and against the things we need to enable us to transmute. But if we have the courage to go through the process, then fly away from our cocoons, all colors blazing, we can look back over our journey and see that everything we had to go through was worth it. Then we can go on to achieve our life's purpose and our dreams.

So, through the human healing process, we develop a conscious awareness of our old selves and our old patterns, and learn new ways of being in the world. Rather like when we have a spring clean and a sort-out of our wardrobe: we decide what parts of ourselves to keep – and what parts need to go in the bin!

But going on a spiritual journey has a price. It is unlikely that the butterfly will remain in contact with his old caterpillar friends, not because there is anything wrong with them as such, but because there is no longer any vibrational resonance between them. He will instead make new friends with the other butterflies. As you do your personal healing work and begin a spiritual practice of some sort, the rate of your *vibration* increases. Let me try to explain it another way.

Imagine a hot-air balloon with its basket on the ground, which is full of sandbags to make it heavy. As we do our personal healing work, it is akin to throwing the sandbags over the side of the basket. Gradually the balloon lifts to greater and greater heights. The more we let go of, the higher we rise. This process is referred to in the wonderful Pixar film *Up*, when the main character, an elderly widower, has to let go of his past in order to fly away to his new future and to safety. (I have noticed that for some reason Pixar produce films which are highly spiritual in content!)

This is why, as you read in the Memories section, when I returned home from one of my shamanic courses, I had done so much energy work and shifted vibrationally so much that nothing fitted me anymore. I didn't feel at home in my house, my clothes felt like they were someone else's, and more importantly, I felt like I didn't belong with my dear friends – I simply was not *resonating* with anything anymore. The biggest challenges on our journey face us then, difficult and painful decisions have to be made, and sometimes the only way to go forward is to make big changes in our environment and in our social circles. Sometimes we have to leave beloved partners behind because we simply do not fit anymore.

Of course, as discussed in the 'As Above, So Below' chapter, because everything is connected, the fact that we have raised our frequency should have the knock-on effect of raising the frequency of those around us, but very often, the people around us refuse to move – or refuse to let us move forward. Therefore, it can sometimes feel like a very solitary journey. This is why *letting go* is such a large requirement of any spiritual journey.

You will also find your tastes change. You may decide to eat more healthily, you may wish to change your décor so it reflects the inner 'you' a little more, and your interests and hobbies may change. Or, like the client in the Practice Notes section, you may suddenly wonder what you are doing living in a situation you hadn't even realized you were in before! The new 'you' on the inside will *have* to be reflected on the outside. It is common for a person on a spiritual journey to end up a 'Billy No-Mates' for a while. But bear in mind that gradually, as your new vibrational 'address' settles, you *will* attract new friends you feel more comfortable with. Enlightenment is all about evolution, not revolution.

So, how easy is this transition? Well, it depends how much you want to change and *what you are willing to let go of*. Most people, however, try to make the journey *while still holding on to everything*. They remain a caterpillar, and through fear of annihilation, just *pretend* to be a butterfly. But how much harder will the journey be for the caterpillar? He will have to drag his fat little body up and down the stems of each flower instead of simply flying to each one. He will try to reach the sweet nectar of life with his short little tongue, and even if he does attain the sweetness, he is not designed to digest it. And however much he fights against it, his little body will always crave cabbage. And the hedgehogs and gardeners will still be a threat, despite his protestations!

Sometimes, by holding on to the old and dragging it along with us we make life, and our spiritual journeys, significantly harder; and at the same time we still fail to reach the dizzy heights of our possibilities, to fly and to become all that we can be.

Put another way, it's a bit like me asking you to go and get me something from my local supermarket while taking my large sofa with you. It may be possible for you to drag my sofa all the way there, but it will be very slow progress; you will get very sweaty, and will probably want to give up halfway. This is what it is like, going through life with all your emotional/physical baggage, when really, you could just dump it and get to where you need to go easily. But in order to do that...

You need to be fully aligned with that which you seek to become, on all levels of your being, and you need to be prepared to let go of everything that has defined you up until this point.

And very often we think that we know the way we are going, but the Universe can have other ideas. During the metamorphosis we can be stripped bare of our old identities, often forcibly. Many people have been pushed into that process by the current 'credit crunch' (many spiritual people will tell you this is the *whole point* of it!). We can be faced with redundancy, the loss of a home, of a loved one, or of our possessions, or sometimes all of it at the same time! This can be very scary indeed because it feels like we are going out of control (again, that is exactly the point!) and losing everything that has defined 'us.' When a person is truly enlightened, there is no 'us,' no resistance to outside events, or attachment to things, places or people. We are more fluid, like a river, which simply flows around each obstacle in its path. What is actually happening during this stripping-away process is that we are being 'de-magnetized' – so that all our old attachments slip away. The process itself can be as difficult or as easy as we make it.

In order for us to make this journey, we require huge amounts of courage, *trust and faith*. We have to be brave enough to let go of our *need for control*, of our need *to know what is happening and where we are going*. So many people wait forever to take steps towards fulfillment because they are waiting to know *what will happen next*. For example, a client will often say, 'I have a very strong feeling that I am meant to sell my house and move on, to drop my past life so that I can move forward.' I ask them, 'So, what's stopping you?' and they reply, 'Oh, I can't do it yet because I don't know where to go.'

Now, I do not deny that this is not an easy position to be in; this has certainly been one of my biggest challenges on my spiritual and healing path – dropping the need to *know what is happening, being able to trust and surrender to the process. (You may recall I said at the outset that I was struggling with all this stuff as you are; I am certainly not perfect!)* But I think that part of the challenge is for us NOT to know where we are going and to act anyway, on our gut feeling. It is about putting the house on the market, making that stand, *following our hearts, not our heads*. This way, we are showing the Universe we are committed to moving forward and then trusting that we will be shown a way forward. Sometimes we *just have to take action* and *then* the Universe or spirit will open up the next step or chapter for us, *after* we have shown our commitment.

These processes can be very tough indeed to face and even harder to experience. We are constantly battling between the desires of the human ego and the urgings of the soul and our Higher Self. On my personal spiritual journey I have found a huge amount of comfort and clarity in the ancient wisdom of the *Tao te Ching* (referred to in the last chapter). I find, whenever I am struggling, that all I have to do is read a few short verses and I am back on track again. I have owned the book for 15 years and

I have to say that every time I read it I find deeper wisdom and messages in the text. Here are a couple more of my favorite chapters to give you a further taste.

[Chapter 9]
Fill your bowl to the brim
and it will spill.
Keep sharpening your knife
and it will blunt.
Chase after money and security
and your heart will never unclench.
Care about people's approval
and you will be their prisoner.
Do your work, then step back.
The only path to serenity.

[Chapter 37]
The Tao never does anything
yet through it all things are done.
If powerful men and women
could center themselves in it,
the whole world would be transformed
by itself, in its natural rhythms.
People would be content
with their simple, everyday lives,
in harmony, and free of desire.
When there is no desire,
all things are at peace.

Let me give you an example of letting go. Very recently, due to financial problems, a dear friend of mine and her husband were forced to move out of a beautiful five-bedroom farmhouse, in the middle of acres of open fields, which they had been renting – to a tiny one-bedroom maisonette in the middle of a housing estate.

I helped them move everything into their new flat, a process which took over 12 hours.

At the end of an exhausting day, I flopped down onto the sofa and closed my eyes for a moment's rest. I opened them again to find my friend manically throwing *unopened* bags of possessions onto the front lawn, to join all the things which were to be taken to the charity shop the next day. I leapt off the sofa, grabbed hold of her by the shoulders and asked, 'Are you sure you don't need these things? Don't you think you should look into the bags and see what's in them?'

She looked up at me so serenely, with an expression of such sublime peace on her face, that in that moment she seemed almost holy to me. Gently she said, 'No, Dawn, I don't *need* these things. This whole process has been a gift to me, because it has made me realize that I don't really need *anything*. I really thought I did, but I can see now that I don't. Every *thing* that I get rid of makes me feel lighter, lighter and freer, and if I could throw away *absolutely everything*, every cup, sock, ornament, *everything* I possessed, then I would do it. I would really like to do it actually – just clear out everything, every last vestige of my past, *of who I used to be* – because this move has changed me.

'Everything makes sense to me now: the things that have happened in the last few weeks, the things I've been called on to do up to this point. I see now that I've been given a golden opportunity to clear myself – and my energy field.

'Of course, I know that if I did throw absolutely everything away I would need to replace certain essentials, but I have learned that I will never, *ever* accumulate so much *stuff* again. Everything I own represents the old me, and holds memories, holds energy – *old* energy, energy that isn't me anymore. That energy is holding me in a certain place, at a certain vibration. *I am on a spiritual path*; I've been on a spiritual path, seeking enlightenment, for years now, as you know. But how am I going to obtain enlightenment with all this STUFF holding me down, holding me back?

'Yes, I've found this experience difficult and very scary indeed. Part of me did start to wonder, *Why is this happening to me?* But then I remembered foremost that I AM on a spiritual path seeking enlightenment, and this experience is part of my lessons, and I have truly learned a lot from it. I trust that this is happening for all the right reasons, I trust in spirit, and I know I'm going to be OK.'

I was greatly humbled by her and her attitude. I realized then that as with the axiom, 'As above, so below, as within, so without,' because she had been doing her personal healing work for years and had cleared up her energy field over a long time, and because everything mirrors our internal state of being, now her *outer* experience – which was represented by her home – had to be similarly cleared of the old, which the enforced move accomplished! Because my friend did not judge her experience of losing her lovely home, she was able to find the gift in it for her and her partner. In fact, because she had totally let go, she only lived in the maisonette a couple of months before various synchronous events led to her living in Andalucía, Spain.

But it is one thing to read about other people's experiences, quite another to go through the challenges ourselves. Doesn't Jesus say that it is 'easier for a camel to pass through the eye of a needle than for a rich man to enter the Kingdom of God?' This does not mean of course that rich people are doomed or evil in any way. My understanding of this saying is that it is hard for most of us to reach the Kingdom of God because we fear giving up money, possessions and security as we have *attachment* to material things. We can't squeeze through the eye of that needle because we want to bring all our *stuff* with us along with our old identities!

And it is impossible to reach enlightenment while we have attachment to things, because they weigh us down. This is why typical figurines of the older, fat-bellied Buddha show him with nothing other than a loincloth to cover his modesty, a small sack of belongings, sometimes a musical instrument, and a great big smile. He is smiling because he has given up his possessions (or his attachment to them); he trusts and has faith.

There is a Buddhist saying, which is quite pertinent in the current difficult economic climate: *'From greed comes grief, from greed comes fear; he who is free from greed knows neither grief nor fear.'*

I once heard it said that 'no one ever reached enlightenment from the comfort of their sofa,' and this is very true indeed as it can be a very uncomfortable process!

When you look at many spiritual traditions and paths towards enlightenment there is a common thread between them all, a common set of principles, and these include some or all of the following:

- The need to quieten down the mind through meditation, contemplation and being present
- A need for acceptance, and surrender to *what is*
- Freedom from attachment and desire, position and possession
- The aim to become heart-centered (Higher Self) rather than head-centered (ego mind).

The above all have one thing in common, and that is that they all serve to quieten down the 'ego.' Now, when I say 'ego,' I don't mean the egotistical side of a person, the side that sweeps into a room and exclaims, 'Darlings, aren't I *fabulous*!' Rather I mean the ego mind, one of the very earliest parts of the human brain to develop. This is also known as the 'reptilian' or 'limbic' brain, and it is the part of us that is responsible for the constant 'chatter' in our heads and our over-concern with our physical and material selves. This part is ancient and was originally designed to keep us safe from dinosaurs; in fact its main aim is to keep us 'safe' – full stop. It should be in service to us, in slavery; however, the ego has been given far too much leeway and the reverse has happened: our ego mind has become the master, and we listen to its inane chatter all the time, controlled by it like puppets on a string, dancing to its repeating tune. Its sole concern is its survival and what are commonly referred to as the 'Four Fs' = Fear, Food, Fighting and er, Sex. It concerns itself with things which affect the 'I,' the personal – our position and our possessions – along with the way we view, or seek to view, ourselves.

It can seem that the ego is evil at times, as so often it stops us from moving forward, but it is to be remembered at all times that it is simply trying to do its job, which is to keep us 'safe.' From my experiences with clients who have become totally governed by their ego minds, 'safety' normally represents being 'stuck,' normally indoors – which, when you think about it, would make you safe from dinosaurs if you were living in your little cave! But this part of our brain is outdated; it cannot seem to understand that staying indoors and keeping 'safe' (i.e. staying in your Known Zone and not trying anything new) can actually be detrimental to us, and that *real safety* means facing fears and not allowing them to dictate your life. It may sound crazy but unless this part of you is on board with your plans, you will not be moving very far ahead! We have to seriously 'retrain our brain'!

All of my current challenges (and if truth be told, pretty much everyone's challenges) are *ego driven*. The mastery of the ego is one of the greatest challenges on a spiritual path towards enlightenment, because we should not be governed by the ego, or our heads, but by our *Higher Selves*, which connect to us via our hearts. This is why so many spiritual paths require us to be 'heart-centered' rather than 'head-centered.'

There are many interpretations of the Higher Self; you can decide what seems right to you, but my sense is that we have a soul or spirit within us, but we also have an 'oversoul' which is huge, exists outside of us, but is connected to us via our hearts.

This oversoul / Higher Self / Higher Consciousness / God-Self – whatever you wish to call it – is the greatest part of us. It is the part of us that understands that we are *eternal*, that we cannot be destroyed, no matter what happens. Sure, our physical form can be hurt and destroyed, but our physical being is *not who we are*. We are energy, and science can prove that energy cannot be destroyed. It can be transformed, it can be moved, *but it cannot be destroyed* – that is impossible. We need to remember this so that it is easier for us to step out of fear, *whatever situation we are in*.

An enlightened person is fully aligned with their Higher (Spiritual) Self, not their ego (physical) self. Our Higher Self also *remembers* what it is that we have come to learn in this lifetime and will try to gently lead us to those realizations. It also has massive intelligence, and can remember every lifetime we have ever had, along with all the skills that we had in those lifetimes. For example, if we were a good pianist in a former lifetime, I believe it is possible to re-access that skill without necessarily taking lessons again in this lifetime, via our heart connection to our Higher Self. It is connected to All-That-Is, not only the Divine, but also the consciousness of the world, the Void, the Quantum Field, to ALL consciousness and all intelligence. When we connect to our hearts, we can know all there is to know.

We have been educated to think that the brain or the mind is intelligent, but all it knows is that which is learned – learned from the wisdom of others – those who have perhaps accessed *their* Higher Self, and utilized their connection to the Quantum Field in order to receive true knowledge. Or most often, it is knowledge picked up from our *conditioning or beliefs*, as children, i.e. 'If I do x, then y will happen.'

If you want to know whether the ego mind or the Higher Self is running you, here is a quick guide. If you are experiencing:

- Fear
- Negative emotion

- Suffering from lack in some way – love, money etc
- Individuality
- Separation

...then you are being governed by your ego mind and you are head-centered.

If you are experiencing:

- Love
- Positivity
- Trust
- Abundance
- Acceptance
- Letting go
- Faith
- Oneness

...then you are being governed by your Higher Self, and you are heart-centered.

The good news is that a) it's not easy for anyone to move away from the control of the mind, so don't feel too badly about it, and b) if you realize that you are being run by your ego mind, then you can do something about it, and use your intent to re-align with your heart center. It is up to *us* to shift our consciousness and our energy down to our hearts and rest in the peaceful energy there. Meditation is an amazing way for us to do this, and one of our biggest allies on our journey towards enlightenment, in my view.

My sense is that the necessary destruction of the ego is what Jesus was trying to teach us on the cross. I believe that He was trying to teach us all, in the most extreme way, about our immortality, and to show us that it is possible to gain mastery of the ego. As we are told, He had a crown of thorns on His head, nails driven through His palms and feet, had been beaten and tortured, and was facing a long, drawn-out death. But ask yourself: despite all this, was Jesus struggling on the cross, hurling abuse at those who tortured Him, crying and feeling sorry for Himself? No, He was not. In fact, He asked His Father to forgive His abusers!

My view on this is that Jesus used the crucifixion to teach us many lessons. Firstly, He knew He could not control what was happening to Him, but He knew He *could* control His reaction to it. Secondly, that He was completely aligned with His heart center and His Higher Self and therefore understood that He *was not His body – that His body was mortal, but that His essence, His spirit, was not.* He knew He was eternal and that in due course He would be released from His mortal body, and be free from pain.

I once read an amazing passage concerning the crucifixion in the book *A Course in Miracles*, which many believe is channeled material received directly from Jesus Himself. I thought it would be good food for thought for you.

I have made it perfectly clear that I am like you and you are like me, but our fundamental equality can be demonstrated only through joint decision. You are free to perceive yourself as persecuted if you choose. When you do choose to react that way, however, you might remember that *I was persecuted as the world judges, and did not share this evaluation for myself.*

Amazing, isn't it? Talk about being an amazing, enlightened, chicken salad person! He is saying that *we* have perceived Him as being persecuted, yet *He* does not view Himself in that way. He does not have *victim consciousness, despite the terrors He endured.* He trusted that everything was in Divine and perfect order. So, here is a big question for you: If Jesus, with ALL that He went through, chose *not* to view Himself as persecuted, could you, with what you have gone through in your life, possibly consider doing the same?

But gaining mastery over the ego is not as easy as it sounds, as many of you who have tried will know. The harder we try to quash the ego mind, the harder it fights back. It must be remembered that the ego mind is *viral* in its make-up – like a virus, it will do anything to survive and its biggest fear is that of being 'killed.' Spiritual seekers and teachers for eons have understood how detrimental the ego mind is to spiritual progression and enlightenment. Ancient cultures were aware of this and, in many traditions, plant medicine has been utilized to assist in the process of the subjugation of the ego mind. As you will have read in the Memories section, I have worked with the Jaguar Shaman of the Amazon who utilize the 'teacher plant' Ayahuasca – also known as the 'Vine of Death' – to help conquer the ego mind and to also gain valuable information about their journey or healing. The Ayahuasca vine has psychotropic qualities when ingested and induces hallucinogenic visions which can last for many hours. The vine is not used as a recreational drug for the sake of the visions themselves, as is commonly done with recreational drugs in today's society, but for the opportunity to detach and master the ego.

The dance with Mama Ayahuasca through the jungle was a spectacular experience for me. But the ceremony the night before, which was carried out on a beach at midnight, was a very different affair. As is so common with Ayahuasca journeys, I experienced complete annihilation of the self during the ceremony, which is the whole point of drinking the vine! I remember that initially I was almost completely consumed by a thousand serpents. Then they left, and the tiny bit that was left of me on the beach was gobbled up by an enormous serpent nearly the breadth of the Amazon River itself. I was pleased that I managed all this without fear or hesitation. To me, my experience the following night was like a reward for my total surrender the night before.

So, a common Ayahuasca vision for those that are overly

attached to their individuated selves, their ego selves, is that of the annihilation of the person's physical being. Often a huge jaguar or serpent will appear in the vision: the jaguar tears the person to pieces, consuming them bit by bit; if the serpent appears, it will swallow him or her whole. This, clearly, can be terrifying as it feels very real. Often you are not aware you are having a vision as you are fully involved in the process; you can also become paralyzed and unable to shout out for help.

Despite taking Ayahuasca for the very purposes of destroying the ego, when actually involved in an annihilation vision, many people try to fight their way out of the hallucination if they can. I remember talking to a friend who had such an experience. He told me glumly that he had valiantly fought off the attack of the jaguar and managed to 'escape' unharmed. However, he told me that after the effects of the plant medicine had worn off, he was very disappointed in himself for not having the courage to allow the dismemberment process to take place. The fact that he had felt the need to *fight off* the attack meant that he was still caught up in ego, in *identity with his form.*

So the purpose, then, of this undertaking is to have the courage and strength to surrender to the process, even if it feels like one is being completely destroyed, and from that place of no-thing, no identity, to find the essential core of one's being, one's true identity. To allow this quietens down the chatter of the ego mind as it has already experienced a death of sorts. Additionally the person is stronger as a result of the process, and more likely to ignore the safety drives of further ego-input. This then is also the 'death' of the old self and the willingness to lose one's control, to face our greatest fear – which is of destruction – in order to find the new, the essential, and to build up our new identity from that place. Shamanic healing is all about death and rebirth – the 'death' of the old self and the old way of being, and the birth of the new self and the new ways of being.

We are indeed highly complex beings – on one level. On

another level, we are very simple beings. Perhaps the greater part of this book has been taken up with the issues that we have with our ego selves, the part of us which *suffers*. But the greater part of us, the Higher Self, is the part of us that we have to be completely aligned with in order to reach enlightenment. When we do that, when we master the ego, then life becomes very easy and very simple – whatever is happening around us at the time. We go from a place of emotional involvement to a place of detached observation and trust; we remain centered in our hearts and in our connection to our God.

Probably one of the biggest shocks that I had in learning about enlightenment is that it is not something attained and maintained on an ongoing basis, like perhaps a university degree. I thought it *was* rather like attaining a degree, in that when I achieved it, that was it: job done; I had it. And I have to tell you that I felt massively aggrieved at this learning. Not only is enlightenment a process that can take a thousand lifetimes to achieve, but when you have finally attained it, *it can be lost*, rather like when the bar of soap flies out of our hands in the shower.

I remember reading a Buddhist story once which really brought home for me the huge undertaking the search for enlightenment is. I can't remember the story exactly, but it goes something like this.

A novice monk asked his Master how long it would take him to reach enlightenment. The Master replied, 'As long as it takes for a crow to erode a mountain by flying across its peak with a silken scarf in its beak. But... the crow only flies once every hundred years.'

Imagine that. All that time, and yet it does not stay with us, if we allow ourselves to be knocked out of balance and centeredness by life! This realization taught me new meaning and wisdom within the well-known saying: 'Before enlightenment, chop wood, carry water. After enlightenment, chop wood, carry water.' What I feel this saying means (and I am more than willing to accept that I may be wrong in this!) is that before we reach enlightenment, we live in the real world of jobs, chores, mortgages, cellulite and the like. After enlightenment – unless we have secluded ourselves in a cave in the mountains somewhere – then we remain living in that same world of daily challenges, stresses and strains; and therefore in the hustle and bustle of daily life we can lose our grip on that golden thread of enlightenment and get caught up once more in human life and its inevitable ego battles. The trick appears to be to hold on to enlightenment while living in the 'real' world – not on some mountaintop somewhere. Being a chicken salad person is essential; loving yourself as a living representation of the Divine is essential; loving others and the natural world as yourself is essential; loving, caring for and respecting your body is essential.

Love is *crucial* to one's journey to enlightenment. I see so many people seeking enlightenment who hate themselves, who flog themselves half to death on their spiritual paths, who become unbalanced and ungrounded, who ignore the needs of their body and soul in the race for spiritual evolution. I know this so well because I have done it myself! But I am older and wiser now and I have come to understand that *searching for or seeking* enlightenment (or searching for anything for that matter) is the one thing that will keep it away from us. Because in the act of *searching* is an *ego* act – the mere fact we are searching implies that we do not believe we already have within us Source energy, that precious aspect of the Divine.

To search *out there* for something that is already within us is futile. But people do not seem to like or understand this concept. Seemingly, they would rather do *anything* than go inside themselves and uncover their diamond heart! People will happily drive themselves crazy reading book after book, attending course after course, buying crystals and all manner of devices. They will listen to gurus and pretty much anyone *outside* of themselves and subject themselves to a whole manner of experiences, instead of simply going within. *Everything you need is within you, always.* There is more knowledge, wisdom and truth within you than within a thousand libraries, if you would just sit with yourself, and center yourself in your heart.

The heart is about *be-ing*; the head is focused on *do-ing*. It is the ego mind that spurs us on to search and seek. The heart knows we already have what we need.

I was interested to read a book recently about the great alchemists, such as Robert Fludd and other seekers of Light. A phrase commonly used within this book was '... he devoted his entire life to the spiritual search.' Pardon me? As one who only spent a *mere* 20 or so years on the spiritual search, I can most assuredly tell you that it is a *waste of time*. Yes, that is a little harsh, I agree, so I will tell you again. Just stop it and *be*. *Searching and seeking* is a waste of time.

What have I learned during those 20 years? Admittedly there have been a few pearls of wisdom gained along the way, but overall, it has been about *frustration and suffering*. A feeling that just as I kick the ball in a perfect arc, the goalposts move. I have endured all manner of things in my search for truth and enlightenment – only to discover that I was *born enlightened*! Imagine that – searching for most of your life for something you already had! If I am being brutally honest, I think I was *more* enlightened *before* I started my search. I was calmer, more at peace with myself and the world, and I experienced true moments of grace. It appears that for a while there, I actually went backwards! So this leads me to make this statement, which I assure you has been very hard won: *The biggest obstacle to one's spiritual development and enlightenment is the spiritual search itself.*

I know that this statement may shock you, but I am convinced that it is true. I am fairly convinced that spiritual progress only comes *after* we give up the search, throw away the books, tapes,

CDs and trinkets. In my own journey, for example, you may recall that it was only when I had absolutely given up on my search that I found my path. I booked a trip to Peru for a holiday. While I was there, I was gifted with the vision of the Inca and was told, very clearly, what it was I needed to do. After years and years of reading and searching, the information came when I was *not* searching, when I was just *be-ing*.

So here is something simple for you to remember if you would, which will hopefully make your journey easier:

If you are *do-ing*, then your ego is in control and you are moving *away* from enlightenment. If you are simply *be-ing*, hurrah, you are on your way!

When we can fully quieten our minds and just *be*, we can experience a moment of grace. But beware! These experiences are seductive and dangerous. Why? *Because experiences of grace can become addictive.* I once met a celebrity who told me he had experienced a moment of great grace one afternoon. He sat in a bliss-like state for a few hours and experienced true one-ness and union with all that is. He said it was the most wonderful experience of his life. However, instead of feeling truly blessed, he went on a massive search in the hope that he could have *another* experience. But these experiences are purely designed to wake us up; when they have done that, they have done their job – they *are not designed to last*. It is actually very difficult for our bodies to contain such huge amounts of energy for sustained periods and it is simply not possible to live in that state permanently.

Liken it to the Queen of England turning up on our doorstep and giving us an ice cube which we perceive to be a stunningly beautiful diamond. We are in awe of it, and of her, and the experience changes our life. But all too soon the Queen has gone back home to Buckingham Palace and the ice cube has melted in our hand. Instead of being grateful for our marvelous experience, we wail over the melting of the ice cube (which was, after all, only doing what ice cubes do); and at the same time the next morning we are pacing up and down our sitting rooms waiting for the Queen to arrive again. And the next morning we do the same thing, and the next, etc, etc, etc. Only she isn't going to visit us again; that was never the intention. And what is more, in our anger, frustration and bitterness (not to mention all the self-hatred) we completely forget the beauty of the ice cube, which was so much like a diamond. Therefore, we have completely missed the point.

Additionally we are at a time in the spiritual development of the world when these experiences are coming thick and fast, because we all need to wake up to what we are doing to the world and start to live differently. Spiritual development has sped up to an unbelievable rate. Please, I beg of you, if you do experience your own moment in Paradise, hold on to the beauty of it, keep the feeling of it in your heart, and try not to become addicted to it. You are *not meant* to reproduce that feeling or have another similar experience. Be grateful for what you have received and move forward in beauty, not in frustration and impatience.

In practice, you of course are going to have to find your own way. If 'be-ing' is going to make you impatient and frustrated, then your humanness will probably dictate that you end up searching for yourself and do-ing. But don't say I didn't try to warn you! Try to bear in mind all the time that the thing you are looking for 'out there' is already inside you. The search, the journey, is an inner one.

It is also *crucial* to remember that the physical body has to be kept in line vibrationally with the vibration of the soul or spirit which dwells within it. So many people disregard the needs of the physical and energetic bodies, incorrectly believing that enlightenment occurs from the head *up*wards. But this is not true. Enlightenment occurs as a process from the head *down*, through the physical body, through the Earth and then back Home to connect with Divine presence. This is very important indeed so please try to remember it.

Additionally, dis-ease *will* occur if the spirit and the physical form are not kept in alignment with each other. This can be done by doing all the things mentioned in the 'Energy Body and Physical Body' chapter. Namely, addressing your personal healing work, eating very healthily, getting out into nature regularly, exercising, meditating, and ensuring you remain grounded and centered. There is a Taoist quote which is particularly relevant here: 'Unless mind, body and spirit are equally developed and fully integrated, no wisdom can be sustained.'

I would also like to mention that I see many clients who are trying to rush the release of 'kundalini energies' via various yoga and meditation practices. Kundalini energy is the natural and very powerful energy which resides at the base of the spine and is often alleged to trigger enlightenment experiences when it is released up the spine to the crown chakra. I have a good few clients – and some friends – who will tell you that encouraging this to happen *before* the body and energy body is ready for it will cause you a lot of psychological damage indeed. Imagine dynamite going off at the base of your spine, causing a huge explosion which ripples up a central tube inside your spine. If this experience occurs naturally after years of spiritual practice and healing work, then the energy channel along the spine will be clear enough for the force of the explosion to leave the body via the crown chakra out into the world, and you will have a wonderful experience. However, if you trigger such an experience before you are ready, then the central tube along your spine will not be clear. (Perhaps one or more of your chakras will be blocked by heavy energy.) The force of the explosion will then rocket up your spine and, unable to escape, will explode within you. If the energy block is in your crown or third-eye chakra then you can literally blow your own mind apart. This is not good, on many levels, so please think carefully and remember that everything will happen when it is meant to.

So please, do not try to rush your spiritual development. Do please bear in mind that the enlightened state is normally the end game for a human being. Once enlightenment is attained the human journey is over... and there is no longer any need for the physical body! GAME OVER! This is why it is the journey that is important. Stay balanced; as my shaman friends say, 'Learn to live with a foot in each world.' You are already that which you seek. My blessings go to you on your journey.

I would like to close this chapter with a beautiful verse written by Marianne Williamson, which sums up the spiritual journey marvelously. May I suggest that you copy it out and keep it in your journal, or on your fridge so that you remember who you truly are at all times, and that it is your duty to let your light shine brightly.

Our deepest fear is not that we are inadequate. Our deepest fear is that we are powerful beyond measure. It is our light, not our darkness, that most frightens us. We ask ourselves, 'Who am I to be brilliant, gorgeous, talented, fabulous?' Actually, who are you not to be? You are a child of God. Your playing small doesn't serve the world. There's nothing enlightened about shrinking so that other people won't feel insecure around you. We are all meant to shine as children do. We were born to make manifest the glory of God that is within us. It's not just in some of us; it is in everyone. And as we let our own light shine, we subconsciously give other people permission to do the same. As we are liberated from our own fear, our presence automatically liberates others.

12. 2012 – The Gateway to a Golden Age

Memories 12.1

It is the summer of the year 2000 and I am at a friend's house as part of a regular weekly spiritual discussion group. My ears prick up as my friend's husband starts to talk about the importance of the year 2012 – more particularly *21 December 2012*. I am puzzled as to why this date – over twelve years in the future – is relevant; after all, we have only recently got over the 'Y2K' fiasco!

He tells us that this date has been prophesied to be the day the world ends, as it coincides with the end of the Mayan Long Count Calendar, and has also been foretold by other cultures. He speaks of natural disasters happening, of odd planetary alignments occurring, and about the collapse of the world's financial and economic systems. He tells us 'something' will come which will destroy mankind, or the majority of mankind. And he mentions the estimated demise *of between 75 and 95% of the global population*.

I argue that this is completely ridiculous – what could possibly happen that could destroy so many people? A global war? A nuclear bomb? And looking at it logically, how could the 5–25% of the remaining population survive with so many dead bodies around them? The problems with bacteria and water pollution would surely kill off the remainder of people. I also assure him that I work for one of the world's largest banks, and that such a global financial collapse is *unthinkable*. I tell him that financial markets have always risen and fallen over periods of time, which is their nature, so total financial collapse is extremely unlikely – and anyway, banks look after each other, don't they?

My friend's husband confirms that he is not sure what will happen, that he does not know how it will all unfold; he has just heard that *something* will happen.

Another friend asks him, 'Assuming what you're saying is true, where can I go in order to ensure that I'm safe?'

He suggests that perhaps the Southern Hemisphere will be OK – New Zealand, South Africa (South Africa *safe*?).

I ask, 'What can we do? Can the process be stopped? How do we prepare?' and he tells us he just does not know; he is just repeating what he has been told.

Everyone in the room appears to be deep in thought and more than a little shell-shocked by his revelations, and the evening comes to a close fairly swiftly. I leave the house feeling very unsettled and in need of many more answers. Although logically speaking I find it very hard to believe in what he has said, something feels like it has been activated within me, a kind of deep knowing, and I feel extremely disconcerted. I look around me as I walk home as if for signs or evidence, but everything seems to be normal, exactly the same as it always has been.

* * *

I am attending a talk in the Sacred Valley of Urubamba, Peru, learning about the Q'ero Indians and their prophecies. I am surprised to hear it predicted that in the run-up to 21 December 2012 there will be a *Pachakuti* – literally a 'turning upside down of time.' The Pachakuti will herald a time when one world ends and another new, transformed world begins. It will be a time of total chaos, but necessary chaos, which will lead us into a Golden Age of a *thousand years* of peace. We are told that we are currently experiencing the Pachakuti, that it has already started, and that it is building up momentum. The translator tells us of the expected 'Inca Child of Light,' who sounds very similar to the Christ child. It is also foretold that holes, or portals, will appear in the fabric of time itself, and that it will be possible for some of us to step through these portals into a new dimension, a new world, which holds a higher frequency of light than ours.

In between now and then, we are told, it is essential for us to work on our own personal healing requirements in order that we may raise our frequency sufficiently. This will have the effect of bringing ourselves into alignment with the higher vibrations of the New World so that we may survive within it. Those who pass through the portals will become the Light of the New World and help create Heaven on Earth for future generations.

* * *

Dream, Spring 2007

I am standing in the middle of the road outside my house. No one else is around, not a soul, for miles and miles around. Everything is very still and silent. I look at all my neighbors' houses. They are all empty, and will remain empty. *No one is ever coming back.*

I realize that I am hungry, and wonder how I am going to get food. I know that in the kitchen cupboards of the houses around me, there will be a lot of food. But it seems disrespectful somehow to break into houses and take food, even though I know that all those homeowners are beyond caring now. However distasteful I find it, I recognize I will have to do a fair amount of breaking and entering in order to obtain food and survive. I console myself with the fact that I will do it as respect-fully as possible.

I feel terribly alone and scared. I hope with all my heart that there will be some other people out there, and that somewhere and somehow they will find me. In the meantime, I have my entire hometown to myself.

* * *

Actual Event

It is the summer of 2007 and I am visiting a friend at her home in
Surrey. My friend is an amazing lady who has spent the last few
years making a film about the need to raise global consciousness,
2012, and the coming of the New World.

We spend most of the day eating lovely food and discussing
the topic of 2012, all the various prophecies attached to it, and
what we believe may happen. I tell her that if indeed there is
going to be a massive loss of life, as some predict, then the only
way that the surviving population will be able to live will be as
the Q'ero predicted – by stepping through portals in time into a
new and higher vibrational dimension. Therefore, it is even more
important to raise our vibration by doing our healing work, so
that we have a chance to survive in that new frequency – if
indeed we are able to step through those portals in time. Of
course this is assuming we survive whatever it is that happens in
the first place!

As we discuss all the theories, I start to notice that the energy
around us in the room appears to be supercharged – crackling
almost – and she notices it too. The hours roll by quickly as we
talk animatedly, and all too soon it is time for us to leave for the
train station.

The journey goes smoothly and I arrive at the station at
4.55pm, in plenty of time for my train which is due to arrive at
5.15pm. As I have time to kill, I visit a little shop on the platform
and buy a refreshing orange juice drink. I then go back out to the
platform and stand in a sunny area and sip the cold refreshing
liquid, enjoying the golden sunlight warming my face.

I then look down at my feet for some reason and notice I am
standing on the yellow 'safety' line which runs the length of the
platform and is very close to the platform edge, so I take one step
back away from it. Hanging from the platform ceiling to my left
is a digital automated sign which details the train departure
times and the various destinations. I am reassured to see that it

reads, '1st Train, Bedford, 5.15pm. On time.' The digital clock at the base of the sign reads 5.01pm so I don't have long to wait at all.

A little bored – and impatient as always – I take a good look around me. About a dozen people have come up onto the platform, including to my left a very attractive man who has his handsome head bent over a newspaper. As I am a person who enjoys beauty, I can't help but look at him. Suddenly, he glances up and catches me looking at him. Embarrassed, I quickly avert my gaze and pretend to look at the clock which now reads 5.04pm. Not long now.

The evening is warm, the sun golden. Many more people join me on the platform and wait peacefully. I sip my drink. I sip my drink again. I see a lion coming towards me. I think it is odd, so I blink a few times and then realize it is a lion on a young man's T-shirt. *Where on earth is my train?* I wonder.

I turn to check the departures sign again and am surprised to see it read: '1st Train, Bedford, 5.50pm.' I tut, and think that the station's computer system must be playing up! The 5.50pm train is not the *first* train; it must the third or fourth train, as *mine* has not even arrived yet!

I look around me casually, hoping to catch a glimpse of the handsome man. I notice that he is not where he was. I have a quick look around me to see if I can see him, but he is nowhere to be seen. Suddenly I realize that *no one* is around me, just the young man in the lion T-shirt, who is leaning against the wall while texting on his phone. I feel very confused! Where is everyone? I look to see if the sign has changed again but it still says: '1st Train, Bedford, 5.50pm.' The time now is 5.22pm. But my train has not been yet! I wonder if the train has been redirected to another platform – perhaps everyone has moved to the new platform and I didn't hear the announcement? But my investigations show that it has not been moved.

And then the realization hits me in the face. I realize that no one is around because *the train has arrived – so close to me I could touch it – lots of people have gotten off, lots more have boarded, and then it has gone, right from under my nose!* Where was *I*? Where had I gone? I knew physically I had remained standing on the platform, I had not disappeared, but 'I' most definitely had *not been here* when the train came. The train that would have been just inches from me!

I feel shaky at the realization and go and sit down on a bench. What has happened to me? As I start to settle down, gradually I start to recall my conversation with my friend, particularly the part about the prophecies which tell of portals in time opening up. Cold realization hits me then and I see that I have been given a message from spirit and a confirmation of my theory. I have just stepped outside of time myself, stepped into another dimension – yet I have absolutely no memory of where I went or what I did when I was there. In fact I didn't even realize I had gone – until I came back; and if it were not for the fact that I was watching the time and a train had come and gone while I was 'away,' I would not have been aware that I had disappeared at all! Where had I been? The enormity of it hits me and my knees start to tremble.

Gradually, more people arrive on the platform and stand around me in the low evening sun. Eventually, the 5.50pm train arrives – enormous, noisy and bright yellow. I board and thankfully sink into a vacant seat. I can hardly believe what has just happened – but I know absolutely that it did happen.

A tall man sits down next to me and rummages around in his briefcase. He pulls out a broadsheet newspaper and shakes it open inches from my face. Right there in front of me on the back page of the newspaper is a large photograph of a lion. I smile. It is true what they say – spirit certainly does move in strange ways!

Practice Notes 12.2

I ask Rainer to tell me about the recurring dream she has had since she was a child, in the hope that it may hold a clue about her relationship problems. She tells me that in her dream she sees London under several meters of water. She is swimming in it, trying to get to Hampstead Heath, which pokes out of the water like a small island.

I try not to react too much to this, and aim to keep my expression neutral. I mention something about water often being a representation of the subconscious and/or the emotions in dreams, so this dream could be showing her that she is struggling to stay afloat with all her emotions. We start to talk about other topics. As she is talking I take a deep breath. Although this is the first time Rainer has mentioned her dream to me, this is not the first time I have heard of it. Other clients have reported having the same recurring dream too.

* * *

Pamela talks rapidly, hardly taking a breath. She tells me she is virtually crippled by anxiety, which has been far worse over the last few years. She speaks of fears that seem to come from nowhere, which have no foundation, but leave her clinging onto her husband in terror. She feels the threat of impending doom all the time, but nothing ever seems to happen.

I ask her to tell me about her home life, and she tells me that apart from a slight financial concern there is no real problem at home. She is very happily married, is fit and healthy, and she has a wonderful relationship with her children. She is very sharp-witted and intelligent and I know she is not suffering from a mental or chemical imbalance, because over the years she has been checked for pretty much everything. She tells me she feels a desperate urge to move house, to get out of the city and go somewhere more rural, with wide-open spaces. She describes feeling a sense of oppression, like the sky is about to fall in on her.

* * *

I return Wayne's phone call after hearing his message on my voicemail. He is a lovely, down to earth, no-nonsense, gruff yet gentle man who works as a sheet metal worker in a factory. He asks me to wait while he goes somewhere more private. He thanks me for calling him back and tells me he has been well and happy since his session with me and that everything has been going well for him over the last year or so.

He then says, 'I don't really know how to say this, so I'll just come straight out with it and hopefully you won't think I'm crazy. The other night I was relaxing on the sofa after a hard day at work, and then suddenly, some sort of *being* turned up, right in the middle of my living room! I don't know if it was an alien or an angel; it seemed more like an alien, I guess, but it wasn't scary at all.

'But the strangest thing is this: firstly I wasn't frightened, just more surprised – totally shocked. Secondly – and bizarrely – it asked me to buy a ton of *camping* equipment. Camping? I never go camping! Why would I need camping equipment? I was so stunned, really. So, I thought I would give you a ring – I just wondered if you had come across this sort of thing before, as I know you see a lot of people.

'It's strange though; even though I'm not a camping man myself, I have such a strong feeling I must do this. I know this sounds completely mad but I just wanted to ask you. Have you ever come across anything like this before with your other clients?'

I sigh and take a deep breath. 'Yes, Wayne, I have.'

* * *

Lulu plonks herself down on the sofa, and tells me she has been struggling with all the heavy energies that seem to be around at the moment. 'Why doesn't everyone else seem worried that the sky might be about to fall in?' she asks me, laughing in spite of herself. I smile and tell her that I feel it too.

She then tells me she has recently been feeling very drawn to learning about plants, particularly medicinal plants and herbs. She has sensed that she has a guide around her, an older man. This man tells her the names of the plants as she passes them in the hedgerows while walking her dogs. She tells me she then feels impulses to go home and learn about the healing properties and medicinal uses of the plants she has just seen, from a book that she felt she must buy some weeks ago. Already she has started to stock her own garden with healing herbs and plants. Although she is a busy working mother with limited spare time, she feels that doing this is highly important for some reason.

She looks me in the eye and says, 'I feel something big is about to happen, Dawn, something huge, and we won't be able to get drugs anymore; we will have to go back to the old ways, and heal ourselves with the things that God has provided for us in the hedgerows. I know I'm being guided to do this, and that I need to learn quickly. It's very important.'

Notes 12.3

I would be quite surprised if you have not heard at least something about the 2012 'topic,' given that there are now even Hollywood films out on the subject – but I will go over the basics here just in case. As you know, I learned about the importance of the year 2012 some years ago now, so it is very easy for me to assume incorrectly that everyone has heard about it. Occasionally clients come to see me and tell me that they are suffering from 'the effects of 2012 and the Ascension Process;' similarly, it is clear that other clients have not heard of it at all.

Before we delve into this topic further I would like to make a couple of points here. Firstly, I would ask you to ensure that you continue reading to the very end of this chapter in order that you may receive a balanced view of the topic. Secondly, as you know, I am all about truth – in fact truth is the very code of my soul. Sometimes, it is hard to *find* the truth, to *really* know what is going on, no matter how hard you try. But I am going to try to give you as much information as I have *today* about the changes which *may* be upon us in our tomorrows, so you have an understanding of the times we are living in. I want you to know and understand the importance of this subject because I feel that we need to act, all of us, all together, as *together* we have such great potential to bring about much-needed change.

And that brings me to my next and probably most confusing point, which is that I want you to bear in mind that, in my view, **no one**, *actually, can write about 2012 with any real authority*. Clearly, 21 December 2012 is in the future – so how can anyone know for sure what will happen, when our future and destiny are being created *by our actions* in every second? Who we are today is not necessarily who we are going to be tomorrow; things change, and action *today* changes outcomes *tomorrow*.

You may well ask: Why are you writing about this topic if you don't know what's going to happen? Because, as I have mentioned before, knowledge is power. My hope is that we all wake up, attend to our personal healing needs, and find love within ourselves for ourselves. Only when we have found love for ourselves can we then radiate that love out to each and everyone – and everything. If we do that, then maybe the Earth will not need to give us a great big slap around the face in order to make us take notice of what we are doing to each other and to the Earth herself. We have already received a couple of warning shots; it is about time we started sitting up and taking notice.

Perhaps the easiest thing to do here is to ask you to break away from this book and take some time out to do your own research on 2012. Why don't you type '2012' into Google or YouTube and then come back to this chapter? I will give you one hour…

* * *

Welcome back! How did that go? I bet you had an interesting – and quite disturbing – search.

In short, my guess is that you will have read about 2012, in particular 21 December 2012, which is the 'end date' or the 'completion date' of the Mayan Long Count Calendar. The Maya were brilliant mathematicians and astrologers and it is said their Long Count Calendar commenced on 11 August 3114 **BCE**. Many books and websites make the Mayan calendar the focus of the 2012 theories. They will tell you that the 'end date' is a time when the Mayan civilization believed the world – *our world* – would end. And because of the highly advanced status of the Mayan culture, the 'end of the world' scenario is being given much more gravity than the Y2K theory.

Mayan mythology indicates that the Maya – a Mesoamerican civilization – originally came from the stars. Many say that their calendar is perhaps the most advanced in the world – not just because of its accuracy over great expanses of time, but because it is in fact a *galactic clock* which shows cosmic cycles and planetary alignments. It is so accurate it even details 'sun spot' activity. Sun spots are areas of great magnetic activity on the Sun, which have the effect of reducing its surface temperature. This creates black spots on the Sun's surface which are visible from Earth. It is said that Galileo gave the first correct explanation of sun spots in 1612. Science has been keeping an eye on sun spot activity ever since, so it is quite amazing that the Maya knew about them all that time ago. In fact, the Calendar is so efficient that lunar and solar eclipses have been accurately predicted, *thousands of years* into the future.

Legend has it that the entire Mayan civilization simply disappeared; they just vanished into thin air sometime in the 9th century. Many would say they 'returned to the stars' but the Mayan culture does still exist today.

As you will have read, theories and predictions (and it is to be remembered there can only be predictions as no one knows for sure what will happen) vary as to the severity of the changes expected to occur in late 2012. At the most frightening end of the scale, some people are predicting that a huge percentage of people – varying between **75% and the entire global population** – will be wiped out in some way or other. Let's have a look at some of those common theories or threats:

- Nuclear attack
- Global war
- Asteroid collision (predicted by Nostradamus)
- Shifting of the tectonic plates (the huge plates of the Earth's crust)
- Increase in the intensity of solar flares
- Earthquakes and tsunamis
- Magnetic reversal of the North and South poles (sounds crazy, I know, but according to science this has already happened many times – according to NASA the last time was apparently 780,000 years ago: see http://science.nasa.gov/headlines/Y2003/29dec_magneticfield.htm)
- A shift in the tilting of the axis of the Earth (the Earth is currently tilted on its axis at 23.5 degrees; some say it will straighten up, i.e. there will no longer be a tilt. This is taken to represent the shifting from the current masculine bias to a more balanced view and the return of the feminine/Goddess energy)
- A rapid melting of the polar icecaps, due to global warming, or an increase in planetary temperature due to increased solar activity
- An increase in sea levels, due to axial or magnetic shifts, or to the melting of the polar icecaps
- Alignment of the planet with the 'dark rift' of the Milky Way

- Entire continents sinking into the sea
- New continents rising from the sea
- Crustal slip/displacement
- A new planet (Planet X / Nibiru) emerging and affecting the Earth's magnetic field
- A shortage of drinkable water
- Famine
- Severe viral outbreaks / plagues
- Bio-warfare
- Dramatic increases in the vibration of the planet, causing sickness and death to those not in vibrational alignment with the Earth
- Alien attack/invasion
- Political/Governmental/Economic upheavals and crises
- Species extinction which has a knock-on effect on mankind

...or a combination of all of the above! *Depressing, isn't it?*

A common phrase I have heard over and over again during the last decade or so is that everything is expected to occur in the 'blink of an eye.' It is interesting to read that woolly mammoths have been found frozen in Siberia, mid step, with their mouths still full of food, suggesting that whatever event brought them to extinction (an asteroid collision?) also must have happened in the blink of an eye.

Outside of the Mayan culture, many other advanced cultures, such as the Hopi Indians and the Inca, all detail an end-point. The Hopi say that they have already lived through and survived four 'great cycles' and that we are on the verge of a transition to the '5th World.' Hopi prophecies state that the seas would rise, the Earth would shake and the Sun would grow hotter, and a 'Great Purification' would take place by the year 2011. The end of this cycle will be marked by the arrival of a new (blue) star. Also they foretell that at this time a figure named Pahana – their 'Lost White Brother,' who again sounds rather like a Christ figure –

will return to Earth and usher in an age of peace.

Given that I am a *Paqo* of the Andean lineage, I must also comment on the prophecies of the Inca. Two points should be noted: 1) knowledge of the prophecies has been lost to the current generation of paqos in the Q'ero nation, and 2) the year 2012 *has not been mentioned specifically.*

The best information on the Incan/Andean viewpoint can be found in the wonderful book *Masters of the Living Energy* by Joan Parisi Wilcox. The Inca believed that in 1990 we would enter the *Taripay Pacha* – the age of 'meeting ourselves again' – which is *said* to last until 2012. Joan writes that during this time period, '... humans have the potential to accelerate our accumulation of energetic power and foster our spiritual evolution.' Before we can fully meet ourselves again, we will pass through a *pachakuti*. If you recall from the Memories section, a pachakuti is a time of great upheaval, chaos or re-ordering which takes place whenever society undergoes a momentous change. The last pachakuti is said to have started when the white man (the Spanish Conquistadors) invaded Peru. This heralded 500 years of materialism, imbalance and spiritual darkness. It is indeed this darkness which will be turned 'right side up.'

As with the other prophecies, it appears that ultimately, *our fate lies in* our *hands.* Joan writes, 'Our choices at a collective level powerfully influence which likely future we will manifest as the "end time" draws near. Human consciousness will have an opportunity to evolve; we will be able to move closer to becoming true light beings.'

Similar to the Hopi prediction of the return of Pahana, it is interesting to note that the Inca also prophesy the return of the Inca Child of Light, a figure similar to Jesus Christ. But this – as with the Hopi/Pahana prophecy – may not refer to *one* Christ-like figure that comes to save us all, *but to the attainment of the Christ-like qualities, the qualities of the highest Light, within us all* – leading to the emergence of a new type of human known as *Homo luminous.*

You may recall in Chapter 1 I commented that 'special' children, who are very sensitive and gifted, are increasing in numbers. Interestingly, I find I am seeing more and more children in my healing practice and they all are exceptionally bright, hugely sensitive and gentle, and generally find fitting into the 'norm' very difficult. My view is (as you will no doubt guess) that these children are sourced from a higher dimension. Perhaps it is these new souls who will guide us all into the New World?

During your internet search on the subject of 2012, you may well have come across a few more well-known prophets:

- The best-known text is in the New Testament of the Bible – John: The Book of Revelation – which speaks of the End of the World, a battle of good versus evil, and a disease that kills a quarter of the Earth's population.
- The Celtic shaman, 'the Merlin' or *Myrddin*, who incidentally is said to have accurately predicted the Nazi Holocaust – spoke of disaster in Britain around this time. He made mention of 'a river burning and turning to blood, London mourning the death of 20,000, and seas rising in the "twinkle of an eye."'
- The Sioux Indian Black Elk was gifted with dreams and visions from a young age and was shown World War I and II, and also World War III, which brought 'dispute all over the Universe.' He also predicted, however, that it would be our current generation which would go on to begin an 'Era of Peace.'
- The dreams of the Ojibwa shaman Sun Bear foretold epidemics, riots, crop diseases, rivers changing course, some areas of the Earth too hot, some too cold, some too wet, some too dry, cities breaking down, and electrical systems failing.

- The Sibylline prophecies of the 6th century BCE foretold that the world would last for 9 periods of 800 years, the 10th generation would begin in the year 2000, and this would be the last. The Sibyl (the oracle) detailed war and fires, followed by a Golden Age.
- Numerical 'Timewave Zero' calculations have been carried out on China's oldest text, the *I Ching*, which is said to have a timeline within it that ceases in... 2012.
- The Yorkshire Oracle of the 1500s, Ursula Southeil, who was more commonly known as 'Mother Shipton,' was said to have accurately predicted the death of Henry VIII, the defeat of the Spanish Armada, the Great Plague, and the ascension of Queen Victoria by name. She wrote her prophecies in poem form (which are available online) and similarly speaks of fires, earthquakes, volcanoes, and floods.

If you are more interested in astronomy than prediction, you may have read articles which state the following:

- At 11.11am on 21 December 2012, the Earth will pass directly into the *Photon Belt*, a massive band of electromagnetic radiation that the Earth is said to pass through once every 11,000 years or so, and it will reside there for one year. Some sites say that as a result of this, *all* life forms will experience greater levels of consciousness and undergo a 'spiritual awakening.' This is because the brain (of which we are said to utilize only 5%), particularly the pineal gland, which is part of the endocrine system, is sensitive to changes in geomagnetic energy. René Descartes (1596–1650), the French philosopher, mathematician, writer and scientist, called the pineal gland 'the seat of the soul,' and indeed it *is* credited with connecting us to both spiritual and worldly planes. So this theory neatly fits into the 'bringing Heaven to Earth' story and also to the Christ-consciousness theory. It is said that a sojourn into the Photon Belt will affect our entire nervous system, which will be recalibrated or rewired. This will lead to increases in abilities and phenomena such as telepathy, foresight, remote viewing, clairvoyance, clairaudience, and clairsen-tience, communication with spirit and other conscious-nesses, and psychic abilities.

- Astronomical calculations for this date indicate a happening which occurs only once every 26,000 years: the alignment of the Sun and the Earth with the very center of our galaxy – the dark rift of the Milky Way (known as the 'mouth of the crocodile' or the 'Great Mother' in Mayan culture).

If you are more of a spiritual person then you may have found the less scary end of the scale and read on New-Age websites talk of:

- 2012 being a time when there will simply be a massive shift in consciousness (without any outside influence, event, or loss of life) which will completely change the way we live our lives, run our businesses, operate govern-ments, families, homes, and how we interact with society, animals and the planet generally.
- Theories that the Earth herself is in a process of evolution and a raising of her vibration, and in order for us and our bodies to manage this shift in frequency we have to raise our consciousness and our vibration too, so that we stay in vibrational alignment with the planet. (Science tells us that two things of different vibration cannot exist in the same place; hence we would need to come into vibrational alignment with the Earth.)
- A return to an age of the Goddess / Gaia (spirit of the

Earth) / the feminine principle – living with respect for each other and the planet. (Shamanism operates on feminine principles.)

- Predictions which say humanity is due for a mass 'kundalini' experience. While personal kundalini experiences are expected to increase, there are others who believe that the Earth herself possesses kundalini energy, which starts at the core of the Earth and rises to the surface of the Earth in a particular location. It is said that every 12,920 years the position of the emergence of the kundalini energy moves, and that the Earth is currently undergoing this process of moving the energy from Tibet to the Andean Mountains. This is particularly interesting for me as my tradition is a mountain tradition based in the Andes!

- Hindu cosmology – which shows that we are currently in the 'fourth age,' the Age of Kali, 'Queen of Demons.' Scriptures say that an aspect of the God Vishnu will incarnate as a savior named Kalki the Avenger, who will destroy the present world, restore peace, and bring in a new age, or *yuga*.

- The 'Ascension Process' – which theorizes that some of us are going through a process in order to shift dimensionally from the 3rd dimension, where we currently reside, to the lighter and brighter 5th dimension. (The 4th dimension seems to be skipped for some reason.)

I have been receiving regular email updates on the effects of the 'Ascension Process,' and these *have* actually been spot-on as far as my symptoms have been concerned over the last few years. They have also accurately described symptoms experienced by many of my clients. Maybe you have experienced some of them without even realizing it? Here is a list of the most common symptoms:

- Rapid heartbeat / Heart 'palpitations' and breathing problems
- Odd ringing or buzzing sounds in ears
- Sudden weight loss or weight gain and food cravings / desire for protein
- Inability to sleep / sleep pattern changes / disturbed sleep / less requirement for sleep
- Increase in frequency and strength of headaches or migraines
- Huge fear seemingly arising from nowhere (I found this to be the worst symptom)
- Feelings of foreboding or anxiety immediately upon waking
- Uncontrollable weeping
- Rashes on skin
- Either significant decrease or increase in vitality
- A *slowing down* of the aging process
- Bizarre memory loss (e.g. forgetting what the kettle is called but knowing what it does)
- Increase in lucid, very real or crazy dreams, or nightmares
- Electrical equipment and cars going wrong constantly
- Sudden inability to deal with your romantic partner – it all feels very wrong for some reason

I do believe that we are *currently* experiencing some kind of change, whether that may be physical, emotional, mental, spiritual or energetic, which could be caused by planetary movements, or shifts in the Earth's vibration, geomagnetics, or a whole host of other things. While the list above may seem fairly exhaustive (and exhausting!), rather than simply having one symptom it is more common for sufferers to experience *all* the symptoms at the same time. I went through a horrible two-year period and I definitely experienced all those symptoms; it was a truly horrendous time for me – and it was also very expensive as I had to fix or replace so many electrical things, and my car had to be practically rebuilt!

The greatest threats to us seem to be solar/planetary/asteroid based, so I investigated NASA's website to see if they had a view on these threats. I came across a section of their website called 'Ask an Astrobiologist,' where members of the public can ask questions and have them answered by a very clever man, in this case, Mr David Morrison, Senior Scientist at NASA Astrobiology Institute (NAI). I have detailed the essence of some of Mr Morrison's answers (shown in italics below) to the most 'Frequently Asked Questions' (FAQs) section of the website – most of which (over a thousand) are concerned with events in 2012. Concerning...

- A planetary line-up? – *This is an internet hoax.*
- Aliens and UFOs? – *Do not exist.*
- A threat of the effects of a planet called Nibiru or Planet X? – *Only a dwarf planet called Eris has been found; however, this poses absolutely no threat to us.*
- The alignment of the Sun, Earth and the center of the Galaxy in 2012? – *This already happens each December – every year – in the constellation of Sagittarius, with no negative consequences.*
- A geomagnetic pole shift? – *If it did happen, it would take around 5,000 years to complete and there is no reason to expect any catastrophic effects of this occurring.*
- The 2012 myths? – *A big hoax, fuelled by Hollywood and mad people on the internet.*
- Increases in solar flares or mass coronal ejections? – *Represent no danger to humans, or to Earth, only to astronauts and satellites.*
- Asteroid collision? – *The last big hit was 65 million years ago which led to the extinction of the dinosaurs; while small hits happen from time to time, no large threat is expected.*
- An axis shift? – *Impossible, has never happened before.*

- Being swallowed by the dark rift of the Milky Way? – *As crazy as the Photon Belt theory.*

So then, it seems that NASA is telling us there is nothing to worry about. I also had a good look on Wikipedia out of interest and found the following gems:

- The Timewave Zero theory / *I Ching*? – Has no scientific credibility. The original numerological end-date was calculated to be November 2012 but according to Wikipedia, the date was moved by the theorist to December 2012 in order to tag on to the Mayan theory.
- The Mayan prophecies? – Academic research does not indicate that the Maya attached any apocalyptic significance to 2012. (This is also confirmed by Carlos Barrios, a historian, anthropologist and Mayan *Ajq'ij* [ceremonial priest and spiritual guide], who says that the world will not end on this date, but that it will be transformed.)
- The Hopi prophecies? – Do not actually mention the year 2012.
- The Bible? – Does not mention the year 2012; it just says those things will happen 'very soon.'
- The Sibylline prophecies? – Similarly 2012 is not mentioned.
- Nostradamus's predictions? – These are actually 'valid' until the year 3797.
- Merlin's predictions? – Apparently Merlin is a fictional character made up by Geoffrey of Monmouth.
- Mother Shipton's prophecies? – Wikipedia states that: 'It is now generally acknowledged that Mother Shipton was largely a myth, and that many of her prophecies were composed by others after her death, and *after the events they "predicted."* The most noted work, by Richard Head, came out in 1684. Head later admitted to inventing almost all Shipton's biographical details.'

So – Who Do We Believe?

It's hard to tell, isn't it, but as you can see from the above, NASA does a good job of stomping all over the 2012 catastrophe theories. I am sure that they *would* indeed tell us the truth if they knew we were on the verge of destruction. Although, as some wise person pointed out to me, if NASA did know something catastrophic was going to happen on a massive scale, wouldn't confirming this cause mass hysteria? So again it comes down to: Who *do* we believe?

If I look purely at my own experiences, I have had the lucid dream about there being no electricity and no people, and a horrible two-year period when I did in fact suffer all the major 'ascension' symptoms – although as you know I am a very sensitive bunny. Then there are all the funny experiences and dreams my clients have had to take into account. Plus, we can often read about people having all sorts of out-of-body, near death, or psychotropic drug-induced visions about 2012 and the changes it may bring. Either way, as you can see, not only is this a fairly impossible subject to write about; it is also difficult to know where to stand on the topic and what we believe may happen – or not happen.

My sense, however, is that *something* is happening right *now*, and soon, either during or after 2012, a 'far reaching' event or series of events will occur, which will have the effect of shaking us all up, one way or another. Let's face it, we need it. Please though, do not go into fear. Fear is a complete waste of energy, and only attracts more negativity to us. I think that one of the biggest threats we face regarding the year 2012 is the fact that so many people now are *expecting* a great disaster to happen, or indeed they are even *hoping* for an Armageddon scenario. And this is not because they are negatively focused, but because so many traditions state that *after* the disaster or the Battle of Armageddon, Jesus, or a similar Christ-like figure, will walk the Earth again. The scary aspect of this is that science shows us that the consciousness of just 1% of the population can affect the masses and bring about great change, so as this topic receives greater publicity, we are at greater risk – just from the *thought forms* of the population! Remember, thoughts create reality – if enough people believe something will happen then they could create some kind of disaster, *even if nothing was actually meant or intended to occur!* This would not be good!

My view is that the world will *not* end on 21 December 2012, and on 25 December 2012 I shall be tucking into my Christmas dinner as usual. Actually, I don't believe that the world will ever end – well... it may do when the Sun dies, but that isn't for another five billion years so we have plenty of time. There *is*, however, far more chance of us blowing ourselves up than the Earth dying. Do I think that we are going to face huge environmental challenges? Yes, actually, I do, because of global warming, and the damage we have already caused to the Earth. Is the Earth evolving? Why yes, as does everything. Everything evolves and everything changes; that is the only certainty in life. The life-and-death process itself is the foundation of shamanism; in fact it is the foundation of pretty much everything!

My view is that if something cataclysmic *does* happen, it will be as a result of our own hand, rather than us being sucked into a black hole or similar. However, I *do* believe that changes in consciousness are happening *now*, and will continue for some time, and that we are in the midst of a transition period, from the old world to the new. Yes, I think the coming few years will mark the end of the world *as we know it, for it, and we, will be transformed, reborn, as long as we let go and allow the necessary changes to happen.* Because really, things have been wrong for far too long. We need to change, and deep down we know we cannot carry on the way we have been doing.

I believe that in the coming months and years, our thoughts, actions, intent and our visions for the future will be instrumental in creating our actual realities. This is because, as I have stated before, the inner creates the outer, our thoughts create our reality – 'As above, so below, as *within*, so *without*.' This is why it is so important not to go into fear over '2012' and instead to focus on the very positive outcomes that could potentially await us. The word 'potentially' is very important here. The potential outcome depends *on us*. What will we choose? We may indeed be faced with some challenges – we already *are* facing some challenges – but it is to be remembered that:

EVERYTHING IS **ALWAYS** IN DIVINE AND PERFECT ORDER

Are things going to get worse before they get better? I would guess so. We are in kind of a big mess. Having said that, my sense is that if a disaster-type scenario does occur, or if aliens do indeed land on our planet, then this will occur in order to force us *to pull together*, to unite, to work together as one, to live with respect for each other, regardless of sexual preferences, color or religious belief, to unify and raise our consciousness. Perhaps, if we could find a way to do this *anyway*, then we could sidestep a big slap from Mother Earth. To be honest, shouldn't we be moving towards this *regardless* of any threat of impending doom? We do not own the Earth. We are allowed to live upon it, and we should be doing that with respect and gratitude. To think otherwise is a bit like asking the fleas on a dog's back, 'Who owns this dog?' and hearing the fleas squeak, 'We do.'

Think about it. This planet is more magnificent, more intelligent than we can even imagine. It has been around for about five billion years; we have been on it for, what, half a million years? Some say that Earth is deemed to be the jewel of the entire Universe and that it is much coveted by other star nations because of its tremendous beauty. Shouldn't we therefore treat it with a bit more gratitude and respect, as societies did in ancient times, instead of raping and pillaging it as we do now? Aren't we supposed to be more *advanced* now? Do we really need a disaster to force us to go back to the shamanic way of being good 'caretakers' of the Earth?

We all need to do less 'do-ing' and have more time to do 'be-ing.' Most of us are spectacularly unhappy; having more *things* isn't going to change that. Our souls need to *be*. I believe the credit crunch is happening to encourage us towards simpler, happier ways of living. It is interesting to see that 'New World' businesses – those which are not solely focused on the making of profit but instead consider the needs of their employees, the environment and the Earth – are seeing increases in business and in staff retention. My sense is that this is the only way business will survive in the future, by focusing on the *good of all concerned, primarily the Earth*. How many companies do things that they know are bad for the end consumer? For example, putting in known carcinogens (cancer-causing chemicals) into soft drinks and diet foods?

Perhaps we will be forced to live more shamanically, *harmlessly*, as we were always intended to live, in small commu-nities, in closer relationship and kinship with others, *and in closer relationship with nature*. It is my firm belief that one of the reasons people suffer so badly with depression nowadays is because of the innate loneliness and separation many people feel. We were never meant to live the way we do now; it is *unnatural*. It's no good having 3,000 friends on Facebook when you are ill in bed with flu and there is no one around to make you some chicken soup! People simply *have* to have close and harmonious relation-ships with other people; it's a basic human need. Many people do not have large family structures around them so they are more reliant on friends than ever. In the New World we will be focused on the good of our community, the good of all, rather than what we can get for ourselves. Like the Q'ero, we will be focused on the 'collective' rather than on the advancement of our own selves and our egos.

As with many of the prophecies, I do feel that the veils between the worlds of spirit and human will continue to thin out and many more of us will experience psychic and spiritual awakenings. I can already see this happening among my friends and clients, so it is likely that this will soon reach the masses. Perhaps we will all become shaman and be able to speak to and communicate with all of life. Quite clearly, we cannot carry on the way that we have been doing, continuing to act selfishly in the belief that we can live the way we do without consequence. We cannot go on treating the Earth – this beautiful planet which **gives us all we need** – with so much disrespect. If indeed we are like fleas on the Earth's back then we must be *really* itching and annoying her by now! Do we really want to upset her so much she simply shakes us off?

Regardless of our race, religion, or sexual proclivities, what is it that we all want anyway? We all want to be happy, we want to love and be loved, we want to live in peace and harmony, and lead healthy and fulfilled lives. We *all* have ordinary human needs. We were cave dwellers once; we lived in community with others. Our hearts need those connections still, and we need love and the support of our community behind us. We need to make considerable changes in the way we live our lives, run our families, homes and businesses, and have a rethink about what is truly important. We need to start listening to the voice of our soul and our Higher Self which resides in our heart. We need to be still enough to hear its voice and take action, to find our bliss and align ourselves with joy – whatever joy is for us. The voice of your soul may ask you to give up those things which up until now have identified who you are. Let me tell you now: that person is *not* who you are – you are far more magnificent than that!

My hope is that we all wake up, stop looking for a quick profit at the expense of a fellow human or the Earth, stop thinking about me, me, me, start treating the Earth and each other with respect, and begin, at last, to use our common sense! We could, all of us, start living in that Golden Age of Peace NOW... if we act quickly.

I believe our future and the future of the planet **is in our hands**. We can all come together now, work together now, to create Heaven on Earth. *Wouldn't that be nice?*

A Healer of Souls – The Short Version
No one says it better than The Beatles:
All you need is love.
All you need is love.
All you need is love,
Love.
Love is all you need.

Acknowledgments

I would like to thank John Hunt and Maria Barry at John Hunt Publishing for all their help and support in getting this book off my computer and into your hands. John, thank you for believing in my work, and for all your words of encouragement.

To Sahar Huneidi (www.psychicsahar.com) – words cannot ever begin to thank you for your support and for the faith that you have shown in me and in my work over the years. This book, and many of the stories within it, would not have been possible without you. Not only are you an amazingly gifted psychic, but you are a wonderful friend! Thank you from the bottom of my heart.

To Nicky Mott – thank you, my sister, for being there and catching me when I fell. I really don't know what I would do without you. I am so grateful for all the love and support you have shown me over the years. I miss you like mad and can't wait to get you back in the UK for a girlie weekend and lots of tea! Tukumunayniyok.

To my mother Patricia Hopkins and my brother Martin Hopkins – thank you for being you and for all that you have taught me. And thank you for letting me be me; I know it can't always have been easy! I love you and hope now I will be able to see much more of you in the future!

To Guy – thank you for all your love, support and under-standing; here's to the start of a fresh new chapter for both of us.

To Claire (and Andy, Cole and Mia) thank you for your love, support and friendship and for all the lovely meals, I couldn't have got through all this without you!

To Dee, thank you for showing me the ways of the Goddess, and for looking after Georgie so well – you are a true friend.

To all my lovely friends – thank you for being there! Now this book is finished I will have time for more fun! A special thank-you to Janey Lee Grace for her friendship, support and encouragement, and of course for Mr Big – twice – I'll never forget it!

To the Q'ero medicine people and the Apu Kuna – please know that I feel honored to be walking this medicine path. Thank you for allowing me to be a part of it. I honor you and give thanks for all my blessings.

And finally... to all my clients over the years. Thank you for your courage and bravery, for facing your fears and for fighting to be all that you can be. You are all an inspiration to me. And thank you to those of you who so generously allowed your stories to be shared within these pages, in the hope that your stories will help others. Good Journeys!

Oh, and to my cat Georgie, who has been a blessing and also one of my greatest Zen teachers. Sorry I have been a rubbish mummy these last few years while writing this book. I promise to play with you more now!

Contact Details

I do hope that you have enjoyed this book and that it has helped you in some way. If you would like to contact me then please feel free to do so.

My website is at www.liberate-online.co.uk

Or you can email me at dawn.paul@btopenworld.com

From 2012 I will be running various health and healing retreats abroad, please go to my website, or to www.pararadishealthretreats.com for information on dates and venues.

A list of the books which have been helpful to me on my journey is provided on my website.

Please visit www.qero.org for more details on the Q'ero – the medicine people of the Andes whose wisdom forms the basis of my work. The Q'ero Ayni Fund is a non-profit fund providing financial assistance to the Q'ero in their mountain villages. It also aims to preserve this beautiful medicine way for the benefit of future generations.

BOOKS

O is a symbol of the world, of oneness and unity. In different cultures it also means the "eye," symbolizing knowledge and insight. We aim to publish books that are accessible, constructive and that challenge accepted opinion, both that of academia and the "moral majority."

Our books are available in all good English language bookstores worldwide. If you don't see the book on the shelves ask the bookstore to order it for you, quoting the ISBN number and title. Alternatively you can order online (all major online retail sites carry our titles) or contact the distributor in the relevant country, listed on the copyright page.

See our website **www.o-books.net** for a full list of over 500 titles, growing by 100 a year.

And tune in to myspiritradio.com for our book review radio show, hosted by June-Elleni Laine, where you can listen to the authors discussing their books.

MySpiritRadio